| | DATE DUE | |
|---|---|---|
| | | |
| | | |
| | | |
| | | |
| | | |
| | | |
| | | |
| | | |
| | | |

# Bloom's Modern Critical Views

## Bloom's Modern Critical Views

*Bloom's Modern Critical Views*

# JOHANN WOLFGANG
# von GOETHE

*Edited and with an introduction by*
### Harold Bloom
Sterling Professor of the Humanities
Yale University

**CHELSEA HOUSE**
**P U B L I S H E R S**
A Haights Cross Communications Company

**Philadelphia**

Introduction © 2003 by Harold Bloom.
All rights reserved. No part of this publication may be
reproduced or transmitted in any form or by any means
without the written permission of the publisher.
Printed and bound in the United States of America
10  9  8  7  6  5  4  3  2  1


Library of Congress Cataloging-in-Publication Data

Johann Wolfgang von Goethe / Harold Bloom, editor ; Pamela
Loos, contributing editor.
    p. cm. — (Bloom's Modern critical views)
Includes bibliographical references and index.
 ISBN 0-7910-7041-7
 1. Goethe, Johann Wolfgang von, 1749-1832—Criticism and
interpretation.  I. Bloom, Harold. II. Loos, Pamela. III. Series.
 PT2177 .G63 2002
 831'.6—dc21

                                        2002008253



Chelsea House Publishers
1974 Sproul Road, Suite 400
Broomall, PA 19008-0914

http://www.chelseahouse.com

Contributing Editor: Pamela Loos

Cover design by Terry Mallon

Cover image © Austrian Archives/CORBIS

Layout by EJB Publishing Services

# Contents

# Editor's Note

My Introduction considers the Goethean vision.

Hans Vaget meditates upon Goethe's achievements as a novelist, while Ehrhard Bahr centers upon the late *Wilhelm Meisters Wanderjahre*, which he sees as a precursor of the modern German novelists Döblin and Broch. The much earlier *Wilhelm Meisters Lehrjahre* is read by Ernst Behler in terms of Romantic poetics.

Wolfgang Wittkowski analyzes the drama *Iphigenie* as a critique of truth-telling, after which Donna Dietrich and Harry Marshall return us to the play in order to argue that "barbarian" Thoas is the authentic hero.

We move to the grand poetic drama *Torquato Tasso*, with a consideration of the play's balance between poetic freedom and order by Hans Reiss.

*Faust II* is seen by John Gearey as an influence upon Charles Darwin, while Tobin Siebers considers *The Sorrows of Young Werther* in regard to the Romantic cult of the suicidal hero.

Goethe's treatment of women in his dramas is found by Sigrid Lange to be a crucial element in the unhappy history of male fantasy, after which Harald Weinrich relates both parts of *Faust* to "the Western culture of forgetting."

*Elective Affinities* is studied as ethical balance by David Constantine, while Ilona Klein returns us to *Werther*, which she views as concealed stage drama.

Brigitte Peucker brilliantly relates the imagery of *Elective Affinities* to "the staging of painting," after which Irmgard Wagner broods upon Goethe's final phase as a poet.

# Introduction

Of all the strongest Western writers, Goethe now seems the least available to our sensibility. I suspect this distance has little to do with how badly his poetry translate into English. Hölderlin translates poorly also, but his appeal to most of us dwarfs Goethe's. A poet and wisdom writer who is his language's equivalent of Dante can transcend inadequate translation but not changes in life and literature that render his central attitudes so remote from us as to seem archaic. Goethe is no longer our ancestor, as he was Emerson's and Carlyle's. His wisdom abides, but it seems to come from some solar system other than our own.

Goethe had no German poetic precursors of anything like comparable strength; Hölderlin came after him, and he has had no rival since, not even in Heine, Mörike, Stefan George, Rilke, Hofmannsthal, or the astonishing Trakl and Celan. But though he stands at the true beginning of imaginative literature in German, Goethe is, from a Western perspective, an end rather than a beginning. Ernst Robert Curtius, to me the most distinguished of modern German literary critics, has observed that European literature formed a continuous tradition from Homer through Goethe. The step beyond was taken by Wordsworth, the inaugurator of modern poetry and also of that line of introspection which goes from Ruskin through Proust into Beckett, until recently the major living writer. Goethe's dates were 1749-1832, while Wordsworth's were 1770–1850, which makes the English Romantic a younger contemporary of the German sage. But British and American poets continue to rewrite Wordsworth involuntarily, and one cannot say that Goethe is a vital influence on German poetry at this time.

From *The Western Canon*. © 1994 by Harold Bloom.

Nevertheless, it should be argued that Goethe's remoteness is part of his enormous value for us now, particularly at a time when French speculators have proclaimed the death of the author and the hegemony of texts. Every Goethe text, however divergent from the others, bears the mark of his unique and overwhelming personality, which cannot be evaded or deconstructed. To read Goethe is to know again that the death of the author is merely a belated Gallic trope. Goethe's daemon or daemons—he appears to have commanded as many as he wanted—is always present in his work, aiding his perpetual paradox that the poetry and prose alike are at once exemplary of a Classical, almost universal *ethos*, and a Romantic, intensely personal *pathos*. The *logos*, or in Aristotelian terms the *dianoia* (thought content) of Goethe's work, is the only vulnerable aspect, since the eccentric Goethean Science of Nature today seems an inadequate conceptualizing of his formidable daemonic apprehension of reality. That hardly matters, for Goethe's literary power and wisdom survive the evaporation of his rationalizations.

Curtius adroitly remarks that "Predominance of light over darkness is the condition that suits Goethe best," and reminds us that Goethe's word for this condition is *heiter*, not so much "joyous" as equivalent of the Latin *serenus*, a cloudless sky, whether night or day. Like Shelley after him, Goethe found his personal emblem in the morning star, but not for its moment of exquisite waning into the dawn, as Shelley did. The serene Goethe is now a temperamental burden for us; neither we nor our writers are tranquil. Goethe's Faust lives to be one hundred years old, and Goethe ardently desired the same for himself. Nietzsche taught us a poetics of pain; only the painful, he brilliantly insisted, could truly be memorable. Curtius ascribes to Goethe a poetics of pleasure in an old tradition, but a poetics of serenity, of unclouded skies, is even closer to the Goethean vision.

"Error about life is necessary for life," a crucial Nietzschean insight, is part of Nietzsche's large (and acknowledged) debt to Goethe, whose idea of poetry centered upon a complex awareness that poetry essentially was trope, and that trope was a kind of creative error. Curtius in his masterwork, *European Literature and the Latin Middle Ages* (1948; 1953 in English), brings together two splendid statements on trope by Goethe. In the "Notes and Essays" attached to the *West-Östlicher Divan*, Goethe comments on metaphor in Arabic poetry:

> to the Oriental, all things suggest all things, so that, accustomed
> to connecting the most remote things together, he does not

hesitate to derive contrary things from one another by very slight changes in letters or syllables. Here we see that language is already productive in and of itself, and indeed, in so far as it coincides with the imagination, is poetic. If, then, we should begin with the first, necessary, primary tropes and then mark the freer and bolder, until we finally reached the most daring and arbitrary, and even the inept, conventional, and the hackneyed, we should have obtained a general view of Oriental poetry.

Clearly this would constitute a general metaphor for poetry, where "all things suggest all things." In his *Maxims and Reflections*, Goethe says of his true precursor (the only one he could accept, because he wrote in a different modern language): "Shakespeare is rich in wonderful tropes which stem from personified concepts and which would not suit us at all, but which in him are perfectly in place because in his time all art was dominated by allegory."

This reflects Goethe's unfortunate distinction between "allegory, where the particular serves only as an example of the general" and "symbol" or "the nature of poetry; it expresses something particular, without thinking of the general or pointing to it." But Goethe goes on to observe that Shakespeare "finds images where we would not go for them, for example in the book ... still regarded as something sacred." To trope a book as something sacred is hardly allegory in Goethe's rather uninteresting sense, but it is allegory as an authentically symbolic mode in which all things again suggest all things. Such a metaphor of the book opens Goethe to his own largest ambitions as a poet, to embody and extend the European tradition of literature without being overcome by its contingencies, and so without losing the image of oneself.

This aspect of Goethe has been best illuminated by his principal twentieth-century heir, Thomas Mann. With loving irony (or perhaps ironic love), Mann composed a series of remarkable portraits of Goethe, from the essay on "Goethe and Tolstoy" (1922) through a triad of essays in the 1930s (on the man of letters, the "representative of the Bourgeois Age" and *Faust*) to the novel *Lotte in Weimar* (1939), concluding with the "Fantasy on Goethe" of the 1950s. Setting *Lotte in Weimar* aside, the most remarkable of these Goethean performances is the speech on the hundredth anniversary of the poet's death: "Goethe as Representative of the Bourgeois Age." For Mann, Goethe is "this great man in poet's form," the prophet of German culture and idealistic individualism, but above all "this miracle of personality," and Carlyle's "godlike man." As bourgeois Representative Man,

Goethe himself speaks of a "free trade of conceptions and feelings," which Mann interprets as "a characteristic transference of liberal economic principles to the intellectual life."

Mann emphasizes that Goethe's serenity was an aesthetic achievement rather than a natural endowment. In the late "Fantasy on Goethe," Mann commends Goethe for his "splendid narcissism, a contentment with self far too serious and far too concerned to the very end with self-perfection, lightening, and the distillation of personal endowment, for a petty-minded word like 'vanity' to be applicable." The charm of this characterization is that Mann describes himself as much as Goethe, both here and in the splendid essay of 1936 on "Freud and the Future":

> The *imitatio* Goethe, with its Werther and Wilhelm Meister stages, its old-age period of *Faust* and *Divan*, can still shape and mythically mould the life of an artist-rising out of his unconscious, yet playing over—as is the artist way—into a smiling, childlike, and profound awareness.

Mann's *imitatio* Goethe gives us Tonio Kroger as Werther, Hans Castorp as Wilhelm Meister, *Dr. Faustus* for *Faust*, and *Felix Krull* for the *Divan*. There are deliberate echoes in Mann's remarks of Goethe's "even perfect models have a disturbing effect in that they lead us to skip necessary stages in our *Bildung*, with the result, for the most part, that we are carried wide of the mark into limitless error." Mann quotes, in several places, Goethe's cruel and central question, phrased in his old age as, "Does a man live when others also live?" Implicit in this question are two superb Goethean aphorisms that between them form a dialectic of belated creation: "Only by making the riches of the others our own do we bring anything great into being," and "What can we in fact call our own except the energy, the force, the will!"

E.R. Curtius's Goethe is the perfecter and final representative of the literary culture that goes from Homer to Virgil to Dante and that achieved later sublimity in Shakespeare, Cervantes, Milton, and Racine. Only a writer with Goethe's daemonic force could have summed up so much without falling into the perfection of death. Our puzzle now is that Goethe, despite his vitality and wisdom, confronts us in his strongest lyric poetry with too undivided a consciousness for us to believe we can be found by that poetry, palpably as powerful as Wordsworth's, yet infinitely less moving. The *Trilogies der Leidenschaft*, or "Passion Trilogies," despite their extraordinary rhetorical intensity, are not poems of the center of our being like "Tintern Abbey" and the "Intimations" ode. The *Prelude* cannot be judged poetry of a higher order than *Faust*, yet it seems by far the more normative work. The great aesthetic puzzle of Goethe is not his lyric and narrative achievements, both of which are unquestionable, but *Faust*, the most grotesque and unassimilable of major Western poems in dramatic form.

HANS RUDOLF VAGET

# Goethe the Novelist: On the Coherence of His Fiction

A century and a half after his death no universal agreement has been reached on the question of Goethe's stature as a novelist. Admittedly, the pivotal position his novels occupy in German literature has never been in doubt. The situation is quite different, however, once we begin to look beyond the German tradition and try to assess Goethe's place in relation to the mainstream of the European novel. Against such a wider horizon the extent of his achievement as a novelist appears diminished or, at least, uncertain. This is particularly obvious in the English-speaking world with its own uniquely rich literary tradition. Here, only Goethe's first novel, *The Sufferings of Young Werther*, has attained a place of pre-eminence in the consciousness of the general educated reader. Apart from *Werther* Goethe appears to be a novelist by reputation only. Small wonder in a culture, from Carlyle and Emerson to T. S. Eliot, that sees Goethe primarily as the Sage rather than the novelist or even the poet.[1] Goethe is of course known as the author of *Faust* and, to a lesser degree, as the poet who inspired Schubert, Wolf, and others to some of their greatest *lieder*. But if regard for Goethe remains high in England and America, it clearly does not rest on an honest appreciation of his fiction; the general public tends to think of him not as a novelist but as a Sage who also wrote some novels.

From *Goethe's Narrative Fiction*. © 1983 by Walter de Gruyter & Co.

If this statement seems exaggerated, consider the following random observations. No complete edition of Goethe's novels in English is available. The translations of the first three, which are available, are unsatisfactory. With the exception of *Werther* no other novel of Goethe's has a firm place on college reading lists outside German departments—whereas the novels of Thomas Mann, Kafka, and Grass, for instance, do. Judging by the evidence of American scholarship Goethe rarely figures in the critical discourse on the genre and the history of the novel. Of *Wilhelm Meisters Lehrjahre* little more seems to be known than the fact, or rather the rumor, that it initiated a new sub-genre of the novel: the *Bildungsroman*—whatever that may be.[2] *Die Wahlverwandtschaften* on the other hand—the best German novel according to Thomas Mann[3]-has not yet become a familiar enough work to create a general awareness of Goethe's finest achievement as a novelist. And *Wilhelm Meisters Wanderjahre*, his most fascinating effort in the genre—comparable to the second part of *Faust* in its artistic freedom and boldness, remains *terra incognita* outside a small circle of specialists. In other words, three of Goethe's four novels have still not arrived, properly speaking, in the orbit of the English language. Is it really any wonder that this author of four major novels is not recognized as a major novelist?

One difficulty we have with the novelist Goethe derives simply from our term "novelist." Both the phenomenon and the term are fairly new—the result of a relatively late specialization in the history of literature. When we speak of novelists we think of figures such as Richardson and Jane Austen, Balzac and Flaubert, Dostoevski and Tolstoi, James Joyce and Virginia Woolf—writers, in other words, who devoted themselves almost exclusively to the novel. To them the novel had become the representative genre of modern literature to which they turned with a heretofore unknown single-mindedness of purpose. Goethe clearly does not belong in their company. He represents another type of writer that reigned from the Renaissance to the 18th century: the universal man of letters. Voltaire rather than Flaubert could be considered his literary relative.[4] Goethe was so many other things besides a writer. And even as a writer he never concerned himself with the novel exclusively for any length of time. He would not on principle privilege the form of the novel, but turn to it only for very specific purposes. Thus the universality of Goethe's literary genius becomes almost an obstacle in any attempt to define him as a novelist.

Another and much greater difficulty arises from the unusual disparity of the four novels. They differ in setting, theme, style, and structure to such a degree that some readers might well take them to be the work of four different authors. The two *Wilhelm-Meister*-novels offer a particularly striking case in point. *Wilhelm Meisters Wanderjahre* of 1829 was meant to be the sequel to the Lehrjahre completed in 1796—and yet a greater change in style, narrative strategy, and ideological position can hardly be imagined. Or take *Werther* and *Die Wahlverwandtschaften*, written 35 years later; they are often compared on the basis of their tragic vision which sets them apart from the other two novels. But again when one reads a page from the early, passionate epistolary novel and then one from the later, much more controlled work one will find it hard to accept that they were written by the same man. It appears that as a novelist Goethe developed by leaps and bounds and not in the slow progression usually associated with him. Whatever the explanation, there can be no doubt that the perception of inconsistency and a lack of clear thematic focus make it difficult to accord to Goethe the title of "great novelist." As long as we have not identified some common critical purpose and some general themes which bind the four works together and render them a coherent novelistic oeuvre, the proposition that Goethe should be considered a major novelist is hard to entertain.

There are of course other factors that have stood in the way of a general recognition of Goethe as a major novelist in the European sense. To begin with, Goethe strikes us as almost too casual about the theoretical demands the novel began to make in the 18th century. He did not write a full-fledged theory of the novel on the scale of Friedrich Blanckenburg or Friedrich Schlegel. The few scattered theoretical remarks he did make have not exactly enhanced his reputation as a novelist. They occur in a brief essay on epic and dramatic literature and in some aphorisms. The essay is based on his correspondence with Schiller at the height of their classicist orientation; strictly speaking, however, it is irrelevant to the concerns of the modern novelist. On the other hand, his aphoristic definition of the novel betrays such disarmingly simple views as to add to our doubts rather than enlighten us. "The novel," he wrote in *Maximen und Reflexionen*, "is a subjective epic in which the author takes the liberty of treating the world in his own manner. The only question then is: does he have a manner of his own? Everything else will fall into place."[5] Can one imagine a more casual attitude to what was to become, before long, one of the central questions of literary theory?

There is also the question of the morality of Goethe's novels, specifically of the *Lehrjahre*. In a literary culture in which the heritage of Puritanism lived on for a long time, the morality of a work of literature has traditionally been a central concern of the reading public as well as of literary criticism. Such a culture cannot easily provide a very hospitable climate to much of Goethe's work. Consider the reaction of Thomas Carlyle, whom a cruel fate had chosen to be Goethe's prophet in the English-speaking countries. Even this most ardent admirer of Goethe's developed an intense dislike of the *Lehrjahre* and grew alarmed at what he thought was the immorality of the book as he worked on the translation which still today passes for the standard English version. According to his letters, from a certain point on he had to force himself to continue his daily chore: so irritated was he by what he was reading.[6] To make matters still worse for Goethe's fortunes in England and America he did not conceal that he considered himself to be a "dedicated non-Christian." Friedrich Schlegel who, in Germany, was endowed with perhaps the finest antenna in matters of religion observed, correctly I believe, that "Goethe is without the word of God."[7] And indeed, his novels display a more or less inimical, though not polemical attitude toward the Christian religion. Furthermore, Goethe's novels exhibit considerable freedom in the treatment of the erotic. This free though not frivolous spirit of the *Lehrjahre* has clearly complicated the English reception of Goethe's novels; George Eliot's defense of the morality of the *Lehrjahre* merely underscores the widespread displeasure with this book in 19th-century England.[8]

And last but not least we must bear in mind that as a novelist Goethe had no clearly identified public. Until well into the 19th century Germany did not possess a large homogeneous reading public with fully developed forms of literary communication and a clearly defined set of social and moral codes. Unlike his French and English contemporaries Goethe never really knew who his readers were. From this there arose a paradoxical situation. Even novels—normally intended for a mass readership—had to be addressed to what was only a relatively small circle of friends. Under these circumstances serious novelists had to attempt to actually create a readership for themselves and to educate it in the art of reading. In this Goethe continued the work of his older contemporary C. M. Wieland. But of his four novels only *Werther* can be said to have succeeded in this mission. The absence of a close, symbiotic relationship between the novelist and his public probably accounts for much of what an English reader might find unusual in Goethe's novels. In their characteristic mixture of the traditional and the daring they seem to display a certain lack of novelistic propriety. On the other hand, however, we may well speculate that it was this independence from a clearly defined, homogeneous readership that facilitated greatly Goethe's inclination to experiment with the forms and conventions of narration. *Wilhelm Meisters Wanderjahre* clearly shows that he used this freedom with increasing self-assurance and boldness; more and more this novel appears to us essentially an experiment in the art of reading.

The task of assessing Goethe the novelist would undoubtedly be easier if we had a clear idea of the inner coherence of his four novels. But there exists as yet no critical consensus on basic points such as the thematic continuity and the development of narrative strategy. This situation has not been improved by the three most recent attempts at a general assessment of Goethe as a novelist. They agree on only one point: that the four novels form a coherent novelistic oeuvre. Opinions differ, however, on the strength and exact nature of their coherence.

Eric Blackall has identified the quest for order as the common concern of all of Goethe's novels.[9] He believes that Goethe's own quest for order in his personal life provided him with a strong impulse for writing novels. He cautions, however, that Goethe was "concerned with a wider conception of order, of which social order is a part, but only a part." Thus Young Werther, for instance, is said to be motivated by a pathological urge to create an artificial order derived from a total absorption in his own thoughts, whereas the book as a whole postulates, according to Blackall, order "as the basic ontological necessity."[10] The structure of the *Wanderjahre*, on the other hand, is determined by an interplay of order and disorder; here the mysterious figure of Makarie represents the highest, cosmic sense of order which is said to embrace and to transcend all its other manifestations within the novel. In the last analysis Blackall defines Goethe's concept of order as an idea beyond all accepted notions of order—social, religious, moral—as a sense of the world that embraces chance and the unfathomable. This supposedly higher concept of order, however, has become so mystical as to be virtually useless for a rational interpretation of Goethe's novels. Since Blackall refuses to restrict himself to the esthetic and political sense of order, his attempts to establish the inner coherence of Goethe's novels remain unpersuasive.

A completely different perspective is provided by Stefan Blessin.[11] As is so often the case when one compares German and American scholarship on the same subject, the two authors are completely at odds with each other without actually engaging with each other. Whereas Blackall explicitly denies the possibility of reading Goethe's novels as social novels, Blessin accepts this premise as a matter of course. And while Blackall declares that Goethe's novels are not concerned with the French Revolution and its repercussions in Germany, Blessin believes that they are—if only indirectly,

What unites the four novels, according to Blessin, is their concern with the internal contradictions of bourgeois society. Goethe's novels, we are told, offer the most complete and penetrating analysis of bourgeois society from its pre-revolutionary stage to the eve of the industrial revolution. For this reason the novels are viewed as the most progressive part of Goethe's work. To substantiate his thesis in the face of massive evidence to the contrary, Blessin must resort to a trick: he simply declares all representatives of the nobility in Goethe's novels as more or less bourgeois at heart. His ultimate goal is to show that Goethe's novels are informed by an original materialist and dialectical concept of history. And this, he suggests, qualifies Goethe as the greatest analyst of bourgeois society before Karl Marx. The implausibility of this elaborate but basically familiar construct is overwhelming.

Compared with Blessin's book Heinz Schlaffer's 1978 essay on "Exoterik und Esoterik in Goethes Romanen" offers a more exciting characterization of Goethe's novels.[12] Schlaffer too sees a close connection between the emergence of a bourgeois society and Goethe's novels. He even characterizes them—echoing Walter Benjamin—as the "Magna Charta of the bourgeois self-consciousness"[13] but emphasizes Goethe's skepticism about the rise of the bourgeoisie. Schlaffer's main point is to remind us that Goethe's novels cannot be regarded as the sacred fountainhead of bourgeois ideals and ideas. In reality Goethe's novels are said to contain serious objections to the ideals they appear to advocate. He thus distinguishes an exoteric and open texture of meaning and one that is hidden and esoteric. On the exoteric level Goethe's novels may be read as poetic pleas for the bourgeois ideals of freedom, self-cultivation, morality, and progress. On the esoteric level, however, they project an essentially pessimistic vision of those same ideals. To Schlaffer, this double-faced profile represents the most essential feature of Goethe's narrative strategy.

In such an esoteric reading the story of Werther, for instance, takes on a completely different complexion from the conventional and from Goethe's own interpretation. Taking the passion of Werther at its most concrete form of expression as a passion for the writing of letters, Schlaffer interprets the novel as a kind of metaphor for the climax and the dying of an almost orgiastic passion for writing. The esoteric meaning of the Lehrjahre also undermines the openly proclaimed humanism of the ideal of "Bildung." Schlaffer, following Karl Schlechta,[14] points out the oppressive and in fact inhuman side of the secret Society of the Tower. The very principles of that society: usefulness, specialization, productivity, capitalism, industrialization, have come to dominate the world portrayed in the Wanderjahre. Here too Schlaffer sees a whole set of hidden objections at work within the novel itself. In contradiction to the apparent plea for the acceptance of the new reality the novel also upholds, according to Schlaffer, the endangered dignity of individualism, of love, and death—especially in the inset novellas.

Although Schlaffer's essay seems to me to be the most stimulating contribution to our topic, he fails to create a strong enough sense of the inner coherence of Goethe's novels. The question of thematic unity is not really pursued, and the structural and technical similarity, of which Schlaffer is convinced, simply does not become visible in concrete formal characteristics. The task of discovering the coherence of Goethe's novelistic work thus remains before us.

In order to discover the inner coherence of Goethe's novels we must try to uncover the hidden connection that exists between their narrative strategy and their characteristic thematic obsessions. There are reasons to believe that Goethe's novels, their great disparity notwithstanding, actually deal in various forms with the same subject matter. What are his basic themes? Why did he return to them again and again? And why did he treat them in the way he did?

To comprehend how and why Goethe as a novelist developed the way he did, we should first look at the endpoint of this development, *Wilhelm Meisters Wanderjahre*. Once we have grasped the structural principle underlying this work we will be able to see that the germs of it were present already in *Werther*.

With regard to Goethe's last novel a fairly broad critical consensus has now been reached on the nature of its puzzling and seemingly careless structural design.[15] Goethe described its basic principle as "Spiegelung," or mirroring. In a letter of 1827, two years before the completion of his last novel, we find the following concise description of this method:

> Since much of what we experience cannot be expressed neatly and communicated directly, I began, some time ago, to resort to a particular method of revealing to the reader the deeper meaning of a work by setting some phenomena off against each other and allowing them, as it were, to mirror each other.[16]

Goethe acknowledges here that the writing of fiction, in the last analysis, is a problem of communication.[17] He emphasizes that his method of communication has to be indirect; but it is indirection of a higher order. What he has in mind is a method of placing the various parts or elements of a given work in such order that they will mutually mirror and gradually illuminate each other. Through this method meaning will be revealed gently, without didacticism, and as in a sudden but perfectly natural illumination.[18]

In view of this statement the seemingly diffuse structure of the *Wanderjahre* can no longer be attributed to the waning of Goethe's creative powers, as was assumed in the 19th century. He obviously knew precisely what he was doing. The statement contains in a nutshell the essence of what Goethe had come to know about the writing of fiction. He no longer believed in the convention of linear plot, and he rejects authorial comment as a viable technique. He also refuses to summarize the essence of a novel at its conclusion or anywhere else—as Schiller had urged in the case of the *Lehrjahre*. Goethe never italicizes in any form the idea, the meaning, or the message of a work for the alleged benefit of the reader. The statement on mirroring even betrays skepticism about meaning as such. It should be noted that the deeper meaning of which he speaks is not to be found in any one of the parts and elements mirroring one another. It must be assembled in the reader's mind from fragments and refractions. It follows that the *Wanderjahre* should not and cannot be read for its plot or various subplots.[19] Its secret meaning lies in the thoughtful and subtly calculated arrangement of the different elements of the narrative that make up this novel, such as: letters, diaries, essays, aphorisms, poems, novellas, reports, and editorials. These elements are not really meant to complement each other; on the contrary, they are intended to comment upon, and to relativize each other—or, as Goethe put it in a note, they are "to work against each other."[20] Most of the longer parts are interrupted at crucial points, broken up and distributed over the length of the book. And yet all persons and phenomena exist in their own right and are allowed to speak for themselves. Hence that wonderful sense of tolerance and impartiality which is a hallmark of Goethe's fiction in general.

Goethe's method of mirroring is intimately connected with two other essential qualities of his fiction: its symbolism and irony. Both devices existed of course before and independently of Goethe, but in his work they seem to have acquired a new and subtle artistic efficacy. It must be granted that some of the irony in the *Lehrjahre*, when it is created through the narrator's comments, does not differ from the manner of Wieland and Sterne. In essence, however, we are dealing here with a new type of irony, as Friedrich Schlegel, the Romantic high priest of irony, was quick to note.[21] In such instances irony emerges from a particular constellation or the relationship between distant parts of the novel without the narrator's ever calling attention to it. This narrative technique is carried much farther in *Die Wahlverwandtschaften* and the *Wanderjahre*. Judging by this development the urbane and talkative narrator of the *Lehrjahre* was not as close to Goethe's deepest artistic instincts as the equally urbane but tightlipped narrator of *Wahlverwandtschaften*. In the *Wanderjahre*, as Ehrhard Bahr has shown, this method has been carried yet a step further to producing an all-encompassing system of discrete and ironic interrelationships.[22]

Goethe's method of mirroring is also related to the well-known symbolism of his fiction. When we speak of symbolism, however, we should distinguish between two phenomena: the symbolic meaning of individual objects such as the mysterious casket in the *Wanderjahre*, or the goblet in *Wahlverwandtschaften*, and a more general esthetic quality of the whole work. The latter type of symbolism results from a carefully designed system of internal correspondences such as we usually associate with late Romanticism. Goethe's fiction anticipates this development. Here I am referring you to one of the aphorisms in the *Wanderjahre* which—like so many other passages— seems to provide a comment on the novel itself:

> Everything that exists, exists in analogy to everything else that exists.[23]

This statement gives us a clue not only to the structure of Goethe's last novel but also to the secret artistic goal of his fiction: the esthetic ideal of symbolism. Goethe's later novels do not fully realize this ideal but they begin to approach it. With the late Romantic symbolism in the wake of Baudelaire Goethe's symbolism shares the ideal of *correspondence* but it remains still untouched by the philosophy of *l'art pour l'art*.

When and where did Goethe begin to use the method of internal mirroring? It is commonly assumed that it was applied only in the works of his last phase, in the *Wanderjahre* and in the second part of *Faust*. In his letter, however, he clearly states that he had been using it for a long time. And indeed it must date back at least to 1979 when he wrote the *Unterhaltungen deutscher Ausgewanderten*. That cycle of novellas is arranged in pairs of parallel stories which mirror and illuminate each other. Goethe again provides the rationale for this method by having one of the characters, the Baroness, comment on it:

> I just adore parallel stories. One points to the other and explains its meaning better than many words could.[24]

This indicates that Goethe had discovered the principle of mirroring by 1795 and that he chose this device in order to reduce the extent of the narrator's role as commentator.

But the beginnings of Goethe's method can be discovered already in *Werther*. Here the story of the "Bauernbursch," the young farm hand who commits a murder out of jealousy, produces a mirror effect in the sense of a "Parallelgeschichte." The obvious purpose of this story is to throw a chilling light on the criminal potential of Werther's passion since he explicitly identifies with the sufferings of the young man.[25] Goethe added the three episodes of this story in the revised version of 1787 but one can see that the idea of a parallel story was on his mind already in the first version of the novel. The story of the farm hand is nothing but an amplification of an earlier story about a former secretary of Lotte's father whose love for Lotte drove him to madness. It is easy to see the purpose of the revision. Goethe wanted to provide the reader with a more critical and "objective" mirror image of Werther. The revision also resulted in a greater emphasis on the editorial role of the narrator. It is interesting to see that Goethe uses the fictive editor not primarily for the traditional purpose of authenticating the story he is telling, but rather in a manner foreshadowing the *Wanderjahre*; there, too, the narrator figures as the editor of a fictitious archive. Already in *Werther* this transparent fiction primarily serves one function: it gives Goethe the opportunity to provide through various mirror reflections a more critical and more complex view of Werther.

In the later novels this method continues to be developed and refined. In *Wahlverwandtschaften*, for instance, two mirrors are set up, as it were, in the second part of the novel: five installments from Ottilia's diary and a complete novella entitled *Die wunderlichen Nachbarskinder*. In the *Wanderjahre* the method of mirroring and, concomitantly, the fragmentation of the plot is carried to the extreme. In this novel Goethe uses different sets of letters, diaries, aphorisms, and an entire cycle of novellas. As a consequence, perhaps the oldest ploy of storytelling, plot, is practically eliminated. Instead the reader is called upon to supply the missing links between the fragments which, in an intriguing manner all seem to mirror each other, and to reflect on their interrelationship. Clearly, by the time Goethe wrote the *Wanderjahre* mirroring had become something different from what it was in *Werther* or in the *Unterhaltungen deutscher Ausgewanderten*. Whereas in the first novel it functions primarily as a device to amplify the central character and to reinforce the main story, in the last novel mirroring actually subverts whatever one might be tempted to take for the "main" story. In other words, Goethe began by using mirroring for the purpose of constructing and reinforcing meaning; in the end it had become a narrative strategy to relativize and to deconstruct meaning. It would be an error, therefore, to read this novel—as has been the custom—as an essentially didactic book of wisdom. The *Wanderjahre*, with its new philosophy of education and gospel of renunciation, its aphorisms and its mystical saint, the puzzling figure of Makarie, merely pretends to be such a book. In the last analysis this novel has become the vehicle for some of the older Goethe's most serene and sophisticated literary games. It has often been remarked that this fragmentation and subversion of the traditional novel structure foreshadows some crucial developments of the form of the novel in the 20th century.[26] This is especially true, it seems to me, with respect to the implied reader who is conceived of in the *Wanderjahre* as the decisive integrating force of the novel. In this respect Goethe's last novel seems to anticipate a basic feature of the *nouveau roman*.[27]

We must return once more to Goethe's own description of his method of mirroring to discover what brought him to it and why it became his most characteristic narrative device. Goethe points out that "much of what we experience cannot be expressed neatly and communicated directly." This statement strikes one as exaggerated, coming as it does from the author of *Torquato Tasso*, *Faust*, and the most eloquent body of poetry in the German language. But it always pays to take Goethe at his word. Accordingly, we must assume that he turned to the technique of mirroring out of sheer necessity—motivated by a keenly felt need. More important, we have to conclude that there were some areas in Goethe's experience so complicated and puzzling to him, so ineffable in the strictest sense of the word, that he needed to deal with them indirectly by mirroring them in repeated reflections and refractions. Once we have identified these areas of Goethe's experience which he found too difficult to communicate directly we will be able to grasp the underlying thematic coherence of his novels. Looking at the inner biography of Goethe and the social circumstances of his life at least two dominant themes can be identified in his novels: the question of his relationship to the nobility, and the problem of dilettantism. These issues concerned him both as a political being and as an artist and thus touch the core of his life and experience.

The question of dilettantism is still poorly understood, its importance to our understanding of Goethe still underrated. One difficulty with it is purely semantic. In Goethe's day the connotations of the term dilettante were more ambivalent and not as negative as they are today. Furthermore, to Goethe's mind the word had a broader meaning. To him it came to denote a certain problematical attitude toward life generally—an attitude based on self-deception. The dilettante as a type came to represent to him the problematical modern hero.[28] Another difficulty is less obvious: as soon as we take the problem of dilettantism in Goethe's life as seriously as he did himself we would have to give up for good one of the most cherished clichés of the Goethe-cult: the belief in his wholeness, as well as that concomitant article of faith—that his greatest work of art was not any one of his literary works but his life.

As the son of a well-to-do burgher of the Free Imperial City of Frankfurt Goethe grew up in a cultural milieu which favored an "allseitige," i.e. comprehensive cultivation of all innate talents, especially in the arts. This philosophy of education still derived some of its inspiration from the Renaissance ideals of the *uomo universale* and the "Complete Gentleman." The Enlightenment discovery that all human beings are endowed with the drive to imitate seemed to lend these ideals some new life. Like so many middle class citizens with an upward social mobility, Goethe's father Johann Caspar, subscribed to this philosophy of education wholeheartedly. Consequently, young Goethe received private instruction not only in all the standard subjects, especially languages, but also in drawing, painting, and sculpture. Characteristically enough, he embraced these forms of creativity with the same enthusiasm with which he turned to writing. As we know from his autobiography, he was unable to decide for a long time whether his true calling as an artist was in poetry or in painting. It is one of the most astonishing aspects of his development that this conflict was not resolved until he was almost 40 when, in Rome, he made one last concentrated but vain effort to perfect his talent. At that time he finally had to admit to himself that he did not posses enough talent. Only then did he realize—with the help of Karl Philipp Moritz—that he had fallen victim to a common self-deception: he had mistaken his great appreciation of the pictorial arts for a sign of true talent—and for actual creativity what was merely the common drive to imitate. Nonetheless Goethe could not bring himself to condemn dilettantism.

The importance for Goethe of this whole experience can hardly be overrated. Of course, I am not thinking here of the countless drawings and sketches that have survived and that fill half a dozen volumes; they represent the least consequential result of Goethe's dilettantism. Of far greater consequence were the indirect ramifications extending to all parts of his work. It could be shown, for instance, that the classicist esthetic program Goethe propagated after his return from Italy, can be viewed in essence as an anti-dilettante esthetics. It is based on the conviction that true art is the opposite of what the dilettante practices and believes. In 1799 Goethe even began, in collaboration with Schiller, a comprehensive treatise on dilettantism in all the arts. He abandoned the project when he saw that the problem could not adequately be dealt with theoretically.[29] The concept of dilettantism is also relevant to an assessment of Goethe's scientific work. He turned to science when he began to realize that as an artist he was unable to master the forms and the underlying laws of nature. In science he simply continued his study of nature with different means—but with the sensibility of an artist. Thus Goethe experienced the dilemma of the dilettante practically all his life: first in drawing, then in science.

In short, the problem of dilettantism constituted one of those experiences that could not be expressed fully and directly in all its ambivalence. Experiences such as these called for fictional treatment. Only in the novel and through the technique of mirroring could he hope to do justice to a phenomenon as troubling and fascinating to him as dilettantism.

We know from the letters of young Goethe that he had an instinctive knowledge of the frustrations of dilettantism long before he really confronted this problem in Italy. He experienced the despair of artistic impotence already in his early twenties, and the shock of this discovery must be regarded as one of his *Urerlebnisse*—one of his most fundamental experiences. I believe that it provided perhaps the most urgent inspiration for the composition of *Werther*. This is not obvious at first reading, but if we look below the surface of the love story and Werther's quarrel with the quality of life in general, we discover a young man despairing of his creativity. Werther cannot live with the realization that his artistic and intellectual gifts are insufficient to mold his life, and that of others, in accordance with his own ideas. Throughout the book Werther expresses his despair over his inability to cope with the world in the manner of a great artist.[30] This despair extends far beyond his dabbling in drawing to the very act of letter writing since it is rooted in the structure of his personality. Werther is the paradigmatic dilettante. Like all dilettantes he mistakes his unusual ability to appreciate art for the ability to produce it. Time and again we are shown that his ideas of a fulfilled life are derived from the experience of literature. Heinz Schlaffer's esoteric reading of the novel has identified the passion of letter writing as the true concern of the book. It seems to me that we need to go a step further: Werther is the dilettante as letter writer. He attempts to recreate as a writer what he has experienced as a reader, and he kills himself in frustration when the discrepancy between reality and his expectations becomes unbearable.

*Die Leiden des jungen Werther* may be interpreted, then, as a magnified projection of Goethe's own, as yet unacknowledged sufferings as a dilettante. He had not yet come to terms with the problem, and this, I submit, accounts to a large measure for the harsh judgment of dilettantism implicit in *Werther*. Once he had become reconciled to his own dilettantism he was able to portray it ironically.

The fact that the character of Wilhelm Meister is conceived as a dilettante is plain to see and needs no elaboration. This time Goethe's *alter ego* aspires to be a great playwright and actor, a second Shakespeare. But he too has to realize that he has deceived himself about the extent of his talent. In Goethe's own account of the beginnings of *Wilhelm Meister* he points out that the problem of dilettantism provided the focus for the book.[31] A comparison between the *Lehrjahre* and its abandoned first version, *Wilhelm Meisters Theatralische Sendung*, confirms this claim. Goethe eliminated most indications of true genius in Wilhelm's youth so as to leave no doubt about the dilettantism of his first steps as a poet.

The crucial point to be made about this novel concerns the extent and depth of Wilhelm's dilettantism. It manifests itself not only in his mistaken desire to become an artist but also in his equally mistaken ambition to attain the culture of an aristocratic personality and thereby realize all his innate possibilities. The letter in which he reveals this ambition has often been read as the quintessence of his novel and of the idea of the *Bildungsroman*, when in reality it can only be meant as the revelation of his quintessentially dilettantish attitude to life. In the end Wilhelm falls far short of his stated goal. He has not achieved Bildung in the intended sense. Nonetheless Goethe refrains from any condemnation of Wilhelm's dilettantism. On the contrary, the novel amounts in essence to an apologia for dilettantism. Goethe demonstrates to the reader—and, of course, to himself—that it is important and fruitful to be a dilettante. Without it Wilhelm would not have attained what he has attained at the end of the novel: a certain maturity, and admission to a circle of superior individuals. Thus Wilhelm's "wrong inclination" is re-interpreted as a "fruitful error;" in Goethe's own terms: *falsche Tendenz* is revealed as *fruchtbarer Irrtum*. This represents an essentially positive view of dilettantism and of erring—reminiscent of the positive connotations of "erring" in *Faust*.

This esoteric reading of the novel suggests, among other things, that the traditional term *Bildungsroman* should not be applied to the *Lehrjahre*. In the end Wilhelm stands before us neither as an aristocrat nor as a bourgeois *uomo universale*. What we witness is a process of a successful socialisation with the focus on the ambivalent role of dilettantism in that process. As Tom Saine has argued, there can be no doubt that Goethe refuses to ratify Wilhelm's idealistic notion of *Bildung*.[32] Instead Goethe shows us how a successful and miraculously rewarding socialisation can be achieved when one's youthful dilettantism is allowed to run its course. I would propose, therefore, that the old label *Bildungsroman* be dropped and replaced by the term "novel of socialisation." It offers a more fitting description of the *Lehrjahre* and sounds less ideologically charged than the term *Bildungsroman*.[33]

Considering the conciliatory view of dilettantism in the *Lehrjahre*, one is struck by Goethe's more radical approach to it in the other two novels. If we took at Eduard, the central dilettante figure in *Die Wahlverwandtschaften*, the change of perspective becomes immediately apparent. Eduard is no longer a young person but a "rich baron in his best years." There is something definitive about his dilettantism. No reader can fail to see that his dabbling in music and landscape gardening is but the outward sign of a much more profound dilettantism. Characteristically, Eduard prides himself on only one point: he considers himself to be a master of loving. It goes without saying that this desperate self-assessment stands revealed as his most painful self-deception. In the crucial scene before his visit to Charlotte's bedroom we are shown that as a lover too he acts as a typical dilettante who merely imitates the example of others.[34] In the end he is reduced to an imitation of Ottilie's death. But whereas Ottilie's action is the result of an admirable self-determination, Eduard's dying lacks all signs of moral autonomy. Ottilie, it could be said, was conceived by Goethe as a genius in the realm of morality, Eduard as a dilettante. Here, dilettantism clearly reveals a negative moral dimension such as Goethe had defined earlier in that abandoned theoretical critique of dilettantism. In this novel, as was noted before, Goethe employs the technique of mirroring to a greater degree than in the *Lehrjahre*. One of the reasons must have been to provide a more complex view of dilettantism. For example Eduard's and Charlotte's landscape gardening in the then modern English style is mirrored in the restoration of the old chapel in the latest Nazarene style. Both are to be understood as complementary forms of dilettantism, just as the architect is to be viewed as a dilettante and variation of Eduard.

At first sight it appears that with the *Wanderjahre*, Goethe finally moved beyond dilettantism to more pressing problems. In a world on its way to industrialization the old ideal of self-cultivation has to be renounced and can not even be entertained as an attractive illusion. The new age demands specialization, and when specialization has become common there is no room left for the luxury of dilettantism. Even Wilhelm now realizes what his true calling is. Only then does he remember the traumatic experience of the drowning of his childhood friend; the depth of his grief finally convinces him that he was meant to become a surgeon. With this Goethe seems to have reached the endpoint in his grappling with this problem. But this is not the case. Not everyone in the novel is ready to practice renunciation as Wilhelm does. His son Felix does not, for instance, nor do the principal characters of the inset novellas. They can be described as dilettantes in a general sense. They are to varying degrees subjective, receptive rather than productive. They are prone to self-deception and error—especially in choosing their lovers and spouses, and they are shown to be in need of guidance and norms.

In short they are dilettantes in the far-reaching sense this concept had acquired for Goethe. These stories not only mirror each other but together they form a colorful contrast to the prosaic picture of the world in which Wilhelm lives. And this reveals the central role of the problem of dilettantism in the unusual design of the novel. Whereas the novellas depict a world populated by dilettantes the main body of the novel unfolds a world in which that central virtue in Goethe's last novel, renunciation, is practiced. In this world the memory of dilettantism and its dangers is still alive; it is perceived not merely as an artistic insufficiency but as a symptom of a pervasive moral and social danger. As such it is diagnosed in the two collections of aphorisms inserted into the *Wanderjahre*. Goethe thus arrives through the method of mirroring at a statement about dilettantism that illuminates both the depth and the paradoxical nature of the problem. Whereas he refrains from condemning the typical dilettante figures in the novellas, every effort is made in the other parts of the novel—through the wisdom of exceptional figures such as Jarno, the Uncle, and Makarie, and even through a new philosophy of education—to make the world safe against dilettantism.

Goethe's novels do not aspire to be social novels in the manner of Balzac and Dickens, or Zola and Fontane. Socially and geographically, Goethe simply was not in a position to write such novels. Germany was without a capital and thus without a flourishing and representative social life to write novels about. Germany's territorial dismemberment as well as her political and economic backwardness proved to be an even greater handicap. Under these circumstances Goethe's interests as a novelist necessarily centered almost exclusively on the private rather than on the public sphere. Despite this concentration on the private, his novels may justly be regarded as the most sensitive monitors of the historical dynamics in the transition from a predominantly feudal and pre-revolutionary and predominantly bourgeois situation. He did not, however, deal directly with the missing link in that historical transition: the revolution. But it was inevitable that he dealt with it indirectly by probing into the causes and consequences of this epoch-making event.

Goethe's reluctant but growing interest in questions of historical change was motivated by his ideological position as well as his social background. His political thinking was shaped primarily by the writings of the conservative Justus Möser, the most influential political thinker in 18th-century Germany and a forerunner, in a sense, of Edmund Burke.[35] Given this fundamentally conservative orientation Goethe naturally abhorred all revolutions. He rejected even the idea of it with the same intensity with which he denied the so-called volcanic theory of the origin of the earth—the two phenomena being intimately connected in his mind. When the revolution did occur in France it became *the* political trauma of his life. This meant that it had become impossible not to deal at least with the ramifications of the revolution in Germany. Goethe did make several attempts to analyse in dramatic form the causes and consequences of the revolution but failed to arrive at a satisfactory solution. This frustrating exercise must have determined him to treat this troubling problem even more indirectly in his novels than he had done in his plays. In the meantime, however, with the appearance of Napoleon, his attitude toward the revolution softened somewhat. Goethe admired Napoleon and remained untouched by the growing nationalism in occupied Germany. He saw in him the executor of the French Revolution and the guarantor of a new political order in Europe. Gradually he would become reconciled to the historical consequences of the revolution and thus modify his ideological position. This staunch and deeply troubled opponent of the revolution began to adopt a more liberal, though essentially still conservative position. Despite this partial reconciliation the revolution remained for Goethe *the* most disturbing political event of his life. It, too, had to be counted among those problematical experiences about which no direct and complete communication was possible.

Goethe's social background proved to be the other decisive factor in his attempt to understand historical change. He was born into a wealthy and socially rising middle class family. In 1782, at the age of 33, he was awarded, at the initiative of his friend the Duke of Weimar, the patent of nobility. As far as one can see Goethe never asked himself consciously whether as a writer he should advocate the interests of the bourgeoisie or the nobility. But one must assume that he felt an allegiance to both classes—or perhaps to none.

Goethe's conservatism, his rise into the ranks of the nobility as well as his administrative responsibilities in the government of Weimar account for a crucial point in his political thinking. He attributed the French Revolution primarily to the moral and political failure of the aristocracy and never really learned to see in it the victorious cause of the middle class.[36] This is a crucial point to remember in any socio-historical reading of the novels. Among other things it should make us skeptical of Blessin's and Schlaffer's interpretations which present Goethe's novels as the *Magna Charta* of the emerging bourgeoisie in Germany. Goethe's peculiar understanding of the French Revolution clearly suggests that we can gain a more adequate perspective on the ideological profile of his novels by considering his portrayal of the nobility rather than his image of the middle class.

In *Werther* the relationship between the middle class and the nobility is at its most antagonistic in Goethe's work. Werther's ideological position is that of an enlightened young burgher who considers himself the equal of the nobility in terms of culture and morality. Hence his name which means "worthier"—worthier, that is, than his modest social rank indicates. The whole bent of his razor-sharp intelligence would qualify him as a rebel against the nobility and absolutism—all the more so, one would think, since he suffers the most painful social humiliation at an aristocratic reception. But young Werther is no revolutionary. He even defends the existing order since he sees quite clearly that he too stands to benefit from it. Although he protests against social prejudices and privileges he counts some aristocrats among the people he admires most. Not even in his first novel can Goethe's position be described as pro-middle-class.

In *Wilhelm Meisters Lehrjahre* the political ambivalence we encountered in *Werther* is significantly modified. The ideological balance is now clearly weighted in favor of the nobility. In one of his comments on the novel Novalis dismissed it as an almost farcical "pilgrimage for the patent of nobility."[37] Novalis' criticism highlights a central point of the novel, but his comment needs explanations. It should be obvious that the arrogant and uncultured type of aristocracy which Wilhelm encounters and blindly admires in book III of the novel, is not intended to be the goal of his pilgrimage. That goal is marked by an entirely new type of aristocracy represented by Baron Lothario and his circle. What distinguishes Lothario from the Count in book III, or from Lothario's uncle, is his willingness, even eagerness to reform the existing social order by renouncing certain privileges of the nobility and by sharing some of these with the middle class.[38] Although it cannot be overlooked that Lothario is ultimately motivated by his concern for the economic and political security of the nobility, he has been charged by Goethe with a comprehensive social mission: he is to show the way to social peace on the basis of a social compromise between the nobility and the middle class in order to forestall any danger of a revolution. Within Goethe's total oeuvre this position marks by far the most generous and optimistic view of the nobility and its reform-mindedness.

It is a mark of the usually underrated thematic coherence of Goethe's novels that with *Wahlverwandtschaften* he continued the examination of the role of the nobility that he had begun in the previous novel. He must have realized by that time that the optimism embodied in the figure of Lothario was not borne out by subsequent historical developments. Consequently he conceived his new novel as a kind of correction, if not a reversal, of the position previously taken ln the *Lehrjahre*. In Eduard we meet a representative of the landed gentry; he is presented to us as the proverbial "rich baron," comparable in social status to Lothario. Eduard, however, is shown to be the exact opposite of Lothario. He selfishly devotes himself to personal happiness without attaining it; he proves to be an alarmingly incompetent manager of the considerable real estate he holds—the economic basis of the nobility; he is determined to uphold the privileges of his class and to refuse social compromises; he is ultimately devoid of any sense of social responsibility for the common weal. Whereas Lothario is endowed with a clear historical consciousness, Eduard, Charlotte, and their friends live as in an enclave without contact with the rest of the world. Seen against the wide and promising horizon projected by the *Lehrjahre*, the nobility in *Wahlverwandtschaften* appears completely unfit for the leading role they are charged to play in society. There can be no doubt that with this novel Goethe wrote off for good the high hopes for social reform he had pinned on the Lotharios of the German nobility. Several factors led to this change of position; the military catastrophe of Prussia in 1806, which brought to light not only the military but also the unsuspected moral and social insufficiency of the nobility, was probably the decisive one.

Somewhat surprisingly Goethe returned to the figure of the rich Baron in his last novel. In the light of the dawning industrialization the role of the still important nobility needed to be reconsidered once more. The new Lothario of *Wilhelm Meisters Wanderjahre* is called Lenardo. Goethe's affection for this type grew with the time; in the final version of the novel Lenardo appears to be the central character next to Wilhelm. There is no character in the book about whom we know more than Lenardo. It is only natural that he also provides the focus for the central socio-historical diagnosis in this reputedly unfocused book. As in the two preceding novels Goethe makes real estate and love the main criteria for the moral and social assessment of the nobility. He connects these two criteria in an ingenious fashion. As a young man Lenardo had unwittingly become the cause of great pain and misery for one of his uncle's tenant farmers and his young daughter whom he only knows as "the nutbrown maid." In order to finance Lenardo's obligatory Grand Tour his uncle had ruthlessly insisted on the payment of their outstanding debts, and when they were unable to pay, evicted them from the land they had leased from him. Lenardo witnesses their suffering, and this unforgettable experience turns into the decisive trauma of his life. Haunted by guilt Lenardo devotes himself after his return to a search for the nutbrown maid in order to make good the injustice he had caused her and her father by the mere fact of his being a young nobleman whose "Bildung" needed to be financed. The fragmented story of this search and the awakening of Lenardo's love—a passion born of conscience—form the nearest thing to a plot in this almost plotless novel. This story links up directly or indirectly with almost all other parts of the novel and culminates in the emigration to America—a project inspired, organized and led by the former Baron Lenardo.

One tends to forget Lenardo's social status as nobleman since almost all we see him do strikes us as decidedly prosaic and bourgeois. This is exactly Goethe's point. Lenardo has left his aristocratic past behind. To him the feudal system has come to mean injustice and domination of people over people. As such it has become the focus of a kind of collective guilt—a guilt feeling on behalf of his whole class. Lenardo realizes too that there is no room left in Europe for the establishment of a new, more egalitarian order. He therefore turns to the New World for a new beginning in America. In this he is joined by Wilhelm who has had to renounce his dilettantish dream of acquiring an aristocratic personality and who is now in the process of becoming a useful specialist such as is needed when a new social order is to be built.

As we try to assess the position of the eighty-year-old Goethe in *Wilhelm Meisters Wanderjahre* we can hardly escape the conclusion that he saw no hope for the nobility to retain its political and social leadership in an age of industrialization and specialization. Twenty years after *Wahlverwandtschaften* with its implicit condemnation of the nobility it would have been inconsistent to return to the counter-revolutionary optimism symbolized long ago in Lothario. All that could be achieved in Europe is the colonization of some distant parts of the continent. Such a colonizing venture is indeed undertaken in the novel by a second group of émigrés led by Odoard, who is also a disenchanted nobleman. This second venture provides an obvious mirror to the more radical plans of Lenardo, Wilhelm, and the Society of the Tower. The prospects for Odoard's venture are clearly less inspiring, if not downright gloomy. In marked contrast to Lenardo, Odoard is characterized as a man whose personal trauma, a mistaken and painful marriage, has not yet heated; he has not yet made his peace with the bitter lesson of renunciation. There are enough indications to assume that Odoard's colonizing project will in essence result in the restoration of the old autocratic order. As far as Europe is concerned, Goethe's erstwhile hopes that the nobility would reform itself and thus be able to retain its leadership role had vanished perhaps somewhat prematurely in view of the continued power of the German nobility in the 19th century. In the end Goethe projected into the New World all his hopes for a new order without a feudal system; he had long since come to the realization: "Amerika du hast es besser." But even the optimism of this new beginning is crucially marred by the prospect of pedantically authoritarian measures to which the new state will have to resort.

## NOTES

1. Cf. William Rose, "Goethe's Reputation in England During His Lifetime," *Essays on Goethe*, ed. William Rose (London: Cassell, 1949), pp. 141–186; Walter H. Bruford, "Goethe's Reputation in England Since 1832," ibid., pp. 187–206; Edwin H. Zeydel, "Goethe's Reputation in America," ibid., pp. 207–232.

2. For a provocative discussion of the whole *Bildungsroman*-tradition see David H. Miles, "The Picaro's Journey to the Confessional: the Changing Image of the Hero in the German 'Bildungsroman,'" *PMLA*, 89 (1974), 980–992; Jeffrey L. Sammons, "The Mystery of the Missing 'Bildungsroman,'" *Genre*, 14 (1981), 229–246.

3. See Mann's essay on *Die Wahlverwandtschaften* in *GW*, IX, 174f: "der größte nicht, aber der höchste [Roman] der Deutschen."

4. Cf. Victor Lange, "Goethe's Craft of Fiction," *PEGS*, 22 (1952/53), 31–63, esp. 33.

5. *Maximen und Reflexionen*, *HA*, XII, 498, No. 938: "Der Roman ist eine subjektive Epopöe, in welcher der Verfasser sich die Erlaubnis ausbittet, die Welt nach seiner Weise zu behandeln. Es fragt sich also nur, ob er eine Weise habe; das andere wird sich schon finden."

6. Cf. William Rose, "Goethe's Reputation in England During His Lifetime," 183.

7. See Friedrich Schlegel, *Literary Notebooks 1797–1801*, ed. Hans Eichner (Toronto: Univ. of Toronto Press, 1957), p. 115, No. 1075.

8. George Eliot, "The Morality of Wilhelm Meister," *The Writings of George Eliot* (Boston: Riverside Press, 1908), XXII, 305–309.

9. Eric A. Blackall, *Goethe and the Novel* (Ithaca: Cornell UP, 1976). Cf. also Hans Reiss' still useful, straightforward analysis of *Goethe's Novels* (Coral Gables: Univ. of Miami Press, 1971).

10. See Blackall, 15, 40.

11. Stefan Blessin, *Die Romane Goethes* (Königstein: Athenäum, 1979).

12. Heinz Schlaffer, "Exoterik und Esoterik in Goethes Romanen," *Goethe—Jb.*, 95 (1978), 212–226.

13. Schlaffer, 212. Cf. also Walter Benjamin's article "Goethe" of 1929, *Gesammelte Schriften*, ed. R. Tiedemann and H. Schweppenhauser (Frankfurt: Suhrkamp, 1977), II, 2, 705–739.

14. See Karl Schlechta, *Goethes Wilhelm Meister* (Frankfurt: Athenäum, 1953). A more fully developed "esoteric" reading of the Wilhelm Meister novels has now been presented by Hannelore Schlaffer, *Wilhelm Meister. Das Ende der Kunst und die Wiederkehr des Mythus* (Stuttgart: Metzler, 1980).

15. The literature on the *Wanderjahre* has mushroomed in the last two decades. Especially useful are: Erich Trunz, introduction and notes, *HA*, VIII; Wilhelm Emrich, "Das Problem der Symbolinterpretation im Hinblick auf Goethe's 'Wanderjahre,'" *DVLG*, 26 (1952), 331–352; Volker Neuhaus, "Die Archivfunktion in 'Wilhelm Meisters Wanderjahre,'" *Euphorion*, 62 (1968), 13–27; Manfred Karnick, *Wilhelm Meisters Wanderjahre oder die Kunst des Mittelbaren* (München: Funk, 1968); Heidi Gidion, *Zur Darstellungsweise von Goethes "Wilhelm Meisters Wanderjahre"* (Göttingen: Vandenhoeck und Rupprecht, 1969); Ehrhard Bahr, *Die Ironie im Spätwerk Goethes* (Berlin: Erich Schmidt, 1972); Jane K. Brown, *Goethe's Cyclical Narratives "Die Unterhaltungen deutscher Ausgewanderten" und "Wilhelm Meisters Wanderjahre"* (Chapel Hill: Univ. of North Carolina Press, 1975).

16. The passage (my own translation) occurs in a letter to K. J. L. Iken of Sept. 23, 1827; *Goethes Briefe*, ed. K. R. Mandelkow, *HA*, IV, 250: "Da sich gar manches unserer Erfahrungen nicht rund aussprechen und direkt mitteilen laßt, so habe ich seit langem das Mittel gewählt, durch einander gegenübergestellte und sich gleichsam ineinander abspiegelnde Gebilde den geheimeren Sinn dem Aufmerkenden zu offenbaren."

17. Cf. especially Karnick's study, passim.

18. Karnick (158ff) and others have pointed out that Wilhelm's letter to Natalie concerning the origins of his interest in the medical profession (II, 11) provides a model example of Goethe's method of mirroring.

19. An interesting attempt was made to do just that by Bernd Peschken, *Entsagung in "Wilhelm Meisters Wanderjahre"* (Bonn: Bouvier, 1968).

20. *HA*, VIII, 582.

21. See Friedrich Schlegel, "Über Wilhelm Meister," *Kritische Friedrich-Schlegel-Ausgabe*, ed. Hans Eichner, II, 126–146.

22. See E. Bahr, *Die Ironie im Spätwerk Goethes*, 88ff.

23. *HA*, VIII, 300, No. 115: "Jedes Existierende ist ein Analogon alles Existierende…"

24. *HA*, VI, 187: "Ich liebe mir sehr Parallelgeschichten. Eine deutet auf die andere hin und erklärt ihren Sinn besser als viele trockene Worte."

25. Cf. Thomas P. Saine, "The Portrayal of Lotte in the Two Versions of Goethe's 'Werther,'" *JEGP*, 80 (1981), 54–77, esp. 67ff.

26. Joseph Strelka, "Goethes Roman 'Wilhelm Meister' und der Roman des zwanzigsten jahrhunderts," *GQ*, 41 (1968), 338–355.

27. Cf. Ehrhard Bahr, "Nachwort" to his new edition of the *Wanderjahre* (Stuttgart: Reclam, 1982), p. 560.

28. See my article "Der Dilettant. Eine Skizze der Wort- und Bedeutungsgeschichte," *JDSG*, 14 (1970), 131–158.

29. For a more detailed discussion see my *Dilettantismus und Meisterschaft. Zum Problem des Dilettantismus bei Goethe. Praxis, Theorie, Zeitkritik* (München: Winkler, 1971).

30. On Werther's dilettantism cf. E. L. Stahl, "Goethe as Novelist," *Essays on Goethe*, 45–73, esp. 50f.

31. See *HA*, VIII, 519.

32. See Thomas P. Saine, "Über Wilhelm Meisters 'Bildung,'" *Lebendige Form: Interpretationen zur deutschen Literatur*, ed. J. L. Sammons and E. Schurer (München: Fink, 1970), pp. 63–82.

33. Cf. Walter H. Bruford, *The German Tradition of Self-Cultivation* (Cambridge: Clarendon Press, 1975).

34. I have discussed this point at greater length in my essay "Ein reicher Baron. Zum sozialgeschichtlichen Gehalt der 'Wahlverwandtschaften,'" *JDSG*, 24 (1980), 123–161, esp. 141ff.

35. Cf. Klaus Epstein, *The Genesis of German Conservatism* (Princeton: Princeton UP, 1966), pp. 320ff.

36. See Eckermann's conversation with Goethe on January 4, 1824.

37. *HA*, VIII, 571.

38. For a discussion of the nobility in this novel cf. my "Liebe und Grundeigentum in 'Wilhelm Meisters Lehrjahren.' Zur Physiognomie des Adels bei Goethe," *Legitimationskrisen des deutschen Adels 1200–1900*, ed. P. U. Hohendahl and P. M. Lützeler (Stuttgart: Metzler, 1979), pp. 137–158.

EHRHARD BAHR

# Revolutionary Realism in Goethe's Wanderjahre

Goethe's novel *Wilhelm Meisters Wanderjahre oder die Entsagenden* of 1829 is usually read as a continuation of *Wilhelm Meisters Lehrjahre*, his earlier novel of 1796. There are good reasons for this practice. The protagonist and many of the characters are still the same. The plot at the beginning of *Wanderjahre* depends on a promise made in *Lehrjahre*, namely, for Wilhelm Meister to travel with his son Felix to Italy to collect his share of Mignon's inheritance.

In 1821 Goethe was provoked into publishing a sequel to *Lehrjahre*, when an author with the obscure name Friedrich Wilhelm Pustkuchen (1793–1834) published his own *Wanderjahre* (1821–1828) which criticized by implication Goethe's handling of Wilhelm Meister's education. Since Pustkuchen's *Wanderjahre* appeared anonymously in order to exploit Goethe's name and reputation, Goethe had to act with speed to displace the false *Wanderjahre* with his own version. Although Pustkuchen's imitation fulfilled its function as a "pacemaker" for Goethe's own work and is largely forgotten today, it is, nevertheless, a convincing testimony to the fact that Goethe's audience expected a sequel to *Wilhelm Meisters Lehrjahre* whose picaresque structure was not difficult to imitate and continue.[1]

Goethe himself had announced his intention of writing a sequel to *Lehrjahre* as early as 1796 in a letter to Schiller, after Schiller had pointed out

From *Goethe's Narrative Fiction*. © 1983 by Walter de Gruyter & Co.

that the concept of "*Lehrjahre*" or "apprenticeship" required a correlative in terms of "*Meisterschaft*" or "mastery."[2] There may have been, in addition to *Wanderjahre* or "journeymanship," even plans for a third Wilhelm Meister novel, a "Meisterjahre."[3]

At any rate, the reviews of *Lehrjahre* indicate that Goethe's audience was fully aware of the title's implication. Some expressed disappointment that the protagonist had not reached his goal in terms of "mastery" in *Lehrjahre*, while others defended Goethe for the same reason, explaining that the novel comprised only Wilhelm Meister's apprenticeship and his journeyman years were still to follow.[4] Audience expectations to that effect were raised, when Goethe announced his forthcoming *Wanderjahre* for the first time in 1810, when he published one of the novellas intended for the later novel. A first and fragmentary version of *Wanderjahre* appeared in 1821, while the final version was published in 1829.

Yet, in spite of the impressive evidence for continuity between *Lehrjahre* and *Wanderjahre*, there are some indications of discontinuity which cannot be disregarded. They compel us to read Goethe's *Wanderjahre* not as a continuation of the eighteenth-century novel *Lehrjahre*, but rather as a nineteenth-century novel which happens to have the same protagonist. The reasons for this change in critical perspective have not a primarily biographical, but a structural basis. To be sure, Goethe had aged by 1829, and he was the same author as of *Lehrjahre* only by name: he had developed his late style (*Altersstil*).[5] But age offers only an explanation, not an analysis.

The title of this paper refers to structure rather than contents. "Revolutionary realism" is conceived in terms of Roman Jakobson's definition as substitution or deformation of a given artistic code in order to achieve a more accurate rendition of reality. In his book on *Fundamentals of Language* (2nd ed. 1971), Roman Jakobson distinguishes between two types of discourse in verbal art: one which is predominantly metaphoric and the other which is predominantly metonymic.[6] In traditional rhetoric, metaphor signifies the transference of "a word from its literal meaning to one not properly applicable but analogous to it," while metonymy represents substitution of the whole for a detail, or "of cause for effect or effect for cause, proper name for one of its qualities or vice versa."[7] These two types of tropes are governed, according to Roman Jakobson, by two different principles: by similarity in the case of metaphor, by contiguity in the case of metonymy.[8] The descriptive terms employed by Heinrich Lausberg are *Sprung-Tropen* for metaphor and *Grenzverschiebungstropen* for metonymy.[9]

Deriving his terms from classical rhetoric, Jakobson considers the "literary schools of romanticism and symbolism" to be determined by metaphoric discourse, while realist literature, according to him, is characterized by metonymic discourse.[10] One aesthetic equivalent of his concept of metaphor is obviously Goethe's symbol.[11] German classicism with its belief in the centrality of the symbol would be included under predominantly metaphoric discourse. Realism, on the other hand, is characterized by "dwelling on unessential details" at the expense of totality. According to Jacobson, a description based on unessential details appears more real to the followers of realism than concentration on a few selected meaningful objects, representing the universal by the particular.[12]

The primacy of the metaphoric process in German classicism and especially in Goethe's *Wilhelm Meisters Lehrjahre* is easily established, if we refer to the well-known symbolism of the novel. The painting of the ailing prince and the figure of Shakespeare's Hamlet are central metaphors for Wilhelm Meister's state of mind. The disorder of the theater world to which he is attracted point to the disorder of his own inner life. The male attire of the three central female characters in Wilhelm's amorous encounters is a metaphor of their androgynous attraction for the protagonist. Mignon's androgyny is a metaphorical allusion to the male and female qualities of poetic genius.[13]

The predominance of metonymy in *Wanderjahre*, however, has gone unnoticed. Even by the standards of Goethe's aesthetics, it is not a symbolic novel, as claimed by Wilhelm Emrich and Eric A. Blackall.[14] Metonymy underlies and actually determines its discourse. It is my thesis that

1.    this change from the metaphoric way to the metonymic way accounts for the discontinuity between *Lehrjahre* and *Wanderjahre*, one of the most radical changes to occur in the history of any literature; and

2.    that the switch to metonymy constitutes a totally new way of rendering reality, or, in Roman Jakobson's words, "revolutionary realism."[15] As Jakobson explains in *Fundamentals of Language*, "the predominance of metonomy [...] actually predetermines the so-called 'realistic' trend, which belongs to an intermediary stage between the decline of romanticism and the rise of symbolism and is opposed to both. Following the path of contiguous relationships, the realist author metonymically digresses from the plot to the atmosphere and from the character to the setting in space and time." As main characteristic Jakobson mentions the realist's fondness of synecdochic details, quoting two examples from

Tolstoj: "In the scene of Anna Karenina's suicide Tolstoj's
artistic attention is focused on the heroine's handbag; and in
*War and Peace* the synecdoches 'hair on the upper lip' and
'bare shoulders' are used by the same writer to stand for the
female characters to whom these features belong."[16] In an
article "On Realism in Art" (1921) Jakobson lists the
following devices in addition to metonymy as characteristic
of "progressive" or "revolutionary realism": fondness of
unessential detail, condensation of the narrative, the elimination of plot, and constant motivation and realization of
literary devices.[17]

I will be arguing that Goethe achieved a similar type of realism in his
*Wanderjahre*, a realism matched in German literature, for example, by
Heinrich Heine in his *Ideen: Das Buch Le Grand* (1826) and by Georg
Büchner in his novella *Lenz* (1835, published 1839). This type of realism was
finally replaced by the "classical realism" or "*poetischer Realismus*" after 1848
which modelled itself on the classical Goethe and his *Lehrjahre* rather than
the old Goethe and his *Wanderjahre*. It took more than a hundred years for
the modernity of Goethe's realism to be recognized by a modern author,
Hermann Broch who declared in his essay on James Joyce that "in
*Wanderjahre* the foundations of the modern novel were laid."[18]

Needless to say, it is not only the structure of *Wanderjahre* that is
modern, but also its content. The revolutionary realism of the content can
easily be established. This is the historical argument in my case. The critical
reception of Goethe's *Wanderjahre* is a history of neglect and misunderstanding. Only the "socialist school" of criticism of the 19th century was able
to realize the revolutionary contents of Goethe's *Wanderjahre*, interpreting it
as a social novel (*Sozialroman*) and a prophetic anticipation of utopian
socialism à la Saint-Simon. In comparison to French socialism, Goethe's
novel was considered a work of "socialist literature" (Ferdinand Gregorovius,
1849), its concepts were found to be in agreement with the "ideals of modern
socialism" (Hermann Hettner, 1852), and one critic (Karl Grün, 1846) even
regarded Wilhelm Meister as a Communist, though he had trouble convincing Friedrich Engels of this designation.[19] But otherwise, negative
criticism prevailed until the middle of this century, ascribing the lack of
classical realism in *Wanderjahre* to Goethe's alleged artistic decline and lack
of imagination in his later years. Until 1950 there was not even a critical
edition of the complete text available. In all previous editions important
sections had been deleted to make *Wanderjahre* conform to the conception of
"classical realism."

The complete text of Goethe's *Wanderjahre* of 1829 consists of three books, including eight novellas, as well as numerous letters, a diary and archival documents. In addition, the novel contains two comprehensive collections of almost two hundred aphorisms each: "Reflections in the Spirit of the Wanderers" (*Betrachtungen im Sinne der Wanderer*), and "From Makarie's Archive" (*Aus Makariens Archiv*), as well as two philosophical poems "Testament" (*Vermächtnis*) and "In the Burial Chamber" (*Im ernsten Beinhaus*), also called "Poem on Schiller's Skull" (*Gedicht auf Schillers Schädel*).

The aphorisms as well as the poems are not integrated into the novel, but form erratic blocks, contiguous to the narrative. Their relationship to the novel can be defined as metonymic. They do not contribute directly to the development of either the plot or the protagonist. For sections of two to almost fifty pages each in the original edition, the plot is interrupted or continued by different material. Action and character are replaced by totally different forms of discourse related to the novel only by association or suggestion. Johann Peter Eckermann's explanation of 1831 that these sections were added by Goethe for the sole purpose of filling the pages of volumes 21–23 of the *Ausgabe letzter Hand*, the last edition of his collected works supervised by Goethe himself, has been proven wrong. These sections were already planned and expressly mentioned in an early outline of 1828. But until 1950 subsequent editors followed Eckermann's model and advice, deleting the collections of aphorisms and the poems.[20] For the reader of the modern novel, however, the metonymic inserts or appendices to *Wanderjahre* pose no problem, because the reader is familiar with such metonymic devices from countless modern novels from Hermann Hesse to Peter Handke, or, on an international level, from James Joyce to Boris Pasternak.

But even the protagonist of *Wanderjahre* can be interpreted as a metonymic figure. Wilhelm Meister is no longer the center of attention as an individual as in *Lehrjahre*, but he becomes a novelistic device connecting a number of small, self-contained narrative units which are independent of one another yet also affect each other. There is no clearly defined linear plot structure. Wilhelm travels with his son Felix from one place to another, from one narrative unit to the other, as the direct or indirect witness of various modes of life. His travels, his encounters and conversations, readings and writings constitute the loosely connected links between the various independent units. The narrator digresses, in Roman Jakobson's words, "from the character to the setting in space and time."[21]

Goethe employed a similar technique in *Faust II*, when he admitted to Eckermann in a conversation of 1831, that he had used "die Fabel eines berühmten Helden bloß als eine Art von durchgehender Schnur, um darauf aneinanderzureihen, was er Lust hat."[22] This statement about the dramatic technique of *Faust II* applies equally to the structure of *Wanderjahre*, despite the great differences between the two works in genre and protagonist. Faust and Wilhelm Meister are to a large degree metonymic figures. Their fate is designed to be secondary to the reader's concern. Their main function within the disconnected plot structure is to direct the reader's attention by association or suggestion away from their problems as individual characters and toward the main themes or phenomena presented in these works. In Goethe's *Faust II* this effect is achieved by the technique, for example, in Act I of having the protagonist hardly participate in the dramatic action and giving him fewer than 200 lines out of a total of almost 2000 lines of dialogue. The audience's attention in Act I, which takes place at the imperial court, is directed towards the theme of the productivity of economic and aesthetic values. In the novel, this effect is created by having the protagonist meet an unimportant and superfluous character, and by the fact that their resulting conversation has no direct bearing on the subsequent plot. Roman Jakobson mentions this device as obligatory in Gogol, Tolstoj and Dostoevskij, pointing out by contrast that in the eighteenth-century novel it can be taken for granted that such an encounter "is of importance either to the hero or, at least, to the plot."[23] This observation can be illustrated by the following example from Goethe's *Lehrjahre*. The reader will remember Wilhelm's early encounters with a mysterious stranger in Books I and II, who later turns out to be the Abbé of Book VII, a representative of the Society of the Tower, secretly guiding Wilhelm's education and fate. In contrast to this carefully designed plot structure in *Lehrjahre*, Wilhelm Meister's first encounter in *Wanderjahre* is of no consequence for the further development of the plot. The external linkage of the encounter to the main plot is quite accidental: Wilhelm and his son Felix meet a character whose life story happens to resemble that of Saint Joseph. Hence he is called Saint Joseph the Second. After spending a few days with Saint Joseph the Second and his family, Wilhelm and Felix continue their journey never to see them again. Saint Joseph the Second never reappears or is mentioned again in the novel. The internal linkage of the story to the novel might be termed metonymic. Saint Joseph's name and the imitation of his legend stand for the model of the family as basic unit of social life and the transformation of its functions in 19th-century society.[24]

*Wanderjahre* is not, like *Lehrjahre*, a novel of individual development and education, or *Bildung*, but a novel about persons functioning in groups. Individual biography which, according to Georg Lukács, is the traditional theme and structure of the novel, is replaced by depiction of human social behavior in general. This constitutes a change in artistic code which Lukács refused to acknowledge, since, as a critic, he represented the school of "classical realism." For him, Goethe's *Lehrjahre* were unsurpassed as a model of realism, while he remained relatively silent about Wanderjahre.[25]

The basic unit of social life in *Wanderjahre* is the family. Marriage and family form the main theme of the interpolated novellas, which present variations in terms of 19th-century transformations and challenges.[26] However, not only the more intimate forms of social behavior, such as love and friendship are depicted, but also the more public forms of human association, such as educational, philanthropic, professional, economic, political and religious groups. They form the major part of the action of the frame. The most important groups include the Pedagogic Province, a kind of educational utopia, the secret Society of the Tower, which in its theory and practice resembles Freemasonry and their utopian goals at the end of the eighteenth century, the League of Emigrants whose members are to found a new society in America, and the League of Immigrants who stay behind in Europe, yet also plan to establish a new type of society in some remote area. Finally, there is the circle around Makarie, a saintly figure, who not only participates in human life on earth, but also in the life of the universe.

Makarie is one of Goethe's most daring literary creations: she is part of the solar system and center of the family of man depicted in the novel; she represents cosmic love regulating human action and affairs on earth. As Eric A. Blackall has said, "Makarie both mirrors and figures in the cosmos."[27] The relationship between her terrestrial and her sidereal existence fits the definition of metonymy: she appears as a nice old aunt, yet is found to be in relationship to the solar system. She is helpful everywhere,

> [...] unaufhaltsam in großen und kleinen Diensten, wandelte sie wie ein Engel Gottes auf Erden, indem ihr geistiges Ganze sich zwar um die Weltsonne, aber nach dem Überweltlichen in stetig zunehmenden Kreisen bewegte (III, 15).[28]

Makarie is connected by contiguity to divine power and fulfills the function of "Liebe ... von oben" within the microcosm of *Wanderjahre*.[29]

The most obvious example of metonymy in *Wanderjahre*, strikingly similar to Anna Karenina's handbag, is the *Besteck*, the case of surgical instruments which Wilhelm had acquired from the surgeon in *Lehrjahre*. Seriously wounded in an ambush by highwaymen in *Lehrjahre* (IV, 5), Wilhelm had been rescued by Natalie, his future wife, and his head wound was attended to by her family surgeon. Once Wilhelm has acquired the surgeon's instrument case as a kind of souvenir, it serves him in *Wanderjahre* as a metonymic reminder of his love for Natalie and the professional training as a surgeon on which he is determined to embark. The first reference to the *Besteck* occurs in Book I, Chapter 4, when Wilhelm pulls "etwas aus dem Busen, das halb wie eine Brieftasche, halb wie ein Besteck aussah." It is claimed by Jarno-Montan "als ein Altbekanntes," and Wilhelm admits that he carries it around "als eine Art von Fetisch [...], in dem Aberglauben, sein Schicksal hänge gewissermaßen von dessen Besitz ab" (I, 4). He asks Jarno-Montan to intervene with the Society of the Tower to plead for his training in a special profession. However, any information about the nature of this training is withheld from the reader at this point. It is almost twenty chapters, before the reader is finally informed of the identity of the mysterious object and its twofold metonymic implications with regard to Natalie as well as surgery. In a letter to Natalie in Book II, Chapter 11, Wilhelm relates the history of the *Besteck* and confesses that he has carried it with him ever since: "Freilich zu keinem Gebrauch, aber desto sicherer zu tröstlicher Erinnerung" (II, 11). Wilhelm considers the *Besteck* not only a "witness" to the moment when his good fortune began, but also as a silent reminder of his future profession as a surgeon. Instead of giving the reader an account of Wilhelm's early interest in medicine and the training in surgery he plans to undergo, the narrator focuses on the instrument case, an unessential, though contiguous object to the study of surgery. Before being informed of the profession Wilhelm is determined to enter, and receiving an account of the actual training in Book III, Chapter 3, the reader is treated to two extensive references to the *Besteck*.

Once its metonymic character is established, a similar case can be made for the central image of *Schlüssel* and *Kästchen*, key and little box or casket. There has been a great amount of scholarly speculation about the meaning of the casket and its key which is even graphically reproduced in Book II, Chapter 2.[30] It has, however, gone unrecognized that the *Kästchen* fits the definition of metonymy as substitution of container for contents. Scholarship has provided us with a whole list of different interpretations, although the contents of the *Kästchen* are never revealed to the reader. Throughout the novel, the casket is never unlocked by any of the protagonists.

Only once is it opened without the key by a jeweler, but immediately closed again with an ominous warning about its secret (III, 17). *Kästchen* and *Schlüssel* fulfill a similar function like Anna Karenina's handbag. As unessential objects they distract from the main events of the plot, while at the same time reenforcing its meaning. The casket is found by Wilhelm's son

Felix in a cavern, but becomes important to Wilhelm's relationship to a young woman, named Hersilie, who is attracted to father and son. When she obtains the key to the casket, she invites Wilhelm in a letter to bring the casket to be unlocked. However, she corrects herself in a postscript to the effect that actually Felix should be invited, since he was the one who found the casket. The mysterious casket then assumes a crucial role in an encounter between Hersilie and Felix, when he tries to open the casket by force and breaks the key. After his parting in anger and despair, Hersilie discovers that the key is not broken, but the two parts are held together by magnetic attraction. Felix is revived by Wilhelm as a surgeon after a serious riding accident which occurred after he has left Hersilie without hope of reconciliation. Casket and key obviously serve to trace the mysterious erotic attraction of father and son to Hersilie, who has to make a choice between the older and younger man.

Another example of metonymic discourse is Lenardo's diary which is crowded with technical details about the home industry of spinning and weaving, while he is on a passionate search of a lost love whom he finally finds among the weavers. She turns out to be a progressive and socially aware entrepreneur who tries to alleviate the social problems caused by the industrial revolution. Upon his request Goethe had received a report on the Swiss home industry from Heinrich Meyer which he had inserted almost verbatim into part I of Lenardo's diary (III, 5).[31] Eric A. Blackall's analysis of these passages as written "in the symbolic mode" misses the point.[32] It is a highly technical description of spinning and weaving, abounding in unessential details. As far as the narrative is concerned, there is nothing even remotely symbolic about information regarding the revolutions of the spinning reel and the amount of yarn produced per thousand revolutions (III, 5). But such information fulfills a metonymic function with regard to Lenardo's search for Nachodine or Susanne, contributing to the realism of the novel. The function of this passage reminds the modern reader of the description of the Dublin water-supply system in James Joyce's *Ulysses*, when Bloom returns home for the ritual hand washing before the abnegation of the Homeric slaying of the suitors.[33]

Absence of linear plot line, condensation of narrative and elimination of plot are essential elements of the narrative strategy of the fictive editor of *Wanderjahre*, who has replaced the omniscient narrator of *Lehrjahre*. There is a conscious attempt made to present almost each narrative unit as a document, either a letter written by Wilhelm or any other character of the novel, or a book, diary or manuscript read by them. Many of the inserted novellas are presented as manuscripts from an archive administered by the fictive editor. The fiction of a central archive, or even several archives, as for example, "Makariens Archiv," and the fiction of the narrator's editorial tasks are essential to the realism of *Wanderjahre*.[34] The amusing tale of "Die gefährliche Wette," for example, is introduced as a text from the archives inserted by the editor without further explanation, "weil unsre Angelegenheiten immer ernsthafter werden und wir für dergleichen Unregelmäßigkeiten fernerhin keine Stelle finden möchten" (III, 8). Other novellas, such as "Der Mann von funfzig jahren," are introduced with great consideration for the public's reading habits:

> Der Angewöhnung des werten Publikums zu schmeicheln, welches seit geraumer Zeit Gefallen findet, sich stückweise unterhalten zu lassen, gedachten wir erst, nachstehende Erzählung in mehreren Abteilungen vorzutegen. Der innere Zusammenhang jedoch, nach Gesinnungen, Empfindungen und Ereignissen betrachtet, veranlaßte einen fortlaufenden Vortrag (II, 3).

At the climax of the novella, the editor, however, interrupts the narrative with the statement that he can no longer proceed by means of depiction, but must switch to narration and reflection, if he is to penetrate the respective moods of the protagonists (II, 5). The final conclusion of the conflict is only summarily indicated by the editor and is largely left to the reader's imagination.

Time and again, the editor intrudes upon the narrative with his comments and plot summaries. The criticism of the theater in the Pedagogic Province meets with the editor's express disapproval, if not censure (II, 8), while parts of the outline of the American utopia are withheld, on the grounds that the editor considers them too controversial (III, 1). The most dramatic example of fragmentary narration is the novella "Nicht zu weit," which is related by the editor in bits and pieces on the basis of an incomplete oral account, while the conclusion of the novella is never told (III, 10).

Toward the end of *Wanderjahre*, the editor admits that the duty of communicating, describing, explicating and condensing has become increasingly difficult:

> Wer fühlt nicht, daß wir uns diesmal dem Ende nähern, wo die Furcht, in Umständlichkeiten zu verweilen, mit dem Wunsche, nichts völlig unerörtert zu lassen, uns in Zwiespalt versetzt. [...] Wir sind also gesormen, dasjenige, was wir damals gewuflt und erfahren, ferner auch das, was später zu unserer Kenntnis kam,

zusammenzufassen und in diesem Sinne das übernommene ernste Geschäft eines treuen Referenten getrost abzuschließen (III, 14).

The device of the fictive editor justifies the fragmentary mode of narration, the abolition of a chronological ordering of the plot, and the constant motivation and realization of literary devices in *Wanderjahre*.

On the basis of the evidence presented, *Wanderjahre* takes the form of a revolution against the given artistic code, as represented by *Lehrjahre*. Goethe seems to have viewed deformation of this code "as a more accurate rendition of reality," while his conservative critics considered this deformation until recently "a distortion of reality," an indication of Goethe's artistic decline and senility.[35] Although metaphor and metonomy cannot completely be separated and there are impressive examples of transitional and combined usage of both tropes, especially since metonomy has a tendency to move in the direction of metaphor,[36] Goethe's comparatively radical switch from metaphor and classicism in *Lehrjahre* toward metonymy and realism in *Wanderjahre* cannot be overlooked and must be considered revolutionary.

While the structure of *Wanderjahre* is undeniably similar to that of the modern novel, the thematic problems of Goethe's last novel prove to be also astonishingly progressive, anticipating major issues of the nineteenth century, including such problems of modern society as those of labor and education, and such general questions as those of religion.[37] A cursory look at Karl Löwith's study of the revolution in nineteenth-century thought from Hegel to Nietzsche will suffice to show that Goethe was not only aware of the pressing problems of his age, but was also an active participant in the debate, shaping the revolution of nineteenth-century thought.[38] This is the first part of the historical argument for revolutionary realism in Goethe's *Wanderjahre*.

The plot situation clearly shows that Goethe was concerned with the relationship of man as a private individual and as a citizen in bourgeois society. This dualistic aspect of man has been the "fundamental problem of all modern theories of the state and society," as Karl Löwith has pointed out.[39] Goethe tried to overcome this incompatibility in *Wanderjahre* through the concept of renunciation (*Entsagung*), thus establishing a balance between the two basic aspects of human existence in modern society. The subtitle of the novel refers to "die Entsagenden," the renunciants, i.e., the group which is able to achieve its balance through renunciation. After Goethe, renunciation and/or resignation became a major theme in bourgeois literature from Balzac to Flaubert, Gottfried Keller, Wilhelm Raabe and Theodor Fontane.[40] The function of society in *Wanderjahre* is "Gleichheit in den Hauptsachen zu erhalten und in läßlichen Dingen einem jeden seinen Willen zu gestatten" (III, 11). This seemingly liberal design nevertheless shows some unmistakable traits of a police state. The American utopia in *Wanderjahre* is highly regimented day and night by telegraphic time signals, and it is described as consisting of people who do not think about justice, but police: "Wer sich unbequem erweist, wird beseitigt" (III, 11). Penalties consist of expropriation and of "separation from civil society": "Absonderung von der bürgerlichen Gesellschaft, gelinder, entschiedener, kurzer und kinger nach Befund" (III, 11).

Other problems treated in *Wanderjahre* concern work and education. Both, according to Löwith, became "the substance of the life of bourgeois society" in the nineteenth century.[41] Goethe described the dangers of the industrial revolution and the threat of unemployment. As one character in the novel explains:

> Was mich aber drückt, ist doch eine Handelssorge, leider nicht for den Augenblick, nein! für alle Zukunft. Das über-handnehmende Maschinenwesen quält und ängstigt mich, [...] Man denkt daran, man spricht davon, und weder Denken noch Reden kann Hülfe bringen (III, 13).

The alternatives offered in *Wanderjahre* are emigration to America and the founding of utopian communes at home and abroad. In his speech to the emigrants, their leader Lenardo explains that people are convinced of the high value of private property (*Grundbesitz*): "Wir [...] sind genötigt, ihn als das Erste, das Beste anzusehen, was dem Menschen werden könne." It is evident that traditional society is seen here as based on the concept of private property. However, this concept is replaced in *Wanderjahre* by the idea of work and achievement when Lenardo adds: "Wenn das, was der Mensch besitzt, von großen Wert ist, so muß man demjenigen, was er tut und leistet, noch einen größern zuschreiben" (III, 9). This new idea of work in *Wanderjahre* comes very close to the philosophy of Adam Smith, Hegel and Marx who defined man in terms of his work: man exists only insofar as he produces.[42]

Education in *Wanderjahre* is no longer a privilege of the propertied classes, but is related in a modern way to work. Man is urged to acquire a useful skill which can be applied for the common good. Thus, Wilhelm becomes a surgeon, a profession which at that time was still considered a craft, almost on a par with the work of a barber. Universal education is renounced in favor of specialization of the individual who, together with others like him, contributes to the functioning of society. Goethe's idea of specialization in education foreshadows the division of labor in modern industrial society.

Finally, the beginnings of nineteenth-century criticism of religion, specifically of Christianity, are reflected in *Wanderjahre*. Religion is transformed into a kind of "secular piety" (*Weltfrömmigkeit*), as it is called (II, 7). In the Pedagogic Province, attitudes of "reverence" (*Ehrfurcht*) are taught; three types of religion are acknowledged: an ethical kind of religion, based on reverence of that which is above us; a philosophical religion, based on reverence of that which is equal to us; and finally Christian religion as reverence of that which is more lowly than us. Christ's suffering and death is withheld from the students of the Pedagogic Province. Christ appears "als ein wahrer Philosoph [...], als ein Weiser im höchsten Sinne" (II, 2). Thus Christianity becomes secularized and transcended by philosophy as in Hegel's writings. Antecedents of nineteenth-century anti-Semitism are to be found in the American utopia where Jews are not tolerated (III, 11).

However, the revolutionary realism of Goethe's *Wanderjahre* becomes evident not only in the problems raised and discussed at length in the novel, but also by comparison with other works of the period and by contrast with the development of realism in Germany after 1848, after the failure and defeat of the political revolution. This is the second part of the historical argument for revolutionary realism in Goethe's last novel of 1829. As possible examples of revolutionary realism in prose, I have mentioned Heinrich Heine's *Ideen: Das Buch Le Grand* of 1826 and Georg Büchner's novella *Lenz* of 1835 (published in 1839). Heine's *Ideen: Das Buch Le Grand* shows all the indications of "revolutionary realism," such as metonymy, avoidance of chronological narration and empirical description. What is presented is not a story with a plot, but "a state of mind," or even "the genesis of political consciousness," as Jeffrey L. Sammons has observed.[43] Personal experiences, ideas and views on literature, history, society and politics are integrated into the text. Le Grand, a French drummajor, is the central metonymic figure of the narrative, and his drum is a metonymic expression of his character and cause. Le Grand is metonymically related to the grand cause of the French revolution and to the defeat of *La Grande Armée* in the Russian campaign of 1812. Since Le Grand does not speak German, he relates the cause of the French revolution and the defeat of the French army by playing on his drum which is finally destroyed by the narrator so that it will not serve any enemy of freedom. The narrator's opposition to the political system is expressed in the form of the destruction of an object metonymically related to the causes of *liberté* and *égalité*.

Büchner's novella *Lenz*, written only six years after Goethe's *Wanderjahre*, was designed neither as a clinical report on the *Sturm und Drang* dramatist J. M. R. Lenz (1751–1792) nor as a case study of schizophrenia, but as a presentation of insanity in verbal art. The presentation, however, is neither metaphoric nor fantastic, but realistic.[44] At the very beginning of the novella, the narrator metonymically digresses from the character of Lenz to the landscape. Lenz's disorientation and changes of mood are related to a metonymic chain of weather changes in the landscape which reflect his anxiety and mental imbalance. However, the relationship between landscape and mental state is not presented as causal. Throughout the novella, all changes of Lenz's psyche are metonymically related to his surroundings. At one time, Lenz feels suffocated by contact with his environment: "Jetzt ist es mir so eng, so eng! Sehn sie, es ist mir manchmal, als stieß' ich mit den Händen an den Himmel."[45] Another time, Lenz feels, "als könnte er eine ungeheure Faust hinauf in den Himmel ballen [...], als könnte er die Welt mit den Zähnen zermalmen."[46] These imagined hostile acts are metonymic gestures directed against God by whom he feels betrayed and abandoned. Not until the end, when his sanity has waned, are the contacts with his surroundings completely severed. Lenz becomes totally indifferent to the landscape through which he travels, when he is brought back to Straßburg. Although he continues to live, the life of his mind has come to its end. The absence of plot and the summary conclusion increase the effects of "revolutionary realism" in Buchner's novella.

The conservative restoration after 1848 with its aversion to industrialization, high finance and bourgeois liberalism affected also the aesthetics of prose and the concept of reality in verbal art. After the defeat of the revolution, there was a realism debate which re-introduced German classicism as its model and emphasized the organization of the individual work of literature as an aesthetic whole. Organized wholeness, as we find it in the novellas and novels by Keller, Raabe and Stifter, was considered a specifically realist element of verbal art. Between 1848 and 1860, literary theory in Germany considered close organization and integration a presupposition for the realistic work of art.[47] The "revolutionary realism" of the older Goethe, of Heine and Bachner was abandoned or transformed according to classical models like *Lehrjahre*, which now became the prime example of the *Bildungsroman*, imitated by the authors of the nineteenth century. The new "classical realism" that emerged after 1848 was marked by predominance of metaphoric (or symbolic) discourse. It was only logical to name it "poetic realism" (*poetischer Realismus*).[48] As Clemens Heselhaus has said, "the revolution in realism became a wasted revolution—like the revolution of 1848."[49] It took the modern novel of a Döblin, Broch and Musil to remind us of the "revolutionary realism" of Goethe's *Wanderjahre* and of his contemporaries.

## NOTES

1.  See Klaus F. Gille, *Wilhelm Meister im Urteil der Zeitgenossen: Ein Beitrag zur Wirkungsgeschichte Goethes* (Assen: van Gorcum, 1971), pp. 209–38.

2.  *Goethes Briefe*, ed. Karl Robert Mandelkow, 2nd ed. (Hamburg: Wegner, 1968), II, 231.

3.  Eric A. Blackall, *Goethe and the Novel* (Ithaca, N.Y.: Cornell University Press, 1976), p. 261.

4.  See *Wilhelm Meister im Urteil der Zeitgenossen*, pp. 32–47.

5.  See Erich Trunz, "Altersstil," *Goethe-Handbuch*, ed. Alfred Zastrau (Stuttgart: Metzler, 1961), I, pp. 178–88.

6.  Roman Jakobson and Morris Halle, *Fundamentals of Language*, 2nd rev. ed. (The Hague, Paris: Mouton, 1971), pp. 91–92. For a discussion of Roman Jakobson's concepts see Henrik Birnbaum, "On the Poetry of Prose: Land- and Cityscape 'Defamiliarized' in *Doctor Zhivago*," *Fiction and Drama in Eastern and Southeastern Europe*, ed. Henrik Birnbaum and Thomas Eekman (Columbus, Ohio: Slavica Publishers, 1980), pp. 55–57.

7.  Richard A. Lanham, *A Handlist of Rhetorical Terms* (Berkeley, Los Angeles: University of California Press, 1968), pp. 66–67.

8.  *Fundamentals of Language*, p. 91.

9.  Heinrich Lausberg, *Elemente der literarischen Rhetorik*, 3rd ed. (München: Hueber, 1967), pp. 66–78. See also Heinrich Lausberg, *Handbuch der literarischen Rhetorik* (München: Hueber, 1960), I, 285–91; 292–98.

10. *Fundamentals of Language*, p. 92.

11. David H. Miles, "Reality and the two Realisms: Mimesis in Auerbach, Lukács, and Handke," *Monatshefte*, 71 (1979), 371–78, esp. 374.

12. Roman Jakobson, "On Realism in Art (1921)," *Readings in Russian Poetics: Formalist and Structuralist Views*, ed. Ladislav Matejka and Krystyna Pomorska (Cambridge, Mass.: MIT Press, 1971), pp. 38–46.

13. See Wilhelm Emrich, "Symbolinterpretation und Mythenforschung," *Protest und Verheißung: Studien zur klassischen und modernen Dichtung*, 2nd ed. (Frankfurt am Main/Bonn: Athenäum, 1963), pp. 67–94, esp. 71–86.

14. Wilhelm Emrich, "Das Problem der Symbolinterpretation im Hinblick auf Goethes *Wanderjahre*," *Protest und Verheißung*, pp. 48–66; Eric A. Blackall, *Goethe and the Novel*, p. 269.

15. "On Realism in Art," pp. 40, 41.

16. *Fundamentals of Language*, p. 92.

17. "On Realism in Art," pp. 41–45.

18. Hermann Broch, "James Joyce und die Gegenwart (1936)," *Gesammelte Werke* (Zürich: Rhein-Verlag, 1955), VI, 206.

19. See *Wilhelm Meister im Urteil der Zeitgenossen*, pp. 306–312

20. See volume VIII of Hamburger Ausgabe, ed. Erich Trunz (Hamburg: Wegner, 1950), pp. 603–607. See also *Wilhelm Meisters Wanderjahre*, ed. Ehrhard Bahr (Stuttgart: Reclam, 1982).

21. *Fundamentals of Language*, p. 20.

22. Conversation with Goethe on 13 February 1831. See Johann Peter Eckermann, *Gespräche mit Goethe in den letzten Jahren seines Lebens*, ed. H. H. Houben, 9th ed. (Leipzig: Brockhaus, 1909), p. 355.

23. "On Realism in Art," pp. 44.

24. See Ehrhard Bahr, *Die Ironie im Spätwerk Goethes: diese sehr ernsten Scherze: Studien zum West-östlichen Divan, zu den Wanderjahren und zu Faust II* (Berlin: Erich Schmidt, 1972), pp. 90–93; Jane K. Brown, *Goethe's Cyclical Narratives Die Unterhaltungen deutscher Ausgewanderten and Wilhelm Meisters Wanderjahre* (Chapel Hill, North Carolina: University of North Carolina Press, 1975), pp. 33–44; A. G. Steer, *Goethe's Science in the Structure of the Wanderjahre* (Athens, Georgia: University of Georgia Press, 1979), pp. 17–33; Hannelore Schlaffer, *Wilhelm Meister: Das Ende der Kunst und die Wiederkehr des Mythos* (Stuttgart: Metzler, 1980), pp. 26–34.

25. Georg Lukács, *Die Theorie des Romans: Ein geschichtsphilosophischer Versuch über die Formen der großen Epik*, 3rd ed. (Neuwied: Luchterhand, 1965), pp. 69–82; Georg Lukács, "Wilhelm Meisters Lehrjahre," *Faust und Faustus* (Reinbek: Rowohit, 1967), pp. 30–46. See also David H. Miles, "Reality and the Two Realisms," pp. 373–75.

26. Cf. Steer, *Goethe's Science*, pp. 17–23. See Bahr, *Die Ironie im Spätwerk Goethes*, p. 93; Schlaffer, *Wilhelm Meister*, pp. 26–34.

27. *Goethe and the Novel*, p. 242.

28. Goethe's *Wanderjahre* are cited by book and chapter, according to the text of the Hamburger Ausgabe, vol. VIII, ed. Erich Trunz (Hamburg: Wegner, 1950). The only English translation available is *Wilhelm Meister's Travel*, transl. Edward Bell (London: Bell, 1902).

29. Bahr, *Die Ironie im Spätwerk Goethes*, p. 173.

30. Volker Dürr, "Geheimnis und Aufklärung: Zur pädagogischen Funktion des Kästchens in *Wilhelm Meisters Wanderjahren*,"*Monatshefte*, 74 (1982), 11–29. For a summary see A. G. Steer, *Goethe's Science*, pp. 130–32.

31. See Weimarer Ausgabe I, vol. 25, pp. 261–71.

32. *Goethe and the Novel*, pp. 267–69.

33. James Joyce, *Ulysses* (New York: Modern Library, 1934), p. 655. I am indebted to William J. Lillyman for this reference. See also Stuart Gilbert, *James Joyce's Ulysses: A Study* (New York: Vintage Books, 1955), p. 372.

34. Volker Neuhaus, "Die Archivfiktion in *Wilhelm Meisters Wanderjahren*," *Euphorion*, 62 (1968), 13–27.

35. "On Realism in Art," p. 41. For the critical reception of *Wanderjahre* see Bernd Peschken, *Entsagung in Wilhelm Meisters Wanderjahren* (Bonn: Bouvier, 1968), pp. 5–9; Klaus F. Gille (ed.), *Goethes Wilhelm Meister: Zur Rezeptionsgeschichte der Lehr- und Wanderjahre* (Königstein/Taunus: Athenäum, 1979), pp. 94–194.

36. See Henrik Birnbaum, "On the Poetry of Prose," pp. 55–57; Heinrich Lausberg, *Elemente der literarischen Rhetorik*, p. 77. Furthermore, the bipolarity of Jakobson's model does not allow for a mutually exclusive choice.

37. See Ehrhard Bahr, "Goethe's *Wanderjahre* as an Experimental Novel," *New Views of the European Novel*, ed. R. G. Collins and Kenneth McRobbie (Winnipeg: University of Manitoba Press, 1972), pp. 61–71; identical with *Mosaic*, 5 (1972), No. 3, 61–71. See also Ehrhard Bahr, "Realismus und Totalität: *Wilhelm Meisters Wanderjahre* als Roman des 19. Jahrhunderts," *Formen realistischer Erzählkunst: Festschrift für Charlotte Jolles*, ed. Jörg Thunecke (Nottingham: Sherwood Press Agencies, 1979), pp. 88–92.

38. Karl Löwith, *From Hegel to Nietzsche: The Revolution in Nineteenth-Century Thought*, transl. David E. Green (Garden City, N.Y.: Doubleday, 1964).

39. Ibid., p. 232.

40. See Arthur Henkel, *Entsagung: Eine Studie zu Goethes Altersroman*, 2nd ed. (Tübingen: Niemeyer, 1964); Bernd Peschken, *Entsagung in Wilhelm Meisters Wanderjahren* (Bonn: Bouvier, 1968); Bahr, *Die Ironie im Spätwerk Goethes*, pp. 122–24. See also Georg Lukács, *Studies in European Realism*, intro. Alfred Kazin (New York: Grosset & Dunlap, 1964), p. 52; Karl Richter, *Resignation: Eine Studie zum Werk Theodor Fontanes* (Stuttgart: Kohlhammer, 1966); Elisabeth Rockenbach Trafton, "Resignation in Wilhelm Raabes Stuttgarter Trilogie," Ph.D. Diss. University of California, Los Angeles, 1978. See also Thomas Degering, *Das Elend der Entsagung: Goethes, Wilhelm Meisters Wanderjahre* (Bonn: Bouvier, 1982).

41. *From Hegel to Nietzsche*, p. 260.

42. See Anneliese Klingenberg, *Goethes Roman Wilhelm Meisters Wanderjahre oder die Entsagenden: Quellen und Komposition* (Berlin/Weimar: Aufbau-Verlag, 1972), pp. 109–113; 198–201.

43. Jeffrey L. Sammons, *Heinrich Heine: A Modern Biography* (Princeton: Princeton University Press, 1979), p. 128; Stefan Blesin, *Die Romane Goethes* (Königstein/Ts.: Athenäum, 1979), pp. 150–57.

44. See David G. Richards, *Georg Bachner and the Birth of the Modern Drama* (Albany, N.Y.: State University of New York Press, 1977), pp. 116–48; J. P. Stern, *Re-interpretations: Seven Studies in Nineteenth-Century German Literature* (New York: Basic Books, 1964), pp. 128–54; Benno von Wiese, *Die deutsche Novelle von Goethe bis Kafka: Interpretationen* II (Düsseldorf: Bagel, 1962), pp. 104–26.

45. Georg Buchner, *Werke und Briefe*, 2nd ed. (München: Deutscher Taschenbuch-Verlag, 1967), p. 77. See also p. 81.

46. Ibid., p. 78.

47. See Helmuth Widhammer, *Realismus und klassizistische Tradition: Zur Theorie der Literatur in Deutschland 1848–1860* (Tübingen: Niemeyer, 1972), p. 144; Helmuth Widhammer, *Die Literaturtheorie des deutschen Realismus (1848–1860)* (Stuttgart: Metzler, 1977), pp. 68–72.

48. See Otto Ludwig, "Poetischer Realismus", *Gesammelte Schriften*, V (Leipzig: Grunow, 1891), pp. 458–62.

49. Clemens Heselhaus, "Das Realismusproblem," *Begriffibestimmungen des literarischen Realismus*, ed. Richard Brinkmann (Darmstadt: Wissenschaftliche Buchgesellschaft, 1969), p. 362.

ERNST BEHLER

# Wilhelm Meisters Lehrjahre *and the Poetic Unity of the Novel in Early German Romanticism*

T he reception of Goethe's novel *Wilhelm Meisters Lehrjahre* of 1795–1796 by the early German romantics was definitely a major milestone in the history of the work and one of the first remarkable public appreciations of the accomplishments of Goethe's narrative fiction after his Italian journey. Although I am not persuaded that an account of this event is essential to our understanding of this novel today, I fully recognize that this reception even in its negative, oppositional aspect can illuminate significant features of *Wilhelm Meister* which otherwise might remain undetected. This confrontation was also crucial to the formation of the romantic literary theory, especially that of the novel. Repercussions of *Wilhelm Meister* were even more successfully manifest in the rise of the romantic novel itself and the appearance of Wilhelm Meister's brothers: Franz Sternbald, Heinrich von Ofterdingen, Godwi, and Florentin.

Specialists have treated this chapter of literary history quite frequently, although with considerably diverse results. They approached the romantic encounter with *Wilhelm Meister* chiefly from the perspective of influence and thereby placed primary emphasis on Goethe's novel and its impact upon the romantics. Only in recent decades did this accentuation shift to the romantic literary theory itself as it emerged in reaction and even in opposition to *Wilhelm Meister*. I should like to go one step further by focusing on the

From *Goethe's Narrative Fiction*. © 1983 by Walter de Gruyter & Co.

differences in the notions of poetic unity generated by *Wilhelm Meister*—or the understanding of this novel by the romantics—and the novel produced during the period of early German romanticism. I should also like to consider a few of these early romantic novels and pose the question as to whether this vantage point of poetic unity justifies our calling them true brothers of *Wilhelm Meister*. This approach would appear to shift even further away from *Wilhelm Meister* and Goethe's narrative fiction, which this symposium is honoring. Yet my objective is to promote, through this comparative analysis, a better view of the individuality of Goethe's novel. Before we can approach the theme of poetic unity in *Wilhelm Meister* and the early romantic novel, however, I will have to summarize briefly how this relationship has been viewed in previous scholarship and also touch upon the question about the position the novel actually occupied in the genre theory of early German romanticism.

We certainly no longer agree today with Rudolf Haym, who in 1870 seriously maintained that virtually the entirety of the romantic literary theory originated with Friedrich Schlegel's reading of *Wilhelm Meisters Lehrjahre*.[1] Arthur O. Lovejoy refused this opinion most convincingly in 1916 by demonstrating that the concept of romanticism had a much older tradition and corresponded more closely to authors such as Boccaccio, Cervantes, and Shakespeare than to Goethe.[2] Since then, critics have come to realize the considerable differences between Goethe's *Lehrjahre* and the goals of romantic literary theory.[3] The edition of fragmentary notes on this novel by Novalis and Friedrich Schlegel even led critics to assume that these early romantics heaped ridicule and vented hostility upon Goethe's *Meister*, while praising the novel publicly for pragmatic reasons. Indeed, the divergencies between the romantics' public statements about *Wilhelm Meister* and their private remarks in letters and notebooks are considerable and can easily make us wonder about the intellectual honesty of these young critics.[4] When Goethe read in an early edition of Novalis' writing that his *Wilhelm Meister* was unpoetic to the highest degree, a "satire against poetry," so much so that whoever took this work truly to heart would not read another novel,[5] he became so enraged that one might justify dating his final rupture with the romantics to this discovery.[6] Recent criticism has been able to ascertain, however, that these discrepancies between public statements and private observations about Goethe's novel have objective reasons, that they derive from a dualistic and quite critical view of this work by the romantics, and that the sensitive reader can very well ascertain reservations, objections, and even opposition in the published statements on *Wilhelm Meister* as well.[7]

Whereas the romantic theory of the novel has now been recognized in its individuality and variance from the model of *Wilhelm Meister*, the particular nature of the romantic novel itself remains an unresolved problem. Still today many critics dealing with *Florentin, Heinrich von Ofterdingen*, or *Godwi*, will pronounce what Caroline Schlegel exclaimed on October 15, 1798, while reading Tieck's *Franz Sternbalds Wanderungen*: "da ist der Wilhelm Meister und zu viel Wilhelm Meister."[8] Most critics still compare the early romantic novel with an ideal which this particular type of prose work did not want to represent at all. Goethe had a distinct sense for the particular beauty of Tieck's prose style[9] and sympathized with him for being measured against standards to which he laid no claim whatsoever.[10] All this demonstrates the overwhelming impression Goethe's *Wilhelm Meister* has made upon German literary history as well as the sense of unprecedented novelty this work must have conveyed to its contemporaries. Friedrich Schlegel captured this revolutionary aspect of the novel in the one lapidary sentence: "Die Französische Revolution, Fichtes Wissenschaftslehre, und Goethes Meister sind die größten Tendenzen des Zeitalters."[11]

Indeed, the first response to this novel among the early romantics was one of spontaneous praise. We are not certain whether the famous phrase— "Morgenröte echter Kunst und reiner Schönheit"—with which Friedrich Schlegel hailed Goethe in 1795 actually refers to *Wilhelm Meister*; most likely this statement relates to his *Römische Elegien*.[12] In several instances Schlegel describes Goethe in these early years, with obvious reference to *Wilhelm Meister*, as representing a new awakening of poetry in prose.[13] August Wilhelm Schlegel demonstrated the truly poetic character of *Wilhelm Meister* by comparing its prose rhythm to the rhyme of poetry.[14] Novalis was of the opinion that all previous novels had to be qualified by an adjective, whereas Goethe's *Wilhelm Meister* was the novel's novel, the novel as such.[15]

Two terms appear most frequently in these early statements on Goethe's *Wilhelm Meister*: "poetic" and "modern." Deviating from the Aristotelian tradition and the authors of the *ars poetica* and strongly inspired by Plato, these critics gave the term "poetic" a new meaning. Poetry, as August Wilhelm Schlegel put it, is not a passive imitation of nature, but an active transformation of reality originating in the creative mind and resulting in a special form of unity shaped by the power of the imagination.[16] Friedrich Schlegel called the poetic unity of a work of literature "structure and arrangement" and derived this concept from the Greek term μορφ επεον;[17] but he usually circumscribed the concept of poetic unity by the term "harmony" and saw the harmony of poetic works as resting upon an inner conformity with themselves.[18] Overemphasizing the poetic character of

Goethe's work in cumulative phrasing, he says in the *Athenäum*: "Goethes rein poetische Poesie ist die vollständigste Poesie der Poesie."[19]

The term "modern" refers to the progressive nature of a striving toward an infinite perfectibility. Such striving has not severed bonds with the past, but maintains the most intimate relationship with the ancients. Yet instead of an imitation of the letter of the ancients in the style of the classicist tradition, this relationship aims at emulating the spirit of classical antiquity. Modern poetry also integrates philosophical reflection with the creative process and unites the author's intellectual, reflective discourse with the fictional process. On this basis Friedrich Schlegel could say in his *Gespräch über die Poesie* of 1800 that Goethe's *Wilhelm Meister* opened a new perspective "auf das, was die höchste Aufgabe aller Dichtkunst zu sein scheint, die Harmonie des Klassischen und Romantischen," and that its author could become "der Stifter und das Haupt einer neuen Poesie ... for uns und die Nachwelt."[20]

This understanding of *Wilhelm Meister* as a profoundly "poetic" work of literature deserves some closer attention in order to grasp the basic difference between the poetic unity of Goethe's novel and that intended by novelistic works of the early romantic movement. From the point of view of the classicist theory, still valid at the time of the reception of *Wilhelm Meister* by the early romantics, it was by all means unusual to consider a prose work like the novel as poetic. The novel was indeed excluded from the poetic genres represented within the canon of the classicist literary theory. This attitude is still reflected in Schiller's and Goethe's correspondence on *Wilhelm Meister*, when on October 20, 1797, Schiller writes, for instance: "Die Form des Meisters, wie überhaupt jede Romanform, ist schlechthin nicht poetisch." He then adds with some hesitation: "Weil es aber ein echt poetischer Geist ist, der sich dieser Form bediente und in dieser Form die poetischen Zustände ausdrückte, so entsteht ein sonderbares Schwanken zwischen einer prosaischen und poetischen Stimmung, für das ich keinen rechten Namen weiß."[21] In sharp contrast to the prevailing doctrine of their own time, the early romantics were ready to recognize as poetry, in the genuine sense of the word, prose works like the novel. Thereby they made an inroad into the dominating classicist doctrine which is hard for us to appreciate today because their view has become a common and established one. The main impulse for this romantic "revolution" of the classicist theory of poetry certainly came from Goethe's *Meister*, as evidenced in Friedrich Schlegel's statement: "Diese wunderbare Prosa ist Prosa und doch Poesie,"[22] and by similar statements made by August Wilhelm Schlegel and Novalis. The reason for this appreciation of the genuinely poetic character of *Wilhelm Meister* was without a doubt Goethe's innovative manner of narration which—through its unique way of foreshadowings, correspondences, symbolization, and irony within the work—created a form of unity shaped by the power of imagination. This awakening of poetry in prose appeared so convincing that Friedrich Schlegel did not hesitate to put this poetry of prose on a par with the highest accomplishment of classical literature and thereby recognized the novel as the most characteristic medium of modern literature.[23]

During the early stage of this reception, the "poetic" quality of *Wilhelm Meister* because of its pronounced imaginative thrust is occasionally equated with the term "romantic." The reason for this association of the "poetic" with the "romantic" lies obviously in the impression, as Karl Robert Mandelkow has pointed out,[24] that just as this novel transcended through its innovative manner of narration the prosaic character of the eighteenth-century novel, it also established through its events the picaresque, adventuresome, and "romantic" atmosphere of the postmedieval and romantic time lost through the rise of the bourgeois age. Yet this appreciation of Goethe's novelistic innovations is accompanied by the progressive realization that this highly poetic and eminently modern novel does not fully correspond to what came to be established for these critics as the "romantic" style. It did not belong for them to that tradition from which they derived their own literary heritage and which they sought to restore. The phrase that Goethe's novel is not romantic is a frequent refrain in Friedrich Schlegel's pronouncements on *Wilhelm Meister* from 1797 until 1808.[25] A subtle distinction between the poetic and the romantic thus arose, and there appeared to be two different types of novelistic unity—one of which seen as poetic and the other as romantic. In view of Novalis' remark that the romantic perished in *Wilhelm Meister*,[26] this observation sometimes assumes a caustic note and comes to mean, as in his letter to Tieck of February 23, 1800, that together with the romantic the poetic quality of *Wilhelm Meister* disappeared.[27] Friedrich Schlegel, in contrast to Novalis, maintained more consistently the poetic character of *Wilhelm Meister* while denying its romantic quality. Yet taken together, these observations strongly evidence that the novel envisioned by this "school" was more and more conceptualized as something basically different from Goethe's creation.

Yet before considering the structural differences between the poetic unity of *Wilhelm Meister* and that of the early romantic novel more closely, I should like to clarify the usage of the term "romantic." The discovery of the close relationship between "Romanpoesie," i.e., the poetry of the novel or the poetry of the romance, and "romantische Poesie," romantic poetry, in the critical terminology of these authors[28] has led critics to believe that the romantic literary theory actually abolished all literary genres by establishing the novel, *Roman*, as the single all-embracing genre for the modern age.[29] As a matter of fact, for Friedrich Schlegel the novel comprised the spirit of modernity to such a degree that he considered this genre to encompass all other genres of modern literature. And indeed, many of the characteristics attributed to the novel could just as well be ascribed to other genres of romantic literature. Yet Schlegel's concept of the novel has a characteristic double meaning and designates, first of all, the spirit of modernity animating all modern genres and, second, a special genre which gained prominence in the modern age and manifested itself through great authors. This double use of the concepts *Roman* and *romantisch* is by no means a terminological extravagancy, but reveals a difficulty deriving from the subject matter itself.

These considerations are closely related to the genre theory of the Schlegel brothers, which because of its strong historical thrust, can also elucidate the distinction between the poetic unity of *Wilhelm Meister* and that of the romantic novel. There was a general tendency in the age of Goethe to deduce the classical epic and the modern novel from the same source, namely, epic narration, and to consider both as special manifestations of the epic genre. Schelling, Hegel, even Goethe held this opinion, still advanced in Georg Lukács' *Theorie des Romans*. With their strong emphasis on the historical moment during the inception of a genre, the Schlegel brothers obviously could not accept such an unspecified and global derivation of the novel. Just like the classical epic, the novel too had its particular historical realm. Considering the history of literature with this sharply delineated historical sense, even Virgil's "epopee" does not share that specific poetic unity which distinguishes Homer's epic. Both creations appear to be built upon completely different principles of poetic unity, and each of them, in the last analysis, is a matchless art object *sui generis*.[30] Attempts to imitate the classical epic in the romantic age, as Ariosto had done, prove that compared to Homer the art of narration had entered an essentially different period in which the poetic unity of the classical epic can no longer be achieved. This becomes evident when in these romantic works a slight persiflage or irony shows up,[31] completely alien to the classical style with its uninterrupted flow of narration.[32] Contrary to Schelling and Hegel who regretted the inability of their age to create a genuine epic, Friedrich Schlegel in his heightened sense of modernity could say: "Umsonst hoffen wir auf einen Homeros," and he doubted whether such longing was at all desirable. For him the time for the classical epic was gone—it had only been at its proper place within its own time.[33]

Thus in his *Brief über den Roman* of 1800 Friedrich Schlegel rejected the common view that the novel has the closest relationship with the narrative and even with the epic genre. He argued that mere narration was only one of the elements of the novel and that he could hardly imagine a novel any other than mixed of narration, song, and other forms. Cervantes provided a perfect example of this feature. Schlegel's central argument, however, concerns the narrative attitude of the author of the novel which for him is fundamentally different from that of the epic narrator, and he says: "Es ist dem epischen Stil nichts entgegengesetzter als wenn die Einflüsse der eignen Stimmung im geringsten sichtbar werden; geschweige den, daß er sich seinem Humor so überlassen, so mit ihm spielen dürfte, wie es in den vortrefflichsten Romanen geschieht."[34] August Wilhelm Schlegel used similar arguments to support the contention that the novel's poetic unity was entirely different from that of the epic. He stressed that Homer is completely without passion in his work and, as Aristotle had already remarked, says as little as possible on his own. Homer's epic is a "ruhige Darstellung des Fortschreitenden," and the hexameter is only the "Ausdruck und hörbares Bild" of this quiet rhythm.[35] The novel represents for Friedrich Schlegel the spirit of modernity in such characteristic fashion that it is actually the only modern genre which can be put on a par with the highest literary achievement of classical antiquity, i.e., tragedy.[36]

As can be expected from this digression into early romantic genre theory, the Schlegelian notion of the novel derives chiefly from historical observations. Cervantes was the main source for the evolving theory,[37] but considering the broad radius of the romantic novel, we should not be surprised to see Dante, Boccaccio, Ariosto, Petrarca, and even Shakespeare listed as representatives of this genre. Next to these "great authors" Schlegel emphasized a number of eighteenth-century writers, perhaps not as prominent as these older models, but excelling through particular features of their literary art such as irony, humor, "geistreiche Form," "Fülle des Witzes," and "Originalität der Phantasie."[38] These are authors like Swift, Sterne, Diderot, and Jean Paul. Schlegel did not consider them as genuine poets but rather as intellectuals who had to develop capricious techniques to work themselves into the art of narration[39]—just as he himself had to do while writing *Lucinde*. Goethe brought about the great turning point in this development by restoring, as a genuine poet, novelistic poetry in prose. Looked at more closely, the history of the modern novel presented itself to these critics in three great cycles.[40] It moved from Cervantes' *Don Quijote* to Sterne's *Tristram Shandy* and then to Goethe's *Wilhelm Meister*. The first cycle is introduced by the so-called "older moderns," mainly by Cervantes, and is truly romantic. The second is represented by authors of the eighteenth century who integrated an intellectual, reflective discourse with a process of fictional creation and thereby united poetry and criticism. The third began with Goethe, whose novel *Wilhelm Meisters Lehrjahre* was deemed modern and poetic, yet not romantic.

When Friedrich Schlegel developed these views about the modern novel in 1797, he had no contemporary model to demonstrate the potentialities of the romantic novel in his own time and had to regress to Cervantes. Indeed, the best he and his brother had to say about the genre of the romantic novel comes forth in their truly outstanding Cervantes criticism.[41] Cervantes is the great master vital for orientation in the present. *Die Musik des Lebens zu phantasieren*, to fantasize the music of life, is the main goal of the romantic novel.[42] Its unity no longer rests on rational, logical, or even teleological principles, but solely on the imagination and the life of fancy. This novel's task is to imitate, as Schlegel puts it in his *Gespräch über die Poesie*, "das unendliche Spiel der Welt."[43] It should render "diese künstlich geordnete Verwirrung, diese reizende Symmetrie von Widersprüchen, diesen wunderbaren ewigen Wechsel von Enthusiasmus und Ironie, der selbst in den kleinsten Gliedern des Ganzen lebt."[44] August Wilhelm Schlegel gave more direct indications as to how such poetic unity based on poetic reflection, wit, and irony should be understood. Referring especially to *Don Quijote*, he said in 1799: "Wenn aber ein materieller Zusammenhang gefordert wird, der die Vorfälle wie Ursache und Wirkung, wie Mittel und Zweck, untereinander verknüpft, so daß alles darauf abzielt, irgendetwas zustande zu bringen, eine Heirat etwa oder andere tröstliche Dinge, wonach der große Haufe der Liebhaber die letzten Blätter eines Romans beglerig umschlägt, so wäre alsdann die Komposition des ganzen *Don Quijote* äußerst fehlerhaft."[45] Schlegel is referring to the recognition that this novel very well consists of facts and events, but does not unite them in logical sequence and presents them according to the laws of the imagination, also defined as "witty" composition. He maintained that for a "genuine novel" the principle of progressive action would be irrelevant. What mattered was "daß die Reihe der Erscheinungen in ihrem gaukelnden Wechsel darin harmonisch sei, die Phantasie festhalte und nie bis zum Ende die Bezauberung sich aufhören lasse."[46] His brother thought that this "great wit of romantic poetry" could not be perceived in individual sections, but only in the structure of the entire work. He maintained that the fascination of romantic poetry by no means related only to persons, occurrences, situations, and individual inclination.[47]

Paul Böckmann has correctly interpreted this essential aspect in the romantic novel as a shift from objective occurrences to subjective modes of integration and from narrative content to the consciousness of the author.[48] The famous "Copernican turn" brought about by Kant in philosophy definitely prepared the way for this new function of literature and undoubtedly influenced its origin. Kant had said that his critical philosophy no longer concerned itself with objects, but with our mode of recognizing objects.[49] Correspondingly, romantic poetry attempted to supplement simple narration by reflection and by what Friedrich Schlegel called the style of expressing poetry.[50] Fichte paralleled this new understanding of poetic creation more directly than Kant when through his transcendental reflection, he reduced the relationship between the Ego and the Non-Ego, man and world, to an interaction of the Ego with itself.[51] As a matter of fact, Schlegel defined this new type of poetry in Fichtean terms as "transcendental poetry," as an act of creation which generated "das Produzierende mit dem Produkt," which portrayed itself with each of its portrayals, and is "zugleich Poesie und Poesie der Poesie."[52]

The emphasis on the author within the act of creation is, however, but one part of this philosophical background and can be considered its Fichtean root. To visualize the full scope of the theory of the romantic novel, we would have to include the further course of idealistic philosophy when Schelling's impulses led the realistic or objective realm of nature to manifest itself and supplement the subjective and idealistic reign of Fichte's Ego. Now man and nature, subject and object, ideality and reality were recognized as equal. Nature appeared as visible spirit and spirit as invisible nature. The former antagonism of these principles was replaced by a conciliatory aura and an amiable cooperation between man and nature. And the romantic conception of the novel came to embrace that intimate relationship of nature and the human mind which actually marks most novels of that period. The symbolic vision created by poetry no longer only related to the mind of the author, but embraced life and existence in their contradictory abundance.

Friedrich and August Wilhelm Schlegel have illustrated these particular aspects of the romantic novel in their comprehensive discussions of Cervantes. In 1797 Friedrich Schlegel wrote into his notebooks: "Wir haben philosophische Romane (Jacobi), poetische (Goethe); nun fehlt nur noch ein *romantischer* Roman," and he added a little later: "*Don Quijote* noch immer der einzige durchaus romantische Roman."[53] But soon thereafter he discovered Tieck's *Franz Sternbalds Wanderungen* of 1798 as a genuinely and contemporary romantic novel and said that this was "der erste Roman seit Cervantes der romantisch ist, und darin weit über Meister."[54]

That for the early romantic critics *Wilhelm Meister* did not represent that type of arabesque unity they appreciated in Cervantes and Tieck, can even be noticed in Friedrich Schlegel's enthusiastic review *Über Goethes Meister* of 1798, which appears to interpret this work as a model of his own literary theory. There is no question that, as Hans Eichner observed, Schlegel painstakingly emphasized everything in Goethe's novel that corresponded to his own theory of romantic poetry.[55] This review is certainly an attempt "to recapture the spirit of the work and to trace its inner development as a poetic and artistic whole."[56] Indeed, the main theme of the essay is actually the aesthetic structure and poetic unity of *Wilhelm Meister*. Schlegel said: "Der angeborne Trieb des durchaus organisierten und organisierenden Werks, sich zu einem Ganzen zu bilden, äußert sich in den größeren wie in den kleineren Massen," and he adds: "selbst der feinste Zug der Nebenausbildung scheint für sich zu existieren und sich eines eignen selbständigen Daseins zu erfreuen."[57] Schlegel believes that it would be beautiful and necessary to fully abandon oneself to the impression of a literary work, but equally important is for him the ability to abstract from everything individual and grasp the general spirit animating the work. The very first sentence depicting how "die Bildung eines strebenden Geistes sich still entfaltet, und wie die werdende Welt aus seinem Inneren leise emporsteigt," already prefaces the "structural pattern" which Raymond Immerwahr has presented as deriving from the relation of the reader to the novel—"a dialectical progression from passive emotional participation, through disciplined critical analysis, to discriminating intellectual interest, and then finally to a moment of ultimate insight."[58] Goethe was one of the first to recognize the orientation of Schlegel's review toward the aesthetic unity of his novel, and he praised the young critic for "immer auf den Bau des Ganzen gegangen [zu sein] und sich nicht bei pathologischer Zergliederung der Charaktere aufgehalten [zu haben]."[59]

Indeed, through his progressive unfolding of the aesthetic organization of the entire novel, his grasp for the correspondences and foreshadowing among the events, and the mirroring of the characters and contrasting figures, Schlegel shows an acute sense for the particular nature of Goethe's narrative technique and its unique manner of symbolizing. Critics are unanimous in praising him for his understanding of the finest shades of nuance in the structure of the novel, but are simultaneously amazed at his apparently complete failure to comprehend the final goal and concretization in Wilhelm's apprenticeship.[60] To be sure, Schlegel was one of the first, as Hans Eichner has observed, to characterize Goethe's novel as a "Bildungsroman."[61] As a matter of fact, Schlegel repeatedly emphasized the idea of "Lebenskunstlehre" as the dominant theme of the novel. Yet confronted with the question of what this "Lebenskunstlehre" actually consists, little more comes to light than "Lebensjahre, in denen nichts gelernt wird, als zu existieren, nach seinen besonderen Grundsätzen oder seiner unabänderlichen Natur zu leben."[62] Schlegel thus takes a lofty position midway the spokesmen for a "universal" and a "particular" idea of "Bildung"—two groups into which the interpreters of *Wilhelm Meister* have been divided.[63] Although in his concluding paragraph Schlegel claims to have penetrated the innermost secret of the novel, he tells us nothing about what he has seen and breaks off his essay adding simply: "*Die Fortsetzung folgt.*" He even distilled Goethe's novel into the ether of pure poetry when he said: "Wie mögen sich die Leser dieses Romans beim Schluß desselben getäuscht fühlen, da aus alien diesen Erziehungsanstalten nichts herauskommt, als bescheidene Liebenswürdigkeit, da hinter allen diesen wunderbaren Zufällen, weissagenden Winken und geheimnisvollen Erscheinungen nichts steht als die erhabenste Poesie."[64]

Of course, from the hermeneutic point of view, Schlegel's relationship to a literary work was not, as Victor Lange observed, "that of an expositor of more or less concealed but nevertheless discoverable and perhaps objective meaning; it is rather that of an intelligent artist in his own right who, by virtue of his receptive sensibility and his close attention to the suggestive poetic detail, is in the position to elucidate, to manipulate, and, on a level of further intellectual differentiation, to reassemble the primary symbols of a poet."[65] Yet critics have actually assumed that Schlegel misunderstood the ending of *Wilhelm Meister* and either unconsciously refused the message of the post-Italian Goethe[66] or replaced classical restraint with romantic irony dissolving Goethe's work into the "ether of joyfulness."[67] I believe, however, that Schlegel had a profound understanding of *Wilhelm Meister* and that his reservation to express himself about it was chiefly motivated by the classical restraint which in his opinion Goethe's novel represented and the feeling of infinity which the romantic novel was to incorporate. Henry Hatfield has provided some interesting evidence for this opinion by pointing to an amazing parallel between Goethe's *Wilhelm Meister* and Schlegel's famous Aphorism 116 of the *Athenäum on* "progressive Universalpoesie." Hatfield refers to the letter of Part VIII, Chapter 5 from which Jarno "reads to the bewildered, almost desperate Wilhelm sentences describing the tremendous range, not to say universality, of man's powers." Because of the striking parallels which exist in the "long, sweeping, cumulative sentences" in both the letter and the aphorism, Schlegel might very well have phrased his aphorism with an eye upon the open copy of *Wilhelm Meister*. Yet as soon as the accent shifts in the letter "from the manifold, indeed universal powers and talents of man to the limitations of any given individual," the parallels cease, and Schlegel's aphorism takes a decided turn towards the infinite.[68]

Although Schlegel had presented his review of *Wilhelm Meister* as the first installment of a series, for him the essay was actually completed.[69] At that time he did not want to say any more about Goethe's novel. It was Novalis who, although not publicly, formulated his polemics "gegen *Wilhelm Meisters Lehrjahre*," which through their sudden vehemence indicate the deep gulf separating the romantic conception of the novel from Goethe's *Wilhelm Meister*.[70] In more conciliatory terms, Schlegel had the same differences in mind when in his *Europa* of 1803 he distinguished between "exoteric" and "esoteric" poetry limiting the former to the "Ideal des Schönen in dem Verhältnisse des menschlichen Lebens," and expanding the latter beyond the human realm into a sphere comprising "zugleich die Welt und die Natur." To illustrate this "Übergang vom Roman zur Mythologie," he cited Novalis' unfinished novel *Heinrich von Ofterdingen* and thereby contributed considerably, although unintentionally, to the disrespect into which Goethe's novel now fell among the new romantic generation.[71] When in 1808 Schlegel reviewed Goethe's *Werke* of 1806, he attempted to remedy the damage by defending it against the reproaches of being prosaic and against unjustified comparisons with other works. Yet he maintained that its center was human "Bildung" and its sphere the poetic, not the romantic, illustrating the romantic novel again with *Don Quijote*.[72]

Instead of delving further into these theoretical considerations, I should like to conclude my discussion of the poetic unity in *Wilhelm Meister* and the early romantic novel by concentrating on two representative novels of the period: Tieck's *Franz Sternbalds Wanderungen* and Novalis' *Heinrich von Ofterdingen*.

Ludwig Tieck's *Franz Sternbalds Wanderungen* of 1798 is the first manifestation of the romantic novel, or its recreation, during the period of early German romanticism. In order to do justice to this frequently maligned novel, we first have to ask ourselves what exactly constitutes the poetic unity of this work. The answer is that *Franz Sternbald* represents the infinite abundance and contradictory variety of life in the medium of the imagination. It represents that particular variation of the romantic novel which I should like to call its fantastic type and which, because of its proximity to the "marvelous," "miraculous," "fanciful," "improbable," "exotic," and so forth, comes closest to the old "romance."[73] The theme of traveling, highlighted in the title, also underscores this feature. This fantastic principle of unity is arrived at, however, through what is almost exclusively the pleasant and benevolent type of imagination and not, as in other works of Tieck, its more sinister, demonic form. We should also note that this fantastic unity is never broken or interrupted by irony and that the work, except for its abrupt ending, does not feature any emergence of the author from his work. Only rarely, and virtually indiscernibly, is the thread of narration interrupted, when the author intertwines elegiac reflections on the "life of youth." In vain do we search for an ironic "smiling down" by the author upon his work, as Friedrich Schlegel had found in Goethe's *Wilhelm Meister*, or for a deliberate destruction of poetic illusion as we might expect from the author of *Der gestiefelte Kater*. Yet we do not listen to a merely naive form of narration. Whoever has the ear for it will notice that the voice of the narrator changes considerably from the first to the second part, i.e., during the transition from the old German past into a timeless landscape. Altogether, although scarcely detectible, a great number of narrative perspectives appear in this novel, specifically called "masks" (190),[74] and manifesting the author's ironical distance and his mastery over his work.

This principle of fantastic and romance-like unity explains the other characteristics of the novel without great difficulty, especially its often recognized lack of content. At first glance, we definitely gain the impression that nothing is actually occurring here. The "action" encompasses a period of about one-and-a-half years (398), and this period with its change of seasons, cities, and landscapes corresponds to Franz Sternbald's inner development, revealing itself in a seemingly erratic roaming which Tieck called "Wanderungen." Friedrich Schlegel, who had a distinct sense for such unsensational happenings, went so far as to characterize the novel as a fantasy on the fantasy when he said: "der romantische Geist scheint angenehm über sich selbst zu phantasieren."[75] The movement in this novel, however, is not circular because the arabesque direction of these travelings assumes the motive of search—of parents, brothers and sisters, the beloved, but also of the own self and its realization.

It corresponds to the particular focus of interest in early German romanticism that this search, development, and finding takes place in the artist. Thus this novel presents us with a young apprentice to the art of painting who in various stages finally achieves mastery in his art.[76] Yet this theme is not germane to my concentration on the particular form of this novel just described as one of fantastic unity and of a romance-like character. What matters here is that the final thrust of the novel transcends Franz Sternbald's maturing as an artist and human being and comprises man and world, art and life, North and South, past and future, ideality and reality. Richard Alewyn clearly visualized this reconciling tendency of the novel when he described the work in terms of converging lines of action aiming at the reunification of the lovers, the rediscovery of the relatives, the disentanglement of all confusion, and the solution of all riddles.[77]

This thrust of the novel is evident in its structure. The two first parts are so fundamentally disparate in their narrative prose, content, and the entire atmosphere that many critics were unable to see any relationship between them at all. To visualize this relationship, however, one has to start from the premise that the transition from the old-German past into the beautiful manifoldness of the Italian Renaissance, which almost looks like a dialectical move into the contrary, is necessary for Franz Sternbald's artistic and personal development. This confrontation leads him to that task of self-discovery and integration in which the two worlds fuse. In order to recognize this goal, we only have to glance at the timid adolescent in the narrow streets of Nürnberg and the light-hearted young man as he appears in Rome with the voluptuous Leonore. This self-realization of the Ego in the sense of an identity of the self and the world can also be seen in the religious tendencies of these two parts. With its praise of Martin Luther and the Reformation, the first represents Protestantism, whereas the second takes a pronounced turn to Catholicism. The solution of this conflict is obviously to be found in a higher synthesis of these confessions. From the point of view of nationalism, the predilection for Germany in the first part changes into an admiration of Italy in the second, a disparity which apparently was to be resolved in a synthesis of northern seriousness and southern light-heartedness.

It is a characteristic mark of this romantic novel that its projected third part was never executed, although Tieck pursued this plan well into late life. Critics naturally considered this hesitance as an inability to reconcile the discrepancy between the two first parts. It has to remain open whether Tieck would have been able to synthesize Nurnberg and Rome, Protestantism and Catholicism, the Ego and the world, ideality and reality, time and eternity. Yet the novel is definitely projected to comprise these grand unifications. Toward the end of the second part, when Franz Sternbald meets Marie, we are led to the threshold of these unifications. Not only Franz, but also Marie, and perhaps also the reader are overwhelmed by the significance of this moment in which the goal of the entire action becomes visible and the ideal, so to speak, becomes real. Yet this also seems to indicate that *Franz Sternbalds Wanderungen* had found its natural conclusion toward the end of the second part and that it was not Tieck's inability, but the inner structure of the work which explains the missing third part. I don't want to maintain that the conception of the novel does not consist of three parts, but believe that the sphere of the third transcends what can be expressed in literature.

Mythology, symbol, and fairy tale are the concepts which the most prominent critics spontaneously employed when they attempted to characterize Novalis' romantic novel *Heinrich von Ofterdingen* of 1802. Solger characterized the novel as a mythical story tearing the veil which the finiteness of this world keeps around the infinite.[78] And for Paul Kluckhohn, *Heinrich von Ofterdingen* was a "symbolical novel" demonstrating the immanence of transcendence in this worldly life.[79] The language is simple and naive and accentuates precisely through its quiet rhythm the transparency of all happenings. Songs and lyrical interludes emphasize the content of respective sections of the work. Dialogues deal with the central topics of Novalis' theory of poetry, philosophy, history, human life, religion, and morality. There is hardly any ironic mood in this novel. Yet of central importance in it is the function of dreams which, however, do not relate to psychoanalysis and spiritualism, but emphasize the relationship to the supernatural. The novel begins with a dream, and at the beginning of the second part a voice named Astralis pronounces the enigmatic words: "Die Welt wird Traum, der Traum wird Welt." Through its blue atmosphere the first dream emphasizes the transparent aura of *Heinrich von Ofterdingen* and the relationship to the transcendent world. And then all of a sudden, there appear, alongside these dreams, symbols, and suggestions of transparency, scenes of the most realistic character and highly developed sense for historical reality. We are in the period of the Crusades, meet merchants and miners, and learn about the work of mining at that time. Penetrating the interior of the world, however, we again move into the mysterious. Yet we are also confronted in this realm with the "King of the metals," gold, which as the basis for money determines the mercantile dealings of the world. This alternating between the worlds of the miraculous and common life, the inner self and the exterior world, is Novalis' literary technique of symbolizing the cohesion of those two spheres.

We have only the first part of this novel with the title *Die Erwartung* and vague sketches for the second. The first part is entirely rounded off and depicts Heinrich's growth as a poet in a series of clearly distinguishable stages. Toward the end of this process, Heinrich is mature enough to gain initiation to the profession of a poet by his fiancée, Mathilde. Mathilde represents the spirit of poetry for him, and her kiss is expected to open Heinrich's lips as a poet. The decisive event, however, that transforms Heinrich into a poet, is not that kiss, but Mathilde's death. Now the boundaries between this world and the transcendent world are taken away, and the poet is equally at home in both realms.

According to his own statements, Novalis had clear conceptions about the continuation of the novel. The novel should "allmälich in Märchen übergehen," we read in one instance and in another: "Der Schluß ist Übergang aus der wirklichen Welt in die geheime."[80] Occasionally, his plans for a continuation of the novel assume such colossal dimensions, however, that doubts easily arise as to whether they could actually be realized. The path of the second part was to lead to the worlds of antiquity, the Greeks and the Orient, to the court of the emperor Frederick II, and finally to the Wartburg. In another version Heinrich is projected to pass through the various realms of nature, the unorganic, organic, animal, and human realms until he is finally reunited with Mathilde. We have to consider, however, that most of these projections are unreliable because we know them primarily through Ludwig Tieck's accounts. Friedrich Schlegel reports that Novalis altered his plans about his novel until the last day of his life.

For a critical examination of the projected continuation of the novel, there is therefore no other authentical source but the first part itself. Yet in an analysis of it, little material comes to light. In one instance, the novel is mirrored within the novel through an antique book in the provençal language. When Heinrich examines the last sections of it, they appear dark and incomprehensible to him, and he has the impression that the conclusion of the book is missing (265).[81] in another instance, Heinrich anticipates Mathilde's death in a dream and then indicates some of the ensuing events with a few strokes. He wanders through a foreign and distant country, hears music, and finds Mathilde. This reunion occurs in a strange surrealistic atmosphere beneath a river with blue waves flowing above the two. Yet the concluding dialogue shows where the true place of their reunion is: "Wo sind wir, liebe Mathilde?—Bei unsern Eltern.—Bleiben wir zusammen?—Ewig, versetzte sie, indem sie ihre Lippen an die seinigen drückte, und ihn so umschloß, daß sie nicht wieder von ihm konnte" (278–279). At the beginning of the novel, leaving his home town Eisenach, Heinrich also has a premonition about where his journey will lead. Delving into the "blue stream" of the distance, he felt "als werde er nach langen Wandertingen von der Weltgegend her, nach welcher sie jetzt reisten, in sein Vaterland zurückkommen, und als reise er daher diesem eigentlich zu."

Of all the novels of early romanticism, *Heinrich von Ofterdingen* is certainly the most ambitious work. Yet we cannot consider it the greatest of early romanticism as Kluckhohn and Dilthey have done. We have only its first part, and this part is clearly a torso, since the center of gravity of the novel evidently lies in its continuation. In its conception, however, *Heinrich von Ofterdingen* can indicate what enormous dimensions the early romantic novel attempted to embrace.

It is clear that these novels are not brothers of *Wilhelm Meister* but cousins at best. It is also obvious why Goethe's *Meister* overshadowed these novels and caused a profound misunderstanding of them. That testifies to the enormous power of Goethe's narrative prose, but also leaves the task for the critic to rescue that which this powerful prose has obfuscated in the understanding of our past.

## NOTES

1. Rudolf Haym, *Die romantische Schule. Ein Beitrag zur Geschichte des deutschen Geistes*, 2nd edition (Berlin: Weidmann, 1906), p. 251.

2. In his essay "The Meaning of 'Romantic' in Early German Romanticism" of 1916, now in Arthur O. Lovejoy, *Essays in the History of Ideas*, 4th edition (New York: Capricorn Books, 1960), pp. 195–196.

3. Melitta Gerhard, "Goethes 'geprägte Form' im romantischen Spiegel," in Melitta Gerhard, *Leben im Gesetz. Fünf Goethe-Aufsätze* (Bern-München: Francke, 1966), pp. 64–78; Raymond Immerwahr, "Friedrich Schlegel's Essay 'On Goethe's *Meister*'," *Monatshefte* 49 (1957), pp. 1–21; Clemens Heselhaus, "Die Wilhelm Meister-Kritik der Romantiker und die romantische Romantheorie," in *Nachahmung und Illusion. Kolloquium Gießen 1963*, ed. H. R. Jauß (München: Eidos, 1964), pp. 113–209; Jacob Steiner, "Äther der Fröhlichkeit. Zur Frage nach einer dichterischen Ironie," *Orbis Litterarum* 13 (1958), pp. 64–80; Henry Hatfield, "*Wilhelm Meisters Lehrjahre* and 'Progressive Universalpoesie'," *The Germanic Review* 36 (1961), pp. 221–229; *Kritische Friedrich Schlegel Ausgabe*, ed. Ernst Behler in cooperation with Jean-Jacques Anstett and Hans Eichner (hereafter *KA*), vol. 2: *Charakteristiken und Kritiken*, ed. Hans Eichner (Paderborn: Schöningh, 1967), pp. LXXI–LXXIX; Hans-Joachim Mähl, "Goethes Urteil über Novalis," *Jahrbuch des Freien Deutschen Hochstifts* 1967, pp. 130–270; Karl Robert Mandelkow, "Der Roman der Klassik und Romantik," in *Neues Handbuch der Literaturwissenschaft*, vol. 14: *Europäische Romantik I*, ed. Karl Robert Mandelkow (Wiesbaden: Athenaion, 1982), pp. 393–428.

4. This applies especially to Friedrich Schlegel and Novalis. On Friedrich Schlegel see *KA*, vol. 16: *Fragmente zur Poesie und Literatur*, ed. Hans Eichner (Paderborn: Schöningh, 1981: formerly Friedrich Schlegel, *Literary Notebooks*, ed. Hans Eichner, London: Athlonem, 1957). On Novalis see Novalis, *Schriften*, ed. Richard Samuel in cooperation with Hans-Joachim Mähl and Gerhard Schulz (hereafter *Schriften*), vol. 3 (Stuttgart: Kohlhammer, 1960–).

5. Novalis, *Schriften*, vol. 3, pp. 646–647, No. 536.

6. Johann Wolfgang von Goethe, *Gedenkausgabe der Werke, Briefe und Gespräche*, ed. Ernst Beutler (Zürich: Artemis, 1949 ff.), vol. 21, pp. 1012–1015 (hereafter *Gedenkausgabe*).

7. *Already Josef Körner, Romantiker und Klassiker. Die Brüder Schlegel in ihren Beziehungen zu Schiller und Goethe* (Berlin: Askanischer Verlag, 1924), but more precisely Hans Eichner in his introduction to *KA*, vol. 2, pp. LXXV–LXXVIII.

8. *Caroline. Briefe aus der Frühromantik*, ed. Erich Schmidt (Leipzig: Insel, 1913), vol. 1, p. 460.

9. *Gedenkausgabe*, vol. 22, p. 227.

10. *Gedenkausgabe*, vol. 24, p. 108.

11. *KA*, vol. 2, p. 198, No. 216.

12. *KA*, vol. 1, p. 260.

13. *KA*, vol. 16, p. 158, No. 857, p. 176, No. 1110.

14. August Wilhelm Schlegel, *Sämtliche Werke*, ed. Eduard Böking (Leipzig: Weidmann, 1847), vol. 11, p. 22 (hereafter *SW*).

15. *Schriften*, vol. 2, p. 642, No. 445.

16. *SW*, vol. 11, p. 189, 193.

17. *KA*, vol. 1, p. 451II,3.

18. *KA*, vol. 18, p. 130.

19. *KA*, vol. 2, p. 206, No. 247.

20. *KA*, vol. 2, pp. 346–347.

21. *Gedenkausgabe*, vol. 20, p. 443.

22. *KA*, vol. 2, p. 133. See also p. 132: "so ist doch auch alles Poesie, reine, hohe Poesie."

23. *KA*, vol. 2, p. 335; vol. 11, p. 160; vol. 16, p. 88, No. 32.

24. Karl Robert Mandelkow, "Der Roman der Klassik und Romantik," in *Neues Handbuch der Literaturwissenschaft*, vol. 14: *Europäische Romantik* I, ed. Karl Robert Mandelkow (Wiesbaden: Athenaion, 1982), p. 394, 400.

25. *KA*, vol. 16, p. 108, No. 289; p. 113, No. 342; p. 133, No. 575; vol. 3, p. 138.

26. *Schriften*, vol. 3, p. 646: "Das Romantische geht darin zugrunde."

27. *Schriften*, vol. 4, p. 323.

28. First presented in Hans Eichner, "Friedrich Schlegel's Theory of Romantic Poetry," *PMLA* 71 (1956), pp. 1018–1041, and later more fully discussed in Hans Eichner, *Friedrich Schlegel* (New York: Twayne, 1970), pp. 44–83.

29. Peter Szondi, "Friedrich Schlegels Theorie der Dichtarten," *Euphorion* 64 (1970), pp. 112–151; Clemens Heselhaus, "Die Wilhelm Meister Kritik der Romantiker und die romantische Romantheorie," in *Nachahmung und Illusion. Kolloquium Gießen* 1963, ed. H. R. Jauß (München: Eidos, 1964), pp. 113–127.

30. *SW*, vol. 11, pp. 194–196.

31. *KA*, vol. 1, p. 334.

32. *KA*, vol. 1, pp. 480–481.

33. *KA*, vol. 1, pp. 332–334.

34. *KA*, vol. 2, p. 336.

35. *SW*, vol. 11, p. 190–192.

36. *KA*, vol. 2, p. 335; vol. 16, p. 88, No. 32.

37. *SW*, vol. 11, pp. 408–426; *KA*, vol. 2, pp. 281–283; vol. 11, pp. 159–162.

38. *KA*, vol. 2, pp. 330–331.

39. Ibid.

40. *KA*, vol. 1, pp. 355–356; vol. 16, p. 158, No. 857.

41. *SW*, vol. 11, pp. 408–426; *KA*, vol. 2, pp. 281–283; vol. 11, pp. 159–162. See on this subject Werner Brüggernann, *Cervantes und die Figur des Don Quijote in Kunstanschauung und Dichtung der deutschen Romantik* (Münster: Aschendorff, 1958).

42. *KA*, vol. 2, p. 283; vol. 11, p. 161.

43. *KA*, vol. 2, p. 324.

44. *KA*, vol. 2, pp. 318–319.

45. *SW*, vol. 11, p. 410.

46. *SW*, vol. 11, p. 411.

47. *KA*, vol. 2, p. 334.

48. Paul Böckmann, "Der Roman der Transzendentalpoesie in der Romantik," in *Geschichte, Deutung, Kritik. Literaturwissenschaftliche Beiträge dargebracht zum 65. Geburtstag Werner Kohlschmidts*, ed. M. Bindschedler and P. Zinsli (Bern: Francke, 1969), pp, 165–185.

49. *Kants Werke*. Akademie Textausgabe (Berlin: de Gruyter, 1968), vol. 3, p. 43: "nicht sowohl mit Gegenständen, sondern mit unserer Erkenntnisart von Gegenständen."

50. *KA*, vol. 2, p. 331.

51. J. G. Fichte, *Gesamtausgabe*, ed. Reinhard Lauth and Hans Jacob, vol. 2 (Stuttgart: Frommann, 1965), p. 414.

52. *KA*, vol. 2, p. 204, No. 238.

53. *KA*, vol. 16, p. 133, No. 575; p. 176, No. 1110.

54. *KA*, vol. 16, p. 206, No. 19: "Sternbald romantischer Roman, daher eben absolute Poesie." See also *Friedrich Schlegels Briefe an seinen Brüder August Wilhelm*; ed. Oskar Walzel (Berlin: Speyer & Peters, 1890), p. 414.

55. *KA*, vol. 2, p. LXXVII.

56. Raymond Immerwahr, "Friedrich Schlegel's Essay 'On Goethe's Meister'," *Monatshefte* 49 (1957), p. 1.

57. *KA*, vol. 2, p. 131.

58. R. Immerwahr, p. 13.

59. *Caroline. Briefe aus der Frühromantik*, ed, Erich Schmidt (Leipzig: Insel, 1913), vol. 1, p. 455.

60. Especially Melitta Gerhard, "Goethes 'geprägte Form' im romantischen Spiegel. Zu Friedrich Schlegels Aufsatz 'Über Goethes Meister'," in Melitta Gerhard, *Leben im Gesetz* (Bern: Francke, 1966), pp. 64–78.

61. Hans Eichner, "Zur Deutung von 'Wilhelm Meisters Lehrjahren'," *Jahrbuch des Freien Deutschen Hochstifts* (1966), pp. 165–196.

62. *KA*, vol. 2, p. 141.

63. First by Hans Eichner, "Zur Deutung von 'Wilhelm Meisters Lehrjahren'," pp. 167–176. See also Erhard Bahr, "'Wilhelm Meisters Lehrjahre' als Bildungsroman," in Johann Wolfgang Goethe, *Wilhelm Meisters Lehrjahre* (Stuttgart: Reclam, 1982), pp. 643–660.

64. *KA*, vol. 2, p. 144.

65. Victor Lange, "Friedrich Schlegel's Literary Criticism," *Comparative Literature* 7 (1955), p. 297.

66. Melitta Gerhard, pp. 77–78.

67. Jacob Steiner, "Äther der Fröhlichkeit. Zur Frage nach einer dichterischen Ironie," *Orbis Litterarum* 13 (1958), pp. 64–68.

68. Henry Hatfield, "*Wilhelm Meisters Lehrjahre* and 'Progressive Universalpoesie'," *The Germanic Review* 36 (1961), pp. 221–229.

69. According to a letter to his brother of December 3, 1800.

70. *Schriften*, vol. 3, pp. 646–647, No. 536.

71. *KA*, vol. 3, pp. 11–12. See on this subject Hans Joachim Mahl, "Goethes Urteil über Novalis," *Jahrbuch des Freien Deutschen Hochstifts* 1967, pp. 130–270.

72. *KA*, vol. 3, pp. 128–141.

73. Hans Eichner suggested the concept of the "romance" as best suited for a characterization of Tieck's novel during the discussion of this paper at the Symposion. See on this topic Hans Eichner, *Friedrich Schlegel* (New York: Twayne, 1970), pp. 51–54.

74. Quoted from the Reclam edition, ed. Alfred Anger (Stuttgart: Reclam, 1966).

75. *KA*, vol. 2, p. 245, No. 418.

76. Most strongly emphasized by William J. Lillyman: *Reality's Dark Dream. The Narrative Fiction of Ludwig Tieck* (Berlin: de Gruyter, 1979), pp. 61–76.

77. Richard Alewyn, "Ein Fragment der Fortsetzung von Tiecks *Sternbald*," *Jahrbuch des Freien Deutschen Hochstifts* 1962, p. 58.

78. K. W. F. Solger, *Nachgelassene Schriften*, ed. L. Tieck and F. von Raumer, vol. 1, p. 95.

79. Novalis, *Schriften*, vol. 1, p. 56.

80. *Schriften*, vol. 4, p. 330.

81. Novalis is quoted from *Schriften*, vol. 1.

WOLFGANG WITTKOWSKI

# Goethe's Iphigenie: *Autonomous Humanity and the Authority of the Gods in the Era of Benevolent Despotism*

It is generally held that the climax of Goethe's *Iphigenie* lies in the heroine's decision to dare to tell the truth. Before taking this difficult step, she quotes the "Song of the Fates," the ancient song in which the Tantalus family express their age-old hatred of the gods. Before that she appeals to the gods: "Save me and save your image in my soul!" At the end of the play, she could react with the same words as Isabella exclaims in Schiller's *Braut von Messina*: "Let the oracles remain in honor, and the gods are saved!"—without any trace of Isabella's horror and bitter irony. But she says neither this nor anything similar, and to me this also seems to suggest irony, albeit irony of quite a different kind.

Today oracles and gods arouse scant interest. Heinz Schlaffer is but one of many who consider that the concept of individual morality lost its relevance as long ago as the nineteenth century.[1] It is, then, small wonder that interest in *Iphigenie*, the drama of humanity, has considerably diminished. In *Neue Interpretationen zu Goethes Dramen*, it is noted with satisfaction that the poet himself did not stay to the end of a performance given in 1825, in honor of his fiftieth year of service to the court, but left after Act III, that is, after Orestes has been purged of his guilt.[2] But this is precisely the event that in 1979 Wolfdietrich Rasch interpreted as the cornerstone of autonomous humanity in *Iphigenie*.[3] This new shift of

From *Goethe in the Twentieth Century*, Alexej Ugrinsky, ed. © 1987 by Hofstra University. Reproduced with Permission of Greenwood Publishing Group, Inc., Westport, CT.

emphasis gave a fresh impetus to the scholarly debate surrounding the play and influenced Dieter Borchmeyer's treatment of German Classicism published in 1981.[4] Like Rasch, he emphasizes the analogy between the gods and absolutist princes. After all, Iphigenie compares Thoas with the gods of the "Song of the Fates," and the latter with absolutist rulers. However, the happy outcome of the play confirms as always "the preestablished agreement of the gods with that which is moral in the human being" as Werner Keller put It in his *Handbuch des deutschen Dramas* in 1980.[5] Hans Robert Jauß celebrates the new concord between man in his newfound independence and the authority of the gods.[6] And, according to Borchmeyer, the "absolutely good divinity that is free from arbitrariness" provides a shining example, an ideal image of "humanity" and of humanitarian rule.[7]

In the poem "The Divine," written between the prose and the verse version of *Iphigenie*, we see the opposite: there the good man provides the "model" that determines the image we construct for ourselves of the unknown gods. This may perhaps explain the fact that in the euphoria of his restoration to sanity and faced with benevolence of the king, Orestes himself, the man of integrity, the man who urges "Let there be truth between us!" gives a highly imaginative reinterpretation of the Delphic oracle and turns the bad gods into good gods. "Like the man, just so his god."[8] It is the good God of Enlightenment theology, a god who desires morality and not slaves, as Rasch put it[9]—somewhat surprisingly, for throughout his book he claims: "Whatever occurs in this drama and is inhuman, evil, unjust, occurs by the will, under the direction or in the name of the gods."[10] And Orestes' generous and good-natured reinterpretation of the oracle is meant to negate all this? Rasch himself does indicate the subjective and arbitrary nature of this.[11] But he overlooks certain implications of Orestes' final speech.

Orestes dismisses the original interpretation of the oracle as a "mistake which a god wrapped around our heads like a veil ever since the time that he obliged us to wander the path here." And indeed when Orestes set out in search of salvation, the oracle gave him no idea of where the journey to Tauris might lead: to the "last abominations" of the house of Tantalus, to the murder of the last male member of the Tantalus race, killed either by his sister or together with her. Orestes fears this when he recognizes his sister, and with good reason. Rasch is the first to have clearly exposed the cunning logic of the fable. Artemis rescues Iphigenie from being sacrificed by Agamemnon, but in such a way that is generally believed that Iphigenie has in fact been killed. This leads to the murder of the father by her mother, to Orestes' matricide of Clytemnestra and to his journey to Tauris,[12] where his sister awaits him, Clytemnestra's daughter and predestined avenger, offspring of a family in which fratricide is a tradition, and, moreover, in her capacity as priestess, the one whose very office it is to wield the sacrificial knife. But she does not exercise this office. The gods made their plans without taking into account the new spirit of humanity that they themselves brought forth.

By intervening at the very moment when Iphigenie saw the sacrificial knife poised above her, Artemis aroused in her priestess a horror of bloodshed that she had meanwhile conveyed to the Taurians. Nonetheless the plan of destruction was still destined to succeed. Apollo ordered the theft of the image of the goddess—a serious crime against religion and state, as again Rasch is the first to make properly clear. Thoas cannot allow this to go unpunished. If he threatens violence, he can always justify it by referring to the will of Artemis. If, however, he shows humanity and does not use violence, then it is his decision and not dependent on Iphigenie's own pious interpretation of her rescue by Artemis as proof that the goddess rejected bloodshed. Here Iphigenie is offering a positive interpretation which parallels Orestes' generous reinterpretation of the oracle. But whether good-natured or not, any interpretation of the will of the gods the characters make is inadequate, since it is always a subjective projection, too, documenting more their own mentality and at the same time their unconscious and involuntary autonomy.

This does not mean, however, that the Gods are nothing more than "internalizations" and "projections" as Borchmeyer assumes.[13] In the events prior to the action of the play, Artemis and Apollo did actively intervene. And in the play itself, Orestes and Pylades see the Erinyes lying in wait for their victim at the edge of the temple precincts. Incidentally, the fact that they remain there does not release Orestes from his torment: he suffers from guilt independently of the feelings of guilt that the gods impose upon him. It is Orestes himself who adds "doubt" and "regret" to the mental torments inflicted by the Furies. And he demonstrates the same autonomy in the way in which he finally sends them all to Hades.

Orestes and Iphigenie give further evidence of autonomous humanity in the way in which they consistently judge the gods according to whether they act benevolently or not. They know how good just gods' actions ought to be. This is particularly important for them because in the mythical world nothing happens without the intervention or approval of the gods. This is the reason for Orestes' bitterness toward them at the beginning, his gratitude after he has been purged of his guilt, his good-natured faith in them at the end. This is the reason for Iphigenie's scarcely restrained bitterness toward Artemis at the beginning, her gratitude at finding Orestes again, her prayer for his redemption, and finally her outburst of Titan-like hatred of the gods when it appears that she is caught in an insoluble conflict: she must either perish with her own people or she must deceive the Taurians and betray their trust in her. In a situation like this, such scruples are perhaps "quite devilishly human" (19 January 1802, Goethe to Schiller). But Goethe does justify them, and he does so in mythological terms. If Iphigenie incurs guilt by outrightly lying, she cannot expiate the curse on the house of Tantalus and atone for the family blood spilled there. And that, after all, is a fundamental reason for her return home. No wonder she is angry with the gods and doubts their goodness. "Save me and save your image in my soul!" That is more an ultimatum than an entreaty. Not every reader has recognized this. Jauß[14] believes, like Benno von Wiese, that Iphigenie takes upon herself the crucial decision to dare to tell the truth trusting in the "gods, to whom the ultimate decision is trustingly handed over."[15] Indeed, Iphigenie's words do appear to justify this interpretation: "On your knees only do I lay it. If you are as true as you are extolled to be, then show it through your support and glorify through me the truth!"

Iphigenie does indeed make the outcome dependent on the will of the gods—it always is in the mythical world anyway. But Iphigenie does not make her own actions dependent on the gods. Thus she puts the gods to a test, and one that has wider implications than she realizes. If the gods do not help her, she will cease to respect them. But if Thoas helps her, then she has not particular reason to thank the gods. And she in fact never does so. Instead, at the end, it is she rather than the picture of the goddess whom Orestes elevates to the holy image that brings salvation. But when Orestes explains that it was in childlike faith that she revealed the truth to Thoas, he is simplifying the situation again—after all, he is not present when it happens. Iphigenie subordinates herself no more to Thoas than to the gods. Only when she is caught out as a liar and accomplice in the attack on the central sacred institution of the state cult does she draw herself up to her full stature and speak as a princess, "Agamemnon's daughter," proud and "great." Instead of the "unprecedented act" of slaughtering—such as that performed in secret by Atreus, in the open, "savagely against savages," by the Amazons—she offers in its place "the impossible": "I have nothing but words." She tells "the truth." She admits to the attack that she and her countrymen have initiated. But in no way does she beg for mercy. She demands mercy. Yes, she warns Thoas that he must not refuse his mercy and that he can and must keep his promise to send her home.

By doing this, she—with Goethe—conceals the crux of the matter. She places the fate of the three criminals in the hands of the king, putting them completely at his mercy. It is the prerogative of gods and kings to show mercy rather than insisting on the letter of the law and imposing the rightful punishment. To put it differently, Thoas is expected to forgive the three sinners and especially his unfaithful priestess. Forgiveness—especially in a world in which revenge is normally taken for granted—would be "the most divine victory of all" (see below). It is the supreme virtue in eighteenth-century German domestic drama. It is true that Goethe does not expressly mention it. When he felt that a word had been overworked, he advised avoiding it for a while, and this may have been the case here. And Thoas uses his capacity to forgive in a thoroughly Goethean manner, that is, quietly and discreetly. He simply continues to show the same trust in Iphigenie that he has always had in her. He believes her without reservation and does not think her capable of any evil motive. Of course he is offended that she has acted behind his back and wants to leave him. But still he sees her suffering rather than her guilt. He calls this "the voice of truth and humanity" and puts up only weak resistance to it.

Thus he instinctively pushes to one side the demands of the gods. Religious law certainly requires of him that he immediately put the temple defilers, and particularly the priestess, to death. Instead Thoas seriously considers letting the Greeks go. A little later he wants to let combat between himself and Orestes decide whether the sacrifice of foreigners should be abolished once and for all. And when he finally remembers that he cannot let the Greeks leave with the image even if he wants to, he also suggests letting "weapons" decide. He does not treat the three offenders as criminals, as his religion demands. For him, religion has lost its absolute validity. His humanity is autonomous too, although admittedly he does not consciously play it off against the gods as Iphigenie and Orestes occasionally do. For that reason he does not give in until he can do so in accordance with the will of the gods.

As we have seen, Orestes creates the conditions for this with his reinterpretation of the oracle. Only his redemption makes him capable or it and, according to Rasch, this above all documents the autonomy of humanity. Rasch (and Borchmeyer follows him in this) denies that either the goddess or Iphigenie have any part in it.[16] According to them, Orestes alone grants himself the absolution traditionally granted to man by the Church. He liberates himself from his intolerable feelings of guilt by suffering in his state of unconsciousness such intensity of remorse that he anticipates the death penalty. This may be true. But how does it come to the second stage, to the reconciliation?[17] Karl Pestalozzi thinks that the reconciliation of the ancestors in the Hades vision is an exact reflection of Orestes' desire for reconciliation. While certainly true, in addition, and above all, it shows that ethical mentality that alone makes reconciliation possible. The pairs and groups consist in each case of the murdered and their murderers. If they are now reconciled and at peace with one another, something extraordinary must have happened, and indeed it really does resemble the "indescribable," which becomes "an event" at the end of *Faust*: the victims of murder must have forgiven their murderers "the inexpiably heavy guilt" and thus have absolved them—as in Schiller's *Braut von Messina* where, as we have already seen, forgiveness is "the most divine victory of all." In this, man actually does exercise a power rightly honored as a privilege of the Church. In the act of forgiveness he releases the sinner from the guilt—"The greatest of evils, however, is guilt" in Iphigenie, too.[18]

Schiller is perhaps the only person to this very day to realize that Goethe in this scene alone has grafted the gentler humanity of modern ethics onto an antiquity otherwise not renowned for such sentiments. And how does he do that? The forgiver reconciles the guilty party with him and with himself, and thus enables him to go on living. "Untainted humanity atones for all human frailties" is a central theme of Goethe's. For Rasch and Borchmeyer, this only applies to Orestes' self-redemption. But his ancestors are included in it, as is Iphigenie. She could feel obliged to close the circle and to take revenge in her turn on the murderer of Clytemnestra, her mother and her own avenger. We may assume that the gods probably bank on this. Instead she neither thinks of doing this, nor that it might even be necessary to forgive her brother. And this is precisely how she in fact does it. That is a degree of forgiveness that we see later in Gretchen and here in Thoas. Orestes, however, experiences his release from guilt in the presence of Clytemnestra in the trance, and of his sister when he comes to himself again: he experiences absolution as the blessing of having received forgiveness. This too is very typical of Goethe. The poet dedicated the lines about the redemption of human sins to the actor who, as Orestes, gave a marvelous performance of this particular scene. Goethe may have considered that, in an era of Restoration and reaction, the program of the Enlightenment, which advocated that its authors trustingly show the absolutist princes "the truth," together with Iphigenie's "casuistry" (Schiller), were too political and in a political sense no longer credible.[19] Yet Orestes' suffering and rehabilitation retained their value, both in human and political terms.

In 1815 Goethe called the end of Act III "the axis of the play."[20] And in 1787 he delayed the first reading by four weeks "on account of the strangeness of the attempt I dared to make with this play."[21] The element of daring is Tantalus. Borchmeyer says that the motif proclaims the Revolution and Goethe's own potential for revolt, but that, since the gods are good, it remains an unresolved aporia and is an artistic weakness.[22] This is an opinion I cannot share. Tantalus' crimes were much smaller than those of his descendants. But they were crimes against the gods, and they did not forgive. That is the difference here between man and gods—and princes. As it says in the play, "Those superior have forged with brazen chains cruel torments for the godlike bosom of the hero." This is Prometheus, the archetype of human autonomy, who, according to *Dichtung und Wahrheit*, together with Tantalus, forms part of the "overwhelming opposition in the background" of *Iphigenie*. In letters written during the years when Goethe was working on the prose version of *Iphigenie*, we find such rebellious statements as the following: "I feel enough courage to vow eternal hatred to the gods when they want to behave towards us as their image, mankind."[23] In the poem "The Divine," it is the good individual who fills the vacuum left by unknown gods. In *Iphigenie* the heroine is consciously good even if the gods should prove not to be, just as in the hymn, "Prometheus." Both poems appeared for the first time in 1785, without Goethe's knowledge, in the correspondence between Loessing and Mendelssohn about Spinoza's pantheism (which many called "atheism"). In an "otherwise most highly enlightened society," wrote Goethe, they brought amazingly archaic ideas to the point of "Explosion," Mendelssohn to his death bed[24] and Goethe "along with Lessing to be burned at the stake."[25]

In the drama the critique never becomes programmatic or ideological. The picture of the gods never becomes absolutely clear to the characters themselves. Men of good will put a positive interpretation on the bad deeds of the gods. In real life that was how one had to deal with the princes anyway. Goethe and his contemporaries liked to believe that in the long run the princes would be forced to conform to their public image, that is, to become good. It was therefore impossible to allow the potential irony and comedy of this to emerge too clearly. After the Revolution, and particularly in the Restoration, even these modest hopes vanished. This is probably the reason why Goethe's love was reserved not for the heroine and heroic truthfulness, but for forgiveness; and particularly for the silent protest of the Tantalus figure, Prometheus, who did not behave in a manner which was "subordinate enough," who was "genuinely tragic" and to whom Goethe attributed the main "appeal" and we can only begin to understand something of it again if we accept that in *Iphigenie* the oracle and the image of the good gods cannot be saved.

## NOTES

1. Heinz Schlaffer, *Faust Zweiter Teil. Die Allegorie des 19. Jahrhunderts* (Stuttgart: Metzler, 1981), p. 8.

2. Fritz Hackert, "Iphigenie auf Tauris," in *Goethes Dramen. Neue Interpretationen*, ed. Walter Hinderer (Stuttgart: Reclam, 1980), pp. 144–168, esp. p. 160.

3. Wolfdietrich Rasch, *Goethes "Iphigenie auf Tauris" als Drama der Autonomie* (Munich: Beck, 1979), pp. 19–23.

4. Dieter Borchmeyer, *Die Weimarer Klassik* (Königstein: Athenäum, 1980), vol. 1.

5. Werner Keller, "Das Drama Goethes," in *Handbuch des deutschen Dramas*, ed. Walter Hinck (Düsseldorf: Bagel, 1980), p. 140.

6. Hans Robert Jauß, "Racines und Goethes *Iphigenie*" (1973), in *Rezeptionsasthetik. Theorie und Praxis*, ed. Rainer Warning (Munich: UTB, 1975), pp. 353–400. For a critique of this essay, see Wittkowski, "Unbehagen eines Praktikers an der Theorie. Zur Rezeptions ästhetik von Hans Robert Jauß," *Colloquia Germanica* (1979): 1–27, esp. pp. 19–23.

7. Borchmeyer, *Die Weimarer Klassik*, pp. 108, 114.

8. Goethe, *Noten und Abhandlungen zum Westöstlichen Divan*. Hamburg ed., C. H. Beck, p. 223.

9. Rasch, Goethes "Iphigenie auf Tauris," p. 180.

10. Ibid., p. 108.

11. Ibid.

12. Ibid., p. 197.

13. Borchmeyer, *Die Weimarer Klassik*, p. 112.

14. Ibid., pp. 108, 114.

15. Benno von Wiese, *Die deutsche Tragödie von Leasing bis Hebel*, 5th ed. (Hamburg: Hoffman & Campe, 1961), p. 108.

16. Rasch, Goethes "*Iphigenie auf Tauris*," pp. 19–23; Borchmeyer, *Die Weimarer Klassik*, p. 114.

17. Karl Pestalozzi, "Goethe's *Iphigenie*, als Antwort an Lavater betrachtet," *Goethe Jahrbuch* (1981), pp. 113–130, esp. pp. 119, 125–129.

18. End of *Die Braut von Messina*. See Wolfgang Wittkowski, "Tradition der Moderne als Tradition der Antike. Klassische Humanität in Goethes *Iphigenie* und Schillers *Braut von Messina*," in *Tradition der Moderne. Festschrift Ulrich Fülleborn*, ed. T. Elm (Munich: Fink, 1982).

19. Schiller to Goethe, 22 January 1802.

20. *Italienische Reise*, 13 March 1787.

21. Goethe to Charlotte von Stein, 20 January 1781.

22. Borchmeyer, *Die Weimarer Klassik*, pp. 113, 112.

23. Goethe to Charlotte von Stein, 19 May 1778.

24. *Dichtung und Wahrheit*, Book 15.

25. Goethe to Friedrich Heinrich Jacobi, 11 September 1785.

26. *Dichtung und Wahrheit*, Book 15.

DONNA DIETRICH AND HARRY MARSHALL

# Thoas and Iphigenie: A Reappraisal

Traditional research has depicted the relationship between Thoas and Iphigenie as essentially one-sided: the rough barbarian (*"der rohe Skythe"*) on the one hand and the pure soul (*"reine Seele"*) on the other. Georg Brandes' interpretation is typical:

> If *Iphigenie* has become perhaps Goethe's most admired play, it is because he impregnated the subject-matter with that pure humanism which reached its zenith in his century. His Iphigenie makes a comforting impression. A rich and refined humanity shines forth from her. Her beauty has prevailed over the gruff Thoas, who aspires to her hand. Her nobility of character has softened the rough customs of the Sythians. Goethe does not present a goddess in the clouds, as Euripides does in his drama of the same name, but rather Iphigenie, as a higher sort of human being, almost becomes a goddess. She is reserved and feminine; but she has a sense of justice, which causes her to stake everything, her own well-being as well as the safety of her loved ones. She can't lie, can't deceive, she has to tell the king the truth and gain his approval of their departure.[1]

From *Goethe in the Twentieth Century*, Alexej Ugrinsky, ed. © 1987 by Hofstra University. Reproduced with Permission of Greenwood Publishing Group, Inc., Westport, CT.

H. A. Korff's similar summation is concise: "Iphigenie herself is the embodiment of noble humanity and genuine humanism. But it comes to her naturally, it is not obtained with difficulty, rather it is innate. She attests to the inner godliness of the world."[2]

More recently, particularly in Ronald Gray's Goethe book of 1967[3] and Wolfdietrich Rasch's *Iphigenie* study of 1979,[4] this interpretation has been modified considerably. Gray finds Iphigenie "egocentric" in her dealings with Thoas, and Rasch argues that she has little to do with Orestes' healing. The object of this paper will be to go even further along these lines by showing that Iphigenie's "humanism" is largely chimerical and that Thoas at least as much as Iphigenie if not more so plays the pivotal role in the resolution at the play's end.

Critics have dealt severely with Thoas' behavior in the first act chiefly because of his decision to reinstate the custom of human sacrifice. Gray, for instance, writes: "Thoas, then, is neither shown as a barbarian to whom sacrifices seem natural—in which case one might feel some greater sympathy—nor as a fundamentally good-natured if rash-tempered gentleman, but as a calculating, exacting man, unreliable in his pledged word, and brutally regardless of Iphigenie's dedicated virginity."[5] Rasch terms Thoas' action a "relapse" and "a serious personal failure, which shouldn't be glossed over."[6]

Yet it seems most logical to argue that Thoas, more or less on the spur of the moment and not with the express wish of pressuring Iphigenie into marriage as Rasch would have it,[7] resorts in this instance to a rather weak bluff, hoping at best to gain more time in which perhaps to captivate her reluctant heart. Emil Staiger comes close to the truth in his analysis of the turn of events, because he also leaves open the possibility that Thoas is not totally serious in his intention to renew the custom of human sacrifice: "Thoas renews the ancient custom. The poet had put the sacrifice aside, in order to tone down and contrast. It is however essential to the further course of action. The relapse can only be justified by the king's feeling deeply hurt and free from all responsibility. Injured love, offended dignity—less would have been insufficient."[8]

It is true, of course, that he can never win his suit—he is much too unaware of Iphigenie's aloof disdain of the Sythians—yet on an emotional level he is willing to try. Moreover, how can it be argued that he applied any pressure at all, when immediately previous to his decision he has told Iphigenie that she is free to return to Greece:

Return then! Let your heart dictate your way
And do not listen to the voice of reason
And careful counsel.[9]

There is never any indication that Thoas is, or ever was, the barbarian that some critics have made him out to be. He first exhibited his goodness by not sacrificing Iphigenie when she first appeared on his shores, an act he certainly should have done had he complied with the ancient custom. Arkas points this out rather clearly:

When some mysterious unfathomed fate
Sent you, so long ago, to serve this temple,
Thoas revered you as a gift from heaven,
He greeted you with honour and delight. (97–100)

The king acted toward Iphigenie "as a gift from heaven" although he did not yet know of the truth about her origin, that is, that the goddess Diana had brought her to his kingdom. Thoas' deportment preceding the marriage proposal is also humble and proper; his words show that he is a patient man who has learned to renounce:

... and I bear
An old desire within my heart, a wish
Not unbeknown to you, nor unexpected.
I long to lead you to my lonely hall
As bride—a blessing to my land, to me! (246–250)

And Iphigenie herself knows that the king has a "generous heart" (270).

Even the actual reinstatement can be read as a minor evil, compared to the tale Iphigenie has to tell, which causes the sensitive king to turn away "in terror" (389). Thoas' sin pales when seen in the light of the past evils of the house of Tantalus and even the Greeks in general, who, after all, inaugurated a long and bloody war, merely to avenge "the rape of lovliest Helen" (414). And the criticism that he knowingly requires Iphigenie to sacrifice her own brother is easily dismissed by pointing out not only that he is not aware that one of the two foreigners is her brother (or even a Greek for that matter), but also that there is no indication he would demand Orestes' death if he knew. Iphigenie herself admits that the king does not force her to carry out the sacrifice when she says:

> But if I should shirk
> This task the king's displeasure laid upon me,
> Then he will choose some temple votary
> As my successor. (936–939)

It is important to remember at this point that Thoas never does choose another priestess, a fact that also supports the contention that the reinstatement is nothing but a bluff. It is also likely that he knows in his heart that Iphigenie will not carry out his "wishes" due to his appreciation and understanding of what Arkas calls her "grace" (135).

Looking at the king's decision from another perspective, that is, comparing it with Agamemnon's sacrifice of Iphigenie, one cannot, with the best will in the world, find it more "barbarian." Agamemnon's deed is actually far *less* civilized in that it involves sacrificing his own daughter, whereas Thoas' is an act of civil defense. The king is, in fact, far more civilized than his own ancestors, as he himself points out:

> If she had fallen to my forebears' hands,
> Been spared their righteous, their most savage fury,
> Her single freedom would itself suffice
> To prompt her thanks, to point her destiny.
>
> The strangers' blood would flow before our alter
> Quickly enough! She'd gladly call
> Necessity her duty then! (1789–1796)

Goethe has Thoas renew the custom as part of a test of Iphigenie's character, which is exactly balanced by the test with which Orestes and Pylades confront her: complicity in robbing the statue of Diana. She is, of course, unwilling and unable to carry out either commission, yet both tests are indispensible for the establishment and maintenance of dramatic tension.

Goethe has an additional object in mind by having Thoas restore the sacrifice, when he has the king refer to it as Diana's will first and then his own:

> But may Diana grant me absolution
> That wrongfully and with deep self-reproach
> I have withheld her ancient sacrifice. (506–508)

The same also applies later, when he reminds Iphigenie that the custom is an ancient one: "It is our law, not I, that orders this" (1831). Goethe wants his heroine to come to terms with the goddess through Thoas directly in these instances, to show that her character is determined not so much from within as from without. Iphigenie's coming-to-terms with the Olympian gods is, after all, a central theme of the play. And her prayer to Diana at the end of the first act shows that she has doubts as to their efficacy, for she is not sure that the goddess will save her and the foreigners; if she were, what need would she have to petition Diana for salvation? Moreover, she has strong reasons for doubting and hesitation at this point, for she knows that the goddess has done nothing to prevent human sacrifice at Tauris before her arrival. Hence, she sees herself being drawn into the same fate that awaits the heirs of Tantalus.

A more efficacious structural device than the reinstatement of the custom is Thoas's promise to allow Iphigenie to return home, even if it is provisional: "If you may hope to find your home again" (293). The king's offer not only shows his nobility at the beginning of the play, but its fulfillment at the end turns him into the play's true hero. As Rasch argues: "The fortuitous conclusion of the drama is therefore already arranged by this promise and is not attained only by Iphigenie's effect on Thoas."[10] One can logically deduce, then, as Rasch does,[11] that the king would have let Iphigenie go had her brother arrived with peaceful instead of hostile intentions. Contrary to accepted opinion of Thoas's character, there is no evidence for the supposition that he would break his promise. It is the Greeks, then, and not the Sythians, who keep Iphigenie imprisoned on the island.

Thoas is the true hero of the play because of the promise he makes and because of the depth and goodness of his nature. It is the true and fatherly knowledge of Iphigenie's strengths and weaknesses that make his presence and voice essential to her salvation at the end and not vice versa, which has been the traditional view. Iphigenie is well aware of the extent of his understanding when she admits, albeit angrily: "You know it, know me! Yet compel me still?" (1854).

Thoas is Goethe's foil, his alter ego; his steadfastness is as essential to Iphigenie's salvation as, say, Antonio's is to Tasso's. When he says: "It is no god that speaks: it is your heart" (493), one hears Goethe's voice guiding Iphigenie along the right path. In the final act as well, Thoas gently brings Iphigenie away from the Greeks' plot toward the truth. As might be expected of him, he respects her words more than the sword of her brother. To her "But I have only words as my weapons, and a man of honour / Would not refuse to heed a woman's pleading" (1863f.) he replies "I heed it quicker than your brother's sword" (1865). A bit later, when she points out that as a mere weak woman she may have recourse to cunning, he checks her with "Be sure that such high judgement finds you guiltless" (1875).

Goethe places Iphigenie on the horns of a dilemma—having to choose between her loyalty to the Greeks on the one hand and to Thoas on the other—in order to test her and ultimately drive her to truth. Goethe clearly wants the king to win this battle of wills, which is illustrated by the simple fact that Iphigenie does not follow the Greeks' plan, but rather the "man of honour" (1864) Thoas, whom she has learned to respect and trust. She cannot go so far as to accept his marriage proposal, but his positive influence over her is clearly more effective than that of deceptive Greeks.

Iphigenie herself is aware of the straightforwardness and honesty of the barbarians, and this knowledge of their goodness also helps bring her around to the truth. She not only calls the king a noble man, she considers Arkas to be "loyal" as well (1523). Iphigenie comes to know these good qualities not so much on her own but rather through her contact with Thoas. In the final act, moreover, she has become so confident in her feelings toward the Taurians that we hear a new voice, one determined to deal with the king's demand: "You summoned me. What brings you here to us?" (1804). Thoas recognizes, however, that Iphigenie's desire to depart with her brother, even as he robs the sacred statue, is surely too much to ask; whereas he (Thoas) has allowed her plenty of time to respond to his wishes, she expects immediate action from him in return. As he laments: "You ask much of me in so short a space" (1988).

That Iphigenie changes from allegiance to the plot to truth in the fifth act cannot be explained away merely by the claim that her inner moral fiber rejects the lie. Rather, she has come to the realization that she is simply not a good liar and wouldn't get away with it. Her attempt at lying fails,[12] again brought on by the king's presence?—"They are—They seem—I think that they are Greeks" (1889)—and she soon must declare the truth. Moreover, Iphigenie does not risk very much by her honesty, for she is sure she will not be punished but rather rewarded by the father-figure Thoas for having told the truth.

Instead of exhibiting strength and nobility in the final scenes, then, Iphigenie really acts more like a child hoping for a reward. In fact, she seemed to foresee such conduct when she earlier said to Pylades: "I see I must be led / Even as a child is led in reins" (1401f.). There is a definite note of childlike defiance at the end of the passage in which she speaks the truth. To the king she says, with a feigned fear of reprisal, for she knows his benign nature well: "Destroy us—if you dare!" (1936). And she places herself further into the child's role in relation to Thoas when she says to Orestes:

> Revere in him
> The king who has become my second father.
> Brother, forgive me, but my simple heart
> Has ventured all our fortunes in his hand. (2003–2007)

Finally, in the last scene of the play, she refuses for the second time the king's request to depart on his terms: "Not thus, my Lord! I may not part / In anger from you, still denied your blessing" (2151f.). As in the first act, when Thoas made a similar request, she has to have her own way and depart on her own terms. The king's famous parting words ("Fare well!" (2174)), then, do not represent a reluctant sentiment of resignation but rather a confident yet disillusioned expression of his essential humanism. He has seen enough of the Greek's treachery to realize that feelings and not words are of the essence. If he has learned anything from Iphigenie, it is from her words "Do not deliberate: act with your heart" (1992).

## NOTES

1.  Georg Brandes, *Goethe* (Berlin: E. Reuss, 1922), p. 265.

2.  H. A. Korff, *Geist der Goethezeit*, 4 vols. (Leipzig: Koehler & Amelang, 1964), p. 160.

3.  Ronald Gray, *Goethe: A Critical Introduction* (London: Cambridge University Press, 1967).

4.  Wolfdietrich Rasch, *Goethes "Iphigenie auf Tauris" als Drama der Autonomie* (Munich: Beck, 1979).

5.  Gray, *Goethe*, p. 76.

6.  Rasch, *Goethes "Iphigenie auf Tauris,"* p. 99.

7.  *Ibid.*

8.  Emil Staiger, *Goethe*, 3 vols. (Zurich: Atlantis, 1952), I: 358.

9.  Goethe, *Iphigenie in Tauris*, trans. John Prudhoe (New York: Manchester University Press, 1966). Hereafter cited in the text by line number.

10. Rasch, Goethes *"Iphigenie auf Tauris,"* p. 107.

11. Ibid.

12. Rasch, *Goethes "Iphigenie auf Tauris,"* p. 162, calls this her inability to tell the *truth*!

HANS REISS

# Goethe's Torquato Tasso: *Poetry and Political Power*

The action of *Torquato Tasso* takes place at a court, the very centre of political power in the sixteenth century and still so in Goethe's own time. Eighteenth-century Europe was still mainly a monarchical continent. Republics were relatively rare and normally governed by oligarchical patrician groups. Even in Britain, where political power was, in the main, wielded by the aristocracy, the court still mattered. But although the ruler of Ferrara, Duke Alfons, and his principal minister Antonio Montecatino are major characters in the play, the plot is not primarily concerned with politics, at least not in the usual restricted sense of the word. Its central theme concerns the vicissitudes of a major Renaissance poet, Torquato Tasso, in late eighteenth-century Germany still ranked among the great figures of world literature, the peer of Homer and Virgil, Dante and Shakespeare.[1] His personal fate is at stake;[2] political questions do not, at first sight, appear to be at issue. No foreign army is imposing its will on citizens bent on safeguarding their own distinct way of life, as in *Egmont*, nor is the conflict between barbaric customs, on the one hand, and natural law and individual conscience, on the other, a major theme of the play, as it is in *Iphigenie auf Tauris*.[3] Yet if we probe more deeply, we discern an intrinsically political problem: has an individual a right to assert his own innate talent or genius, or even merely his own preferences, if in doing so he violates established rules and customs?

From *The Modern Language Review* 87, part 1. © 1992 by The Modern Humanities Research Association.

Court life has always been hierarchical. Before 1789 the poet, too, had a firm place assigned to him in the social order of the court, just as he had in society at large, though the writing of poetry was frequently thought of not as a way of life but as an activity pursued in leisure hours. The position occupied by a poet at court imposed obligations on him. He was expected to pay attention to the wishes of his patron and, on appropriate occasions, even write at his command. He was Poet Laureate, not only in name but in fact. In some ways, thus, he was imprisoned in a golden cage, but he would not necessarily, or even usually, have felt himself to be so confined. That would have been so only if he had had to work under a truly tyrannical patron or if he wanted openly to flout convention. In general, there is no reason to assume that poets were irked by the status assigned to them by convention. A poet knew his place in the scheme of things. If it restricted him in some ways, it also gave him assurance and security; it enabled him to follow his calling. He knew the public for which he was writing, and he was well aware what that public expected of him. He did not have a political role, strictly speaking. For him, politics, in the modern sense of the word, was out of bounds. In Germany, unlike in France or England, a writer was not able to participate in politics or even to influence public opinion in any substantial way.

Even if *Torquato Tasso* is not a political play, any individual's reaction to the arrangements made by society can be termed political. In that sense, Tasso is confronted with political choice. Conflict may arise between the poet's need to assert his individuality and the social conventions of the day, or the demands made upon him by the powers that be. From the beginning of the play it is unmistakably clear what kind of poetry the court expects Tasso to deliver: it is to create an imaginary world. This is implied by the pastoral dress worn by the Princess and Leonore Sanvitale, as well as by the setting, the country palace garden graced by the statues of Virgil and Ariosto. A realm of make-believe is set up in which poets are crowned with laurel wreaths and live far away from the hustle and bustle of practical life.[4] The poet is treated as a useful ornament, to suit the court's wishes. Admittedly, Tasso is not at the beck and call of a tyrant. The court of Ferrara in the play, in accordance with eighteenth-century ideals, is a place where high-minded men and women have congregated. (That reality in the eighteenth century and even more so in the sixteenth was markedly different need not be laboured!) Yet however civilized the Duke and his entourage may appear in the play, they lack understanding of the feelings and needs of someone as different from them as Tasso. They are, perhaps inevitably, content to accept the social and political *status quo*. They believe it to be in their interest to do so. Indeed, they cannot conceive an alternative way of living.

The Duke, in particular, wishes to be considerate and understanding, but he always remains the sovereign ruler, certain of his rights over his subjects and over a protegé such as Tasso (Borchmeyer, p. 76). He expects Tasso to complete his epic poem *Gerusalemme liberata*. Tasso has to carry out this task with dispatch to prove himself worthy of the Duke's patronage. He has to write the poem not to satisfy an inner urge but to reap benefits for his patron. The poem is to enhance the Duke's glory and his political standing in the realm of politics, in consonance with the Renaissance (and indeed the Baroque or Rococo) view of a prince's position. To that end the Duke feels he has the right to guide and order Tasso's life. His attitude is paternal, but is entirely in keeping with the practical reality of political life which the Duke as a ruler has to respect.

Tasso is a difficult subject, but since a renowned poet is a rare commodity, he is to be treasured. He needs, therefore, generous treatment and special consideration. The Duke is a humane ruler. He wishes to foster culture. He seeks to understand Tasso. But there are limits to his understanding, because of his position and political interests. Leonore expresses the view that it is a matter of ducal policy to have great literary men at the court, for patronage can pay handsome political dividends:

> Und es ist vorteilhaft, den Genius
> Bewirten: gibst du ihm ein Gastgeschenk,
> So läßt er dir ein schöneres zurück.
> Die Stätte, die ein guter Mensch betrat
> Ist eingeweiht, nach hundert Jahren klingt
> Sein Wort und seine Tat dem Enkel wieder.
>
> (l. 77)

Poetry produces fame. The ruler's status is assured both for the present and for posterity. Even the Princess, who is far less concerned with official cultural policy, reflects this view when she alludes to her delight in listening to the poet for whom 'die fürstliche Begier des Ruhms' (l. 129) has become material for his poetry. Patronage gives rights analogous to feudal or property rights. Tasso is a good investment which the Duke does not wish to lose:

> Ich bin auf ihn als meinen Diener stolz,
> Und da ich schon für ihm so viel getan,
> So möcht' ich ihn nicht ohne Not verlieren.
>
> (l. 2851)

The Duke fears that Tasso might be enticed away to another court:

> Er will verreisen; gut, ich halt' ihn nicht.
> Er will hinweg, er will nach Rom, es sei!
> Nur daß mir Scipio Gonzaga nicht,
> Der kluge Medicis ihn nicht entwende!
> (l. 2839)

The Duke is proud of Tasso; for he is *his* poet, to whom he has been exceptionally kind. But Tasso is, he thinks, also anything but easy to deal with. He is suspicious of others, by no means always justifiably so. His judgement is often clouded. Almost superhuman forbearance is required, at times, to cope with his moods. Yet the Duke is neither insensitive nor foolish and knows that he cannot control Tasso's mind:

> Ich kenne nur zu gut den Sinn des Mannes
> Und weiß nur allzuwohl was ich getan,
> Wie sehr ich ihn geschont, wie sehr ich ganz
> Vergessen, daß ich eigentlich an ihn
> Zu fordern hätte. Über vieles kann
> Der Mensch zum Herrn sich machen, seinen Sinn
> Bezwinget kaum die Not und lange Zeit.
> (l. 2865)

While always believing in the rights due to his patronage, he realizes that it is wrong to expect short-term results. As an experienced man of the world he knows that Tasso has to be carefully handled:

> Nicht alles dienet uns auf gleiche Weise;
> Wer vieles brauchen will, gebrauche jedes
> In seiner Art, so ist er wohl bedient
> (l. 2939)

But the limits of his tolerance are set by political convention. He expects Tasso to remain his subject, even when he has left Ferrara. Tasso is merely on leave: 'wie ich dich / als *mein*, obgleich entfernt, gewiß betrachte' (l. 3012).

The Duke always expects the reward due to him. Therefore, he will keep the manuscript of the poem until it has been copied. He concedes that Tasso may polish the verses, but should do so speedily so that the Duke may garner the public acclaim which he expects and needs: he wants results. He is impatient, although he should know that it takes time to produce an epic such as the *Gerusalemme liberata*, which runs to more than 15,000 verses. Moreover, court etiquette has to be observed. Therefore the Duke has to punish Tasso for drawing a sword, even though he knows that Antonio should have gone to greater lengths to avoid a quarrel. Indeed, the Duke does not really investigate the nature of the quarrel property. Admittedly, the punishment is lenient. The Duke is not insensitive to Tasso's feelings. He knows that Tasso will feel illuminated and the punishment will, although light in itself, appear harsh, far more severe than it really is. Yet he must punish Tasso because he feels obliged to uphold convention, though he is willing to exercise clemency with dispatch. Similarly, since it would run counter to convention and his political interests, a dynastic ruler would never be able to acquiesce in his unmarried sister having a love affair. Tasso himself does not at first rebel against the Duke's rights as a patron. He tells the Princess:

> Er ist mein Fürst!—Doch glaube nicht, daß mir
> Der Freiheit wilder Treib den Busen blähe.
> Der Mensch ist nicht geboren, frei zu sein,
> Und für den Edlen is kein schöner Glück,
> Als einem Fürsten, den er ehrt, zu dienen.
> Und so ist er mein Herr, und ich empfinde
> Den ganzen Umfang dieses großen Worts.
> Nun muß ich schweigen lernen wenn er spricht
> Und tun wenn er gebietet, mögen auch
> Verstand und Herz ihm lebhaft widersprechen.
>
> (l. 928)

Of course, this speech teems with the rhetoric of courtly convention. Yet it indicates differences of opinion between the Duke and Tasso. But this does not mean that Tasso is already aware that he will later cut himself loose from the Duke's patronage. He is still acting as befits a court poet. For on his first appearance he brings the poem which he has just completed, his masterpiece, *Gerusalemme liberata*, to the Duke as an act of homage. He appears genuinely to feel that the work owes its completion to the Duke's protection, which enhanced its worth (l. 402). He knows that he needs the court, for it alone provides an appropriate audience (Borchmeyer, p. 74). Yet his words make it plain that he views poetry differently from the way the Duke and the courtiers see it. In providing sustenance the Duke elevated him to 'einer schönen Freiheit' (l. 418). But he is mistaken in his appraisal of the Duke's attitude. He wrongly believes that the Duke shares his view of poetry and possesses genuine empathy for its intrinsic worth and intention.[5] In the course of the action, Tasso becomes aware of the gulf which separates his conception of poetry from that of the court. He becomes convinced that it is the poet's duty to write poetry as he alone thinks fit. A poet must not be coerced, be it directly or indirectly, to write his poetry to order. Moreover, he must be allowed to lead that kind of life which he considers necessary for the writing of poetry. Thus, Tasso's view of a poet's freedom runs counter to what the court expects a poet to be like. The individual and the powers that be are potentially (and as the play develops, actually) locked into conflict with one another.[6]

At first Tasso deceives himself in believing that he will be able properly to play the role of a courtier. He wants to belong to the court, but he finds he cannot be subservient for long. Soon he strongly resents the whole tutelage entailed by patronage. Outwardly, he accepts completely the system of courtly rules and etiquette and the Duke's right to impose his will; inwardly, he yearns for freedom and self-determination. But he does not want solely to dwell in the world of poetic dreams. When Antonio returns from Rome, proud of his diplomatic success, Tasso wants to participate in the world of action. Given his temperament and experience, it appears an unrealistic, indeed, absurd wish, for it does not arise from an understanding of the world of practical life. It is a cry of the heart, symbolizing his yearning for another mode of existence. It makes him espouse the grievous, indeed potentially pernicious, error of applying aesthetic criteria to political situations:[7]

> Was mir noch jetzt die ganze Seele füllt,
> Es waren die Gestalten jener Welt,
> Die sich lebendig, rastlos, ungeheuer
> Um *einen* großen, einzig klugen Mann
> Gemessen drelit und ihren Lauf vollendet,
> Den ihr ein Halbgott vorzuschreiben wagt.
>
> (l. 789)

Equally utopian is his belief that Antonio could, if he so chose, give him lessons in statecraft, as if that subject could be taught. Tasso cannot acquire those gifts which nature has denied to him, the gifts needed to survive and even to prosper in the jungle of public life. Indeed, his vision of the golden age where the instinctive response of all citizens guarantees a harmonious social and political life is naive. He conjures up a world of innocence and harmony, a Rousseauist view of the state of nature. This conception of 'erlaubt ist, was gefällt' (l. 994) amounts to wishful thinking about politics.[8] The Princess appropriately corrects this unrealistic view by asserting that rules of conduct have to apply in public life. 'Erlaubt ist, was sich ziemt' (l. 1006) is the right approach. Of course, her view is limited. If the rules of conduct are too severely applied to public life, individuality can be repressed, creativity and change inhibited, if not excluded.

Lack of realism is not the prerogative of poets, nor does it necessarily form an integral part of a poet's personality. Goethe was a first-rate administrator and could, if he so wished, handle others well. Tasso is quite different. How unrealistic Tasso's approach to politics is can be gauged when he tempestuously seeks to gain Antonio's friendship. He does not know how to handle a practical situation. However, Antonio does not respond sensitively either. Indeed, for once the skilful diplomat is at sea. He does not know how to deal with a situation where the conventional rules of conduct, within whose framework he operates like a past master, are flouted. But statesmen ought to be able to prove their mettle in unusual situations. In mitigation, it could be argued that Tasso presses his demands heedless of Antonio's feelings and position. However, both men are at fault, Antonio more so; for as the Duke comments:

> Wenn Männer sich entzweien, hält man billig
> Den Klügsten für den Schuldigen.
>                    (l. 1619)

Tasso does not spell out what he wants from Antonio when he asks for his friendship. Antonio feels that Tasso wishes to participate in his political activities, and sees no point in agreeing to Tasso's request. Like most politicians he is keen on preserving his power and sees no need for compromise, let alone for a generous action based on impulse. Politicians do not give way unless it is in their interests or they are forced to do so. Therefore, Antonio stonewalls. Tasso insists on his right to be ranked among the nobility, not because he is noble by birth (that he was a member of the minor nobility in historical fact is not mentioned). He claims to belong to the nobility because he possesses nobility of heart. This view was not unknown in eighteenth-century Germany. For instance, it was advocated by Johann Michael von Loen, Goethe's great-uncle, in his tracts *Der Kaufmanns-Adel* (1742) and *Der Adel* (1752). Goethe himself held a similar view when, as a Frankfurt patrician (which he was not), he claimed to be of a rank equal to that of the nobility. Of course, the still strongly hierarchical society of the eighteenth century did not accept that rank could be determined by personality.

Tasso's quarrel with Antonio is rooted in his belief in his right as a poet to enjoy an equal standing with a cabinet minister. He feels quite correctly that Antonio denies that status to him. That conviction brings him to the point where he feels it necessary to break the court's rules and draw his sword. He thus commits a serious offence, a resort to (potential) violence, out of place in, and indeed abhorrent to, a courtly society. Antonio does not understand Tasso. For him he is a youth, a misguided enthusiast.[9] He lacks experience and judgement, the criteria by which men ought, so he avers, to be appraised. Antonio considers Tasso to be an idler who believes he can reap rewards without effort. Antonio fails to grasp how hard a taskmaster poetry is. Yet he has a point in arguing that poetry is not a guide to action:

> Wie leicht der Jüngling schwere Lasten trägt
> Und Fehler wie den Staub vom Kleide schüttelt!
> Es wäre zu verwundern, wenn die Zauberkraft
> Der Dichtung nicht bekannter wäre, die
> Mit dem Unmöglichen so gern ihr Spiel
> Zu treiben liebt.
>
> (l. 1487)

The Duke takes Antonio to task for misjudging the situation. On being thus reproached, Antonio immediately agrees to put matters right, for his master's word is for him a command. His own convictions do not matter. In any case, we never learn what his innermost thoughts are, since he does not appear alone on the stage. He changes his attitude to fall in line with that of the Duke. If he is at odds with his master's views he is wrong and must adapt his tune as quickly and deftly as possible. Antonio knows where power lies and will do all he can to make sure that his master is satisfied with his conduct. He never contradicts the Duke. Of course, he is not free from desires and impulses. He seeks 'den Lorbeer und die Gunst der Frauen' (l. 2020). But the laurel which he seeks cannot be that granted to the poet. It must be that of the statesman, as Leonore points out. He enjoys the confidence of his master; he can see the fruits of his diplomatic or political activity. Therein lies his reward. It is much more tangible than the fame of a poet, for the results are immediately evident. Posterity may give a poet far greater fame, but politicians need reward in the here and now. Women, too, respond to Antonio, but he is, as Leonore tells him, far too self-contained to need them.

Antonio is quite content to live by conventional wisdom. If he furthers his interests, he usually does so by stealth, by apparently complying with the Duke's wishes. Whatever his feelings may be (and they are not spelt out) his overwhelming ambition to enjoy political and diplomatic success always prevails. His friendly gesture at the end of the play can be interpreted in the light of this attitude. He follows the course charted by his master, for he knows that the Duke's mind is set not on punishment but on reconciliation. His final action is both humane and adroit.[10] just as he had skilfully explained to the Duke how his mission to placate Tasso and make him stay in Ferrara failed, so he shows sensitivity in offering Tasso support in his moment of travail. Yet the image of the rock applied by Tasso to Antonio also intimates his limitations. Tasso's attempt to venture into uncharted seas, even at the risk of being shipwrecked is not for Antonio. In comparison to Tasso, Antonio appears, so to speak, a landlocked being. Therefore, the conflict with the powers that be does not arise, since he never runs any risks.

The Princess and Leonore, too, accept the rules of practical life completely. The Princess renounces her love because she feels the need to comply with the rules as they prevail at court. Her love for Tasso is, in fact, entirely circumscribed by social conventions. For her there is no other way of dealing with the situation. She is never tempted to flout court rules. Propriety conditions, if not her feelings, at least their expression. She implies that conflict can be avoided by accepting the rules on traditional conduct as a guide. She relies on custom and courtesy, a word derived from the realm of courtly society. Since she is not passionate by nature she has little difficulty in complying with convention. She does not share Tasso's view of art. For her the task of art is not to make an impact on life but to be a substitute for it.[11] Hers is a passive response. Her feelings and personal wishes must be subordinate to traditional conduct.

Leonore Sanvitale does not wish to run counter to convention either. On the contrary, she uses it for her own advantage to take Tasso away from her friend, the Princess. She does so deliberately, though she rationalizes her selfishness by claiming that she is not harming her friend, who is bent on renouncing him in any case. She stifles any qualms which she may have about depriving the Princess of Tasso's company by saying that he will be absent only for a while; she will allow him to return to Ferrara, and the Duke's glory will not be impaired. But it never occurs to her to consider Tasso's own wishes. She is keen on having her own way and enjoying the renown of being celebrated by a famous poet.

Wie reizend ist's in seinem schönen Geist
Sich selber zu bespiegeln!

(1. 1928)

For a married woman, a love affair in Renaissance court society was acceptable, provided etiquette was preserved.

All four characters (the Duke, Antonio, the Princess, and Leonore) pursue their own ends and are blinded by the (conventional) belief that Tasso's interests must coincide with theirs, since he is bound to share their outlook on life. Their enlightenment is limited by their conventional understanding of life which denies Tasso the right to make his own decisions. Thus, each of Tasso's friends (and they believe they are his friends) abuses his or her position by seeking to make Tasso do what he or she wants him to do. They believe they know better what is good for him than he himself does. They seek to impose happiness upon him, and produce revolt. Their actions recall Kant's criticism of paternalism in politics; if a ruler sets out to make his people happy he brings about either tyranny or rebellion, since his conception of happiness is likely to differ from that of the people. The Duke treats Tasso as a subject who has to obey; for Antonio he is, at least till the last scene, a pawn in a political game; for Leonore, he is a pawn, too, but in a private one. The Princess allows her feelings to be smothered by external rules. Each of them harms Tasso without actually wishing to do so.

But what about Tasso? Does he accept the politics of the *status quo*? His attitude is ambivalent. On the one hand, he respects Alfons as his master. On the other hand, he finds it impossible to accommodate himself to those court rules which run counter to his inner nature both as a man and as a poet. When he believes the Princess returns his love he is prepared to defy society and assert the supremacy of feeling and individual self-realization over social and political customs and convention. This view is, at bottom, an enlightened view of the world. Tradition is to be judged at the bar of individual development.

Not only as a man but as a poet, Tasso objects to finding himself in chains. No wonder that his voice rises to strident tones. His reaction is extreme, but he finds the pressures intolerable and hence commits errors of judgement. He feels coerced to revise his work speedily. Moreover, he does not want to write conventional poetry, but wishes to speak with his own voice. He has the highest conception of poetry and therefore feels that poetic perfection should not be sacrificed to utilitarian considerations, such as his patron's wish for glory. Yet he is caught on the horns of a dilemma. On the one hand, only he knows what is right for his poetry. On the other hand, he needs recognition by the very men and women from whom he wants to free himself. He needs a patron and an audience. Yet to write the poetry that he wants to write he needs freedom from constraint by convention. He needs political rights in the wider sense of the word.

Thus, Tasso's problem is that of being confronted with two irreconcilable courses of action: to respect tradition and to pursue freedom. The court society to which he belongs cannot offer him both—but he needs both. In this conflict lies the source of his tragedy. It cannot be resolved within the confines of practical action. Only by poetic creation can he respond successfully. As a man, he is condemned to silence; the pain inflicted upon him by events is too great. But as a poet he can speak; he speaks for all those who are in chains but find that art can tell of their sorrows. Tasso's experience reflects Goethe's own problem, though it would of course be foolish in the extreme to identify the unworldly Tasso with Goethe, the man of practical experience and diplomatic skill. Yet Goethe was well aware of the political conflict between man's urge for freedom and his need to respect tradition. As a student of Justus Möser he accepted his master's conservative assessment that tradition has to be heeded if conflict is to be avoided. But he also knew that tradition must sometimes be challenged in the name of individuality and creativity. Traditional patterns could thus be reformed. Without such reforms revolt will sooner or later ensue. An isolated individual who challenges the conventions of his society is likely to be harmed. But a poet can speak for the individual who is overwhelmed and may, through poetry, in due course be able to modify and change tradition. By means of his work he can affect public opinion and modify attitudes. Yet *Torquato Tasso* does not preach. None of Goethe's great works does that, for to have done so would have been implicitly to connive with the court's view that poetry should serve an ulterior end. Yet he knew that poetry could make an indirect impact. As he remarked in *Dichtung und Wahreit*:

> Ein gutes Kunstwerk kann und wird moralische Folgen haben,
> aber moralische Zwecke vom Künstler zu fordern, heißt ihm
> sein Handwerk verderben. (III, 12)

Goethe himself experienced this conflict between freedom and tradition. It is in this context that we may understand his well-known words spoken to Eckermann on 6 May 1827, 'daß Tasso Bein von meinem Bein und Fleisch von meinem Fleische ist'. They reflect the problem which he encountered at the court in Weimar. On the one hand, he accepted its conventions and traditions; on the other hand, he found this world increasingly restrictive,

threatening to stifle his creative powers. He wanted to reform political life
but found himself unable to do so: hence his need to escape to Italy. But even
if he escaped to live a life dedicated to the pursuit of individual experience,
he never severed his links with the duchy of Weimar. He stayed a Privy
Councillor and left it to his poetry to convey his doubts about conventions,
as well as his attachment to and respect for his patron and employer, his
sovereign, Duke Carl August of Saxe-Weimar-Eisenach. He escaped from
tradition to return to it. The relationship between the two men was not
always easy, but it lasted.

But Goethe did not merely side with Tasso. He also recognized that if
a poet (or for that matter, anyone) lacks balance and judgement, he will
unavoidably incur suffering. He knew that the demands of the real world
cannot be set aside lightly. A man of genius, too, has to learn to live with
them. (There is of course not the slightest suggestion of his acquiescing in
inhuman acts or outright tyranny.) But it may appear to him impossible to do
so: hence the 'Disproportion des Talents mit dem Leben' of which,
according to Caroline Herder (March 1789), Goethe spoke. Not only genius
but also practical life has rights that need to be respected. Those in power
cannot always accommodate an individual's wishes, since they have to cope
with political realities. Goethe saw both sides of the question. He presented
a complex picture of reality, and that makes the play so inexhaustible a work
of literature. It is also the best way in which a poet can further the process of
enlightenment.[12] Goethe amply did so in *Torquato Tasso*.[13]

## NOTES

1. Wolfdietrich Rasch emphasizes Tasso's high reputation before 1800
(*Goethes Torquato Tasso. Die Tragödie des Dichters* (Stuttgart: Metzler, 1954),
pp. 39–40).

2. This view is generally accepted; see Rasch, *Goethes Torquato Tasso*,
and Elizabeth M. Wilkinson, 'Goethe's *Tasso*: The Tragedy of a Creative
Artist', *Publications of the English Goethe Society*, n.s. 15 (1946), 96–127
(reprinted as 'Goethe's *Torquato Tasso*. The Tragedy of the Poet', in *Goethe:
Poet and Thinker*, by Elizabeth M. Wilkinson and L. A. Willoughby (London:
Arnold, 1962)), pp. 75–94, both of whom take this view.

3. See my article '"Theological" Politics in Goethe's *Iphigenie auf
Tauris*', in *Patterns of Change: German Drama and the European Tradition.
Essays in Honour of Ronald Peacock*, ed. by Dorothy James and Sylvia Ranawake

(New York, Frankfurt a.M., and Berne: Lang, 1990), pp. 59–71, where I put forward that argument.

4. Dieter Borchmeyer emphasizes this point (*Höfische Gesellschaft und französische Revolution bei Goethe* (Kronberg/Ts: Athenäum, 1977), p. 71).

5. See Borchmeyer, p. 74, where this is stated very clearly.

6. T. J. Reed analyses the contrast between the two views of the world ('Tasso und die Besserwisser', in *Texte, Motive und Gestalten. Festschrift für Hans Reiss*, ed. by John L. Hibberd and H. B. Nisbet (Tübingen: Niemeyer, 1989), pp. 103, 105).

7. T. J. Reed convincingly argues that it is wrong to assume that the court society, the establishment, is right and Tasso wrong, and that a case can, therefore, be made out for Tasso's attitude towards the court (pp. 100–02). But however justified Reed's criticism of the court establish-ment is, due weight ought none the less also to be given to the practical political situation to which the Duke must pay attention.

8. See Reed, p. 102, where he speaks of a tacit conspiracy by the members of the court directed against Tasso. This is at best only partly true. The members of the court are not mistaken in all facets of their appraisal of Tasso's character and abilities. For instance, there is no evidence in the play that he is suited to carry out administrative or political tasks. Compare Ronald Peacock, *Goethe's Major Plays* (Manchester: Manchester University Press, 1959), p. 106; Peacock even considers Tasso's 'absurd disregard of the realities of the situation' as a central feature of his character. To take a critical view of Tasso's suitability for active participation in political life does not necessarily mean siding entirely with the establishment's view of his aspirations. I differ from Reed, who suggests (p. 89) that the word 'Gelassenheit' sometimes carries a negative association in the play.

9. See Reed, who makes this point convincingly (pp. 108–09).

10. In his justified criticism of Antonio's attitude Reed does not take account of his humane stance at the end of the play (pp. 100–01).

11. Gerhard Kaiser emphasizes this aspect of the Princess's attitude ('Der Dichter und die Gesellschaft in Goethes Torquato Tasso', *Wanderer und Idylle* (Göttingen: Vandenhock & Ruprecht, 1977), p. 202). See also Hans Rudolf Vaget, 'Um einen Tasso von außen bittend. Kunst und Dilettantismus am Musenhof von Ferrara', *Deutsches Vierteljahrsschrift für Literaturwissenschaft und Geistesgeschichte*, 54 (1980), 232–58 (p. 241). Vaget writes: 'Kunst dient ihr als Lebensersatz, an dem sie sich in der Einsamkeit erquickt.'

12. See Reed, 'Tasso und die Besserwisser', pp. 108–11; he rightly emphasizes the importance of Enlightenment ideas in the play.

13. A conversation with T. J. Reed spurred me on to draft this paper some months before I heard an English version of his 'Tasso und die Besserwisser' at a conference of University Teachers of German in Great Britain and Ireland at Sheffield in April 1988. I revised my argument in the light of his essay. Since Reed's views were expressed in an essay which appeared in the *Festschrift* dedicated to myself and for which I am most grateful I hope that it does not appear churlish to differ with him over some aspects of his argument. I trust that he will accept my comments as an argument *inter amicos*, both of whom are concerned to promote ideas first mooted by the Enlightenment and formulated by Immanuel Kant. My thanks are also due to John Hibberd for his useful scrutiny of my text.

JOHN GEAREY

# Faust II *and the Darwinian Revolution*

In a footnote to the Introduction of his *Origin of Species*, Darwin cites Goethe as among those earlier thinkers whose views in one way or another had anticipated his own. 'It is rather a singular instance of the manner in which similar views arise at about the same time, that Goethe in Germany, Dr. Darwin [his grandfather] in England, and Geoffroy Saint-Hilaire ... in France, came to the same conclusion on the origin of species, in the years 1794–95.' That is precisely my point. Whatever the differences in the concept of evolution that Goethe and Darwin separately espoused, and however significant those differences would eventually prove to be in subsequent scientific thought, they nevertheless partook of the common revolution in thinking that was occurring in the age.[1] Darwin refers here, of course, to Goethe the scientist, but we note that he chooses to single out for recognition not any particular accomplishment of his early contemporary, but his general method or approach. The equivalent in art of method or approach in science, however, is form. While the scientific thought of the age played an important role in the creation of *Faust* almost from the beginning, it is to the form rather than the content of that thought that the second part of the work owes its unusual genius and with which the present chapter, for the most part, is concerned.

From *Goethe's Other* Faust. © 1992 by the University of Toronto Press.

Darwin said of Goethe: 'He has pointedly remarked that the future question for naturalists will be how, for instance, cattle got their horns, and not for what they are used.'[2] We ask how *Faust II* came to have its form and not what purpose it served.

The question may seem idle, just as when applied in the scientific realm its implications are not at first clear. But the same distinction between the concept of creation by design and by adaptation that caused a revolution in thought when brought to bear in the natural world has a bearing also in the world of art. Not that the future question for criticism should be how a work of art got its form. Creation by design has been so persistent an assumption in the tradition that it seems almost a definition of art. It is only when a distinct departure from the norm takes place in a radical assertion of content over form that we can speak of a true variant having come into being and meaningfully ask the question.

*Faust II* provides such an opportunity, perhaps unprecedentedly. For the sense of form is the product of tradition, and what deviates significantly from the tradition will appear unformed and thus unartistic, unless establishing itself, the deviant in turn becomes absorbed in a new progression which gradually identifies, clarifies, and justifies its existence. This was the case with Romanticism. The tradition creates form and form is created by the tradition, after the fact. There are, to be sure, exceptions. One thinks of Dante's *Divine Comedy*, a work which no more evolved formally (its content is another matter) from a literary past than it produced a new poetic medium for the future. But Dante was creating within a framework of inherited moral and metaphysical values which he accepted, and reflected in his poem. Without the guide of form his meanings can be surmised from the suppositions underlying his work. Goethe was attempting in *Faust* to create a new set of values from a new set of suppositions. Here structure emerged not as a vehicle for the expression of ideas but as a mode of experience outside of which the new suppositions and values were not to be conveyed. It has been said of *Faust* that it does not express a philosophy so much as it creates a modern myth.

We have *Faust II* in transit. If we read the work against the past it seems propelled by its otherness away from the tradition and yet not toward any subsequent development that might serve to identify its purposes and explain its differences. This, again, is in regard to form, not matter. If there have been developments in art that throw *Faust II* into new perspective, they have come not from drama, or for that matter from literature, but from the visual arts. Here the revolution in form has succeeded not only in creating but in establishing new modes of perception. A kind of literary cubism does in fact suggest itself in the interrupted sequences and broken surfaces of *Faust II*. Goethe was conscious of this problem of re-creating reality in art: 'Since much of our experience does not allow itself to be expressed directly, I have long since used the device of conveying more hidden meanings by juxtaposing images one against the other and as it were mirroring themselves.'[3] It was as if the deeper currents in the age, or the deeper potential of the Faust theme which was its herald, had already prompted in the late Goethe a development that would subsequently emerge as a general and broad concern: the imitation in art of reality perceived, not by the eye but in the mind.

Goethe did not plan an original or experimental design for *Faust*. He placed little importance on originality, which he was more likely to see as mannerism. Experimentation of the kind that the early German Romantics championed in their esthetic theory, if less in poetic practice, he scorned. His own originality derived not from novelty but from the ability to express wholly and truly what in others almost invariably appeared fragmentary or forced. The fundamental nature of his genius rested upon this wholeness of mind which we admire more than we can imitate. In his experimentation he also shunned novelty, choosing his models from classical or traditional, folk or popular literature. Rarely did he look to innovate. Only in his early, *Sturm und Drang* period do we find exceptions.

But how to account for the dramatically disjunctive structure of *Faust II*, for its apparent lack of wholeness, if it is not the product of originality or experimentation? It is the result of an evolution. The work from its inception seems to have followed an inner law or laws that more than considerations of art determined its course. Goethe often spoke of the work as if it had a life of its own. In a letter to his publisher, it is a 'witches' creation'—*ein Hexenprodukt*.[4] At the height of his classical period, which *Faust* spanned, as it spanned all other stages of his development in its long years in the making, he could refer to it in a letter to the art historian Hirt as a 'barbarism' from which he would happily be free.[5] To the end the work remained 'the strangest the world has seen or will see,' as he wrote to the composer Zelter.[6] And while Part II, with its five-act format and its verse forms derived from classical traditions, presents itself superficially as a balanced conclusion to a tumultuous beginning, in fact it represents a far more radical departure from the norm than Part I and gains its balance only through a revision, a re-seeing, of the dramatic form at a depth that meter, rhyme, and the division into acts do not touch. Yet the departure and the newly discovered vision were not the product of design so much as the result of demands and constraints upon the work that, gradually but inevitably accumulating, had somehow finally to be confronted and resolved. The form of *Faust II*, one might say, is what remained after all other matters had been settled except the matter of form.

Yet the play is not formless. 'Content brings form with it; form is never without content,' Goethe himself wrote in the plan of 1800. Moreover, he held to this tenet, if that is what it may be called, this fact of art that becomes apparent and gains meaning only in the event of a mutation in form. Such an event was *Faust II*, a triumph of content over form which yet brought form with it.

How this occurred, and how it was possible, are questions that will concern us in general and in detail throughout this study. For the triumph of content over form, as I say, is the process of evolution itself. In citing Darwin and the evolutionist mode of thinking I was not merely using modern concepts to describe a phenomenon as easily understood simply as development and change, but seeking to identify the matrix of thought that produced both *Faust II* and *On the Origin of Species*, a revolution in art and a revolution in science.[7]

The age as a whole had eaten of the tree of scientific knowledge. Not only Goethe, who practiced science, but the poets of his and the later generation that his lifetime spanned show a remarkable awareness of the scientific developments in their times.[8] Remarkable, because we are often inclined, wrongly, to think of this era that we call Romantic as distancing itself from the world of science. We think rather of the *philosophes* of an earlier generation as joining the poetic and the scientific in their thought. But it was in natural history, as we noted at the outset, that the great advances of the age occurred, so that the so-called Romantic poets and writers in pursuing the subject that was in fact their characteristic concern—Nature— had their science where their interest lay. An affinity in structure rather than in content of thought again suggests itself in the separate fields. Thus, Schiller, who was exceptionally unconcerned with science, seems nevertheless through sheer application of his contemporary intelligence to have uncovered in history, and in the analysis of history in his dramas, the same kind of developmental contexts that were emerging in science to explain the phenomena of the natural world. The moral dilemma posed by the new understanding was the distinctly modern feature he brought to the concept of tragedy and yet, with its implications of determinism, historicism, and relativism, the feature that repulsed him. The dilemma drove him back, as we noted in the preceding chapter, upon an idealistic moral position, a position prevalent *in* the age but, by its absolutist nature, not truly *of* the age. Similarly, Herder, who gained that title he is sometimes accorded of 'father' of modern history precisely through the importance he placed on historical development as a determinant in human action, failed to draw new moral conclusions from the base he had newly conceived for human behavior. Herder, it is true, was a pastor and his moral precepts were tied to religion. But it is also true that he did not write dramas, which is a form of expression, a mode of discourse that demands a moral resolution in a way that history and science do not.

In *Faust II* Goethe fully absorbed the implications of the science and thought of his day and drew the ultimate conclusions. It was not that his science went deeper than that of his literary contemporaries, though surely it did. But whereas Balzac, for example, cited the work of the celebrated naturalists of the era, Buffon, Cuvier, and Geoffroy Saint-Hilaire, as analogous to his own great undertaking in *The Human Comedy*,[9] Goethe made the bridge with science in principle. The extent to which the form of *Faust II* deviates from the dramatic tradition is a measure of the depths at which his thought conflicted with the view of human action on which the traditional dramatic forms were predicated. There is no suggestion of such a departure for the novel in *The Human Comedy*.[10] Nor do we find in general in Goethe a radical morality radically portrayed. *Faust* is alone in pressing the question,[11] though less in its capacity as a philosophical poem than in the condition of its being. The pact, or wager, it concludes with the Devil requires that it demonstrate in its action what it presumes in its thought, and that thought was different from any thought that had come before.

The Renaissance has been described as a secularization of an essentially religious frame of mind inherited from the Middle Ages.[12] Goethe, as if in an inevitable next step, sought a naturalization of the abstract moral and metaphysical principles of the preceding age through the scientific understanding that was the mark of his own age. His view did not preclude what had come before, rather it reinterpreted or, better, co-interpreted the ways of God to man in terms of the laws of nature. The Prologue in Heaven of Part I had already set the pattern. From the higher vantage point it afforded, but now in the physical sense, Goethe was able to effect the transmission of his science into poetry by the description from eternity of the earth in its turbulent, almost violent atmosphere that was the arena in which the action would play itself out. The description is as physically accurate as it is poetically striking and dramatically relevant. The point is not its scientifically conceived accurateness, however, nor its expressive beauty, but its reminder that the physical and the poetic are one, or, at least, they strive to be one. Goethe in the essay *On Morphology* stated: 'One forgot that science had developed out of poetry; one did not consider that after a revolution in time the two might again meet on a higher plane, to their mutual advantage.'13

Appropriately, then, *Faust*, Part II begins with what has been called a 'prelude on earth.'14 The contrast helps to relate the two parts—an impression Goethe attempted to reinforce in any minor way as he faithfully developed the theme in his work at the expense of its dramatic continuity. But the importance of this second prologue lies again in its physical, and thus philosophical, positioning of man. The Faust who, standing on earth, looks to heaven, to the sun, in order to know and to see, must turn away blinded, as if in a scientific confirmation of the religious or philosophical concept that certain truths are not allowed to man. Faust turns his back to the sun so that he may see by its reflected light: 'So let the sun behind me stand.'15 This position of man in the universe, in 'die große Welt,' which is the composite world of times and places in the play, determines the nature and development of its action just as the glimpse of the turbulence in his physical setting anticipated the inner life of the individual in 'die kleine Welt' of Part I.

A transformation and naturalization of morality also occurs immediately in Part II. The Faust who has sinned so greatly in the Gretchen tragedy is not made to repent and so proceed as hero and protagonist in a new action. He is made to sleep. Sleep 'removes the burning shaft of keen remorse,' as does repentance; sleep 'bathes him in the dew of Lethe's stream,'16 restoring him to life, as if nature were causing with time what morality causes through sentiment. Not that the transforming of the philosophical and the moral into the physical and the natural introduces a new vision in which the scientific grasp or basis of reality would substitute for the abstract and diffused concepts in earlier thought. *Faust* in fact ends with a religious epilogue. But the religiously colored ending is no more a concession to the historical setting of the theme than is the biblically allusive Prologue in Heaven, as fitting as both might be. Nor, conversely, does it represent a final, transcendent vision. Like the poetic and the scientific, the moral and the natural, it is yet another metaphor, a co-interpretation.

The structure of Part II is designed to bring the audience or the reader, but not Faust, to that recognition. 'Everything transitory / Is but a metaphor,' as the Chorus Mysticus says in summary at the end of the play. His progress will be the reliving of the deeper antecedent experience that brings him to an ultimate resolution, a 'final wisdom' in his time, as if he were a child of the collective unconscious. Our progress is a growing awareness of that process.

*Faust II* is there more for us, as *Faust I* was there for the hero. At times we observe with him events in which he himself has little active part. The action itself, by its nature, is almost always at one remove, for us in the sense that we are experiencing illusion or poetry, for him in that he knows that the substance of his life is not 'real' but the product of magic. When he attempts to make real his union with Helen of Troy, initially at the end of Act I and again at the end of Act III, his attempts are frustrated. If we in turn try to grasp an objective reality behind the symbolism in the play, or behind a physical reality a metaphysical truth, we will be similarly misled. These terms will have become metaphors, and magic will have joined their ranks. Magic is here another word for poetry, which also creates from nothing.

Yet, as allusive, imaginative, recondite, and, at times, playful as *Faust II* may be, its underlying theme is that of time and place. This is not the time and place of traditional drama, to be sure. Nor is it the time and place of historical fact, which would have compromised the purpose of the play in moving its hero through different worlds of thought and states of mind. For these worlds were conceived not simply as products of earlier causes in a continuity leading to a present but as truly evolving, with a life and development in their own right, and in that sense free. The fantastic countenance of the work, its literary cubistic aspect, reflects the need that Goethe felt to keep these worlds distinctly separate so that they would better tell against one another and against the world and state of mind that would ultimately obtain for Faust in his moment of decision in *his* time and place. That was the purpose: to resolve within a single sphere of existence a problem separately and differently resolved in other spheres in the play; to frame the moral choice within always deepening and broadening contexts.

What these contexts were will be discussed when they emerge separately. I mention here time and place only to suggest that Goethe's poetic rendering of the past has less to do with poetry and fantasy than with his understanding of history as influencing the unconscious no less than the conscious actions of men, that is, his understanding of history as culture. In this understanding lay an answer to the question that had initially been raised in *Urfaust*, that is in the early period of revolt when Goethe himself, like Faust, saw little use in a knowledge of history, if indeed it were attainable. There the past seemed 'a book with seven seals' and our attempts to explain other times a futile effort resulting in a mere reflection of our own times.[17] Part II, through the medium of poetry, breaks the seal and penetrates the past in a way that it may be known and absorbed. When we enter the world of classical antiquity, for example, we hear the steady and measured rhythms of greek tragedy, the iambic trimeters; when Helen joins Faust in the modern world she notes its rhymed speech, that symbolic expression of a state of mind poised between remembrance and anticipation—the modern, the romantic state. The two worlds are there in their very verse forms.

How did the work come to have its form? I repeat the question, not rhetorically with a view to summarizing the answers already stated or implied, but in order to make a final point. For while our present discussion has indicated the many reasons why traditional forms could not serve Goethe as his drama took on more and more the colorings and suppositions of a new era in thought, still it has not suggested what form could and did serve.

*Faust II*, we said, is not formless. Yet its structure in depth, its juxtaposing of material and motifs in abrupt and unforeseen sequence, casts the whole into such extraordinary and unique relief that we are made, not so much to see its content in a new light, as to alter our mode of thinking in order to be able to 'see.' It is not surprising that when the work first appeared, in 1832, it was not judged with much understanding. Instead it was viewed against the past, and a manner of thinking born of the past was used to judge it. The lack of dramatic cohesion in the play was attributed to the waning powers in the aged author who had after all brought himself to complete his *Faust* only in the last years of his life.[18] An inversion of this critique found willfulness rather than lack of clarity (though both might be symptoms of senility) in the face that *Faust II* presented and, in recognizing the multiplicity of perspective afforded the work by its apparently total freedom of form, at the same time denied that freedom as such to art. 'Every work of art must convey its infinite meaning in finite form.'[19] Nor did later critical literature on *Faust II* answer the questions raised by the initial reaction. The tendency was to resolve the problems presented by the text within the larger frame of reference that is Goethe himself in his works and total development. The censure was gone but the sense of esthetic displacement, which is the initial and persistently striking feature of our experience of *Faust II*, remained.

For the challenge from the beginning was not to uncover a hidden design either within or outside the work that would create new and elaborate harmonies. The challenge, I believe, was to pose the question that was impossible to pose from within an esthetic that presupposed design and purpose as the beginning and the end, the goal, of creativity. Not why *Faust II* took its unique form, but how, was to be the question. For, once posed, an answer would lie close to hand.

The answer lay in the motif of magic. The element of magic, so indigenous to the theme and in such potentially radical opposition to the concept of order as to attract the young *Sturm und Drang* Goethe when he first conceived *Faust*, grew as the work itself grew. What had served mainly as accompaniment to the action in Part I became its mover and shaper in Part II and thus its dramatic expression. From the background in the play, magic emerged as foreground and altered the mode of perception. One senses Goethe himself attempting to resist this poetic development as he time and again plans and then abandons scenes and motif which would have created links with logic and traditional thought. It was as if he had deliberately to suppress those conceptual instincts that were part of his times and his literary heritage in order to allow creative urges that anticipated the future to hold sway. The transition from the 'little' to the 'great world' required more than a mere extension of time and place, as it proved. The relation of cause and effect had also to be adjusted if a new sense of life and view of things were to emerge. In true evolutionary fashion, the element of magic in the play both allowed and forced this adjustment. It provided the freedom to create patterns and juxtapositions of reality that exist in the mind but not in time, while establishing in the process an order of thought from which there was no return in the play.

Goethe does not use magic to account for the unaccountable in *Faust II*. So employed, the motif only reestablishes the order it is designed to upset. So employed, nothing changes in the world in which magic has occurred and the perception of that world remains the same. But Goethe was intent on altering perception. Mephistopheles alighting in the first scene of Act IV in seven-league boots that would account for the great distances he is supposed to have traversed is the exception. The rule is the fate of Helen. Evoked as a phantom by Mephistopheles, she then materializes in her own realm, only to vanish literally into the air when she takes leave of Faust. Magic giveth and magic taketh away. Not that the inexplicability, the mystery, of these occurrences was the purpose in their design. Nor was the transitoriness of things their intended meaning. The world of *Faust II* is presented in abrupt disjunctions, phantasmagorically, but not on the assumption that there exists in essence outside the work a world similarly designed. The play is not an imitation, a representation. Yet it is also not a fantasy. The past, or rather the pasts, it evokes are meant as real, as realities in poetic guise, and it is only against the background they form that the final resolution in the play gains its true significance. But the presentation of this past is unusual in that it offers neither a continuous action, in the manner of history, nor a concentrated action, in the manner of drama. It presents rather the past contained in the present, multilayered, as it exists in the mind, as it exists in culture.

Magic made possible the transfer of this vision to the stage.[20] But in the process, and in the necessity, of suspending time and the laws of cause and effect, which magic by its nature prescribes, it also replaced the sense of history or life or drama as progression by a new sense or experience of the constant emergence of things within a context. By evoking the past within the present, realities within a reality or, if one will, illusions within the illusion or fiction that is the work of art itself, magic created or induced a way of seeing no longer compatible with the traditional view (whence the disjunction) but suggestive of the altered mode of thought in the new age. Magic effected here in the realm of poetry what the new concept of time had brought about in the science of the day, an opening onto a world of the past vastly expanded in its relation to man, a 'große Welt.' I am not speaking of Darwin and the specialized concept of evolution but of the more generalized development that had occurred earlier and created what we called at the outset of this chapter the structure or form in the thought of both Darwin and Goethe, and in the poetic no less than the scientific writings of the latter. The phenomenon of emergence in the physical, plant, and animal worlds was his concern from the beginning in his scientific work and it found its least sober, perhaps, but most illuminating expression in his search for a plant primeval from which all plant life had emerged, his *Urpflanze*. Yet life as constant emergence within a context was a model of thought he had encountered as well outside the realm of science, in the realm of history. The concept of history as culture that we associate with Herder and further identify in Goethe is an evolutionist concept simply in its view of the unfolding of events not as progression but as process. In its modern, laboratory sense the word 'culture' means growth in a medium.

The form or structure of *Faust* as a whole, to repeat, evolved. The very fact of a second part to the work was less the result of design than necessity. It was not the desire to explore a universe newly measured and history newly conceived that prompted the journey into the great world. The central action alone, the issue of good and evil, when re-seen and developed within the new mode of thought produced of itself the kind of expanding contexts not found in earlier forms of drama because not present in earlier forms of thinking. Like the phenomena of nature, good and evil were no longer to be conceived abstractly or absolutely, created once and for all in the nature of man as the universe itself had been created once and for all at some beginning in time. A Faust drama in one part was not to be written any more, as it were. Just as magic had emerged from its mainly poetic and atmospheric role to transform the conceptual and perceptual character of the play, the moral issue, newly conceived, transformed the concept of the hero and the nature of the dramatic action. There is every evidence that the Faust of *Urfaust* was not conceived as a representative hero, as a symbol of Western man, which he became only later. The great world was not created as an arena for the actions of a representative Faust, therefore, so much as he became that figure by his presence and his actions in that great world. The moral issue determined the dramatic development, not the dramatic, the moral, which is the case in traditional drama that offers objective reality as a confrontation in which the actions of the hero or heroine are tested and not, as here, as a context in which they are understood. This distinction becomes more important when we attempt to define the moral character and justify the salvation of Faust, whose actions are too often seen simply as the product of an individual will rather than the expression at a given stage of a cultural evolutionary process. The proliferation of dimensions that comprises *Faust II* reflects this process; and to read only its last act as a fitting conclusion to Part I, which is often done when the work is read in translation and one seeks its 'essential meaning,' is to miss the point.[21] Its meaning, and its drama, if a different type of drama, lie in the comprehensively imagined worlds that surround and define the action and project it beyond. *Faust* does not come to a conclusion so much as it reaches a point that can be declared a present. It brings us to where we are in time, which is the only conclusion possible in an evolutionist mode of thought.

Goethe did not need Darwin in order to carry out his evolutionist intention in *Faust II*. An awareness of the mechanics of evolution, which was the achievement of Darwin and alone rendered the theory scientific,[22] might well have hampered him. The fantastic creatures, half-man, half-beast, who pass through the Classical Walpurgis Night in playful tableau might have lost their suggestive powers had they been made to resemble a scientifically imagined reality. Instead, Goethe adapted, he 'naturalized,' myth. He placed his sphinxes, centaurs, griffins, pygmies, and other legendary creatures in a perspective that was concerned with the emergence of earth forms and physical beings and thus included them in his grand theme of a developing universe. We think of science too often as preceding poetry in the arrival at truth and indeed praise those poets who are even aware of its discoveries.[23] It is rare that we can identify, as here in the example of Goethe, Darwin, and evolution, the truer picture of a new sense of things, a 'truth' coming into being in separate realms in its separate ways. Not that Goethe contributes to science with his parade of creatures from myth. This is Goethe the poet, not the scientist, speaking. But he contributes to the evolution of thought, as he leads us to discover in these projections of the primitive mind the element of animal interrelatedness that will eventually become scientific theory. If science and poetry come together in Goethe, it is because he believed they emerge from a common source. They were, after all, combined in him.

But *we* need Darwin in order to understand *Faust II*, if not in its content, in the particulars of its form. We are dealing here with a work that not only reflects a mode of thought but is itself best understood within that mode. We spoke of magic as a mechanism in its evolution, as a factor or motif given in the legend but made now to serve not only a new but a necessary function. Magic opened up a world hidden by the traditional imitation or representation of reality in art, the very world or context within which the new sense of the human condition alone could be portrayed. Or, more accurately, it reopened a world in which the spiritual and abstract under-pinnings and antecedents of experience once had their place and filled it with natural causes. The completed *Faust* stands in that relation to the *Divine Comedy*. Paradoxically, the broadest movement in literature from Dante to Goethe was toward a verisimilitude or realism which, at least in drama, came to exclude more and more of the reality that was considered more and more the truly real. In *Faust II*, magic interrupted the progression to reveal a new real world.[24]

Goethe did not deliberately create a disjunctive whole in *Faust* so much as he omitted or discarded elements of dramatic and thematic continuity that would have served to 'complete' the work, but at the same time belie its content. A completed form implied a completed world. Many of the plot factors and motifs contained in the plans, sketches, notes, and verse jottings to *Faust*, as we shall see, will suggest familiar and traditional links in motiva-tion and logic, and their abandonment an uneasiness with just such explicit design. But it was not by default alone that the great disjunction of form, and thus the great freedom of allusion, arose in *Faust II*. Rather the development in the composition of the work, its internal evolution which produced the external form, was itself the determining factor.

Long before Act I, Goethe had conceived and in part written a *Helena*, a planned 'Interlude to Faust,' which, altered, eventually became Act III. Begun in his classical period, the *Helena* was an uncompromising imitation of ancient tragedy, with a Chorus and in classical meters. Goethe had thus fashioned a separate world in its own right, which was not to be joined artistically, but only conceptually, to the other worlds in *Faust*, including the world of Part I. In the awareness of this fact and this necessity, we sense, unable to join, he began artistically and formally to put asunder. He now created each world in its own right and with its own laws of composition, each 'a little world standing on its own.'[25] He would trust, as he said when the work was finally completed, that 'the idea of the whole will present itself to the intelligent reader, though he will not be lacking in transitions to supply.'[26] Like magic, the *Helena* had functioned as an evolutionary mechanism. The part had not been inspired and created by the design, the design was inspired and created by the part.

Yet this 'supplying of meaning,' an expression Goethe used as well in reference to *Wilhelm Meisters Wanderjahre*,[27] was to be no mere esthetic exercise. The becoming aware of what one unconsciously knows through culture, through the living but disjunctive experience of the past, was also a moral imperative: 'Would thou possess thy heritage ... render it thine own.'[28] *Faust II* brings us through the past, in its broadest and deepest human sense, to a present, but not in the manner in which we experience history, or experience knowledge that is presented already possessed and therefore not for our own possessing, but as poetry and culture are experienced. We noted above that poetry, like magic, provided an appropriate means of expressing the vision in *Faust II* of evolving views of life, views that are to be understood as changing in time. We may now say that it was the only means. For in this way *Faust* itself, as poetry, as cultural artifact, takes its place in the very development it was created to describe.

## NOTES

1. The meaning of the word 'evolution' is itself evolving. It is thus perhaps best to speak of the concept as an 'evolutionist sense,' as does Günter Martin in a recent article, 'Goethes evolutionärer Sinn' (*Goethe-Jahrbuch*, vol. 105 [1988], pp. 247–69). Martin suggests that the difficulty we have in distinguishing between the strictly scientific and the more philosophical implications of the concept derives from the modern tendency to falsely separate the human from the physical sciences, thus obstructing understanding of an earlier age when this was not so clearly done. Goethe believed in what would later be called epigenesis, a theory of development that envisions a chain of new formations from a common beginning; the Darwinian theory envisions evolution as a series of mutations. The German words *Neubildung* and *Umbildung*, 'new formation' and 'transformation,' perhaps make the distinction most clearly. Before Darwin, the 'theory of evolution' was understood as a development or expansion of a pre-existing form (in effect, a homunculus) and was also called Preformation, a term which relates the idea of evolution to concepts dating back to Empedocles. Caspar Friedrich Wolff (1733–94) was the first to propose the theory of *Epigenese* against *Preformationstheorie* in Goethe's time and that surely had something to do with the satire in Act II. Yet Goethe saw the human being as the crown of creation, for all that he may have regarded nature and the

surrounding world of culture, politics, and art as eternally evolving. This is in contradistinction to Darwin and to Nietzsche. See, e.g., George Wells, 'Goethe and Evolution' (*Journal of the History of Ideas*, vol. 28 [1967], pp. 537–50). For Goethe's writings in geology and morphology, see Douglas Miller, ed. and trans., *Goethe: Scientific Studies* (New York, 1988).

2. This note appears in the second edition of *On the Origin of Species*. Darwin does not quote Goethe directly, but from Karl Meding, *Goethe als Naturforscher in Beziehung zur Gegenwart* (Dresden, 1860). Goethe does not in fact make his own analogy with cattle and their horns but rather in scientific terms which Meding obviously rendered more familiar in the interest of popularization.

3. In a letter to the Islamic scholar K. J. L. Iken, 27 September 1827.

4. To Cotta, 2 January 1799.

5. To Aloïs Hirt, 25 December 1797.

6. Karl Fr. Zelter, 6/7 June 1828.

7. See Gertrude Himmelfarb, *Darwin and the Darwinian Revolution* (Garden City, NY, 1962). Her title suggested my chapter heading.

8. See Alexander Gode-von Aesch's excellent *Natural Science in German Romanticism* (New York, 1941).

9. In the preface (1842) to the series of novels under that title. In *The Wild Ass's Skin*, ch. I, is the remark: 'Is not Cuvier the greatest poet of our century?' The contrast with the English Romantic poets is interesting. 'Much of the new poetry tended to devote itself to revealing man's inner nature ... This position tended to make poetry and science antagonistic, or to render one a continuation of, or development from, the other. The former point of view was supported by Coleridge and his followers, who regarded these spheres as entirely antithetical. Wordsworth, on the other hand, felt that even "the remotest discoveries of the chemist, the botanist, or mineralogist, will be as proper objects of the Poet's art if the time should ever come when these things shall be familiar to us ... as enjoying and suffering beings"' (Ralph B. Crum, *Scientific Thought in Poetry* [New York, 1931], p. 129). See also Frederick Burwick, *The Damnation of Newton: Goethe's Theory and Romantic Perception* (Berlin and New York, 1986).

10. Balzac does plan a series of 'études analytiques,' 'études philosophiques,' 'études des moeurs,' which were to illustrate the principles of human behavior.

11. *Die Wahlverwandtschaften* also derives a radical morality from a scientific premise, but the novel is not radical in its artistic form.

12. Robert Ergang has written that 'the secularization of life, thought and culture is the essence of the Renaissance' (*The Renaissance* [New York, 1967], p. v).

13. *Zur Metamorphose der Pflanzen*. Schicksal der Druckschrift, 1817 (Artemis edition, vol. 17, p. 90).

14. Stuart Atkins in his discussion of Pleasant Landscape in *Goethe's Faust: A Literary Analysis* (Cambridge, Mass., 1964), p. 101.

15. My translation of 'So bleibe denn die Sonne mir im Rücken' (l. 4715).

16. 'Entfernt des Vorwurfs glühend bittre Pfeile' (l. 4624) / ... 'Dann badet ihm im Tau aus Lethes Flut' (l. 4629).

17. In the original version: 'Was ihr den Geist der Zeiten heßt, / Das ist im Grund der Herren eigner Geist, / In dem die Zeiten sich bespiegeln' (ll. 224ff.).

18. Otto Pniower, in 'Fausts zweiter Teil,' *Dichtungen und Dichter: Essays und Studien* (Berlin, 1912), p. 74, is most dogmatic on this point. Wilhelm Emrich sees this approach to the question as typical of nineteenth-century German criticism of *Faust II* (*Die Symbolik von Faust II* [Bonn, 1957], p. 66).

19. Friedrich Theodor Vischer acknowledges the 'Unendlichkeit der Perspektive' in *Faust II*, but warns: 'Jedes Kunstwerk soll in endlicher Form die unendliche Bedeutung tragen, keinem soll diese Perspektive fehlen; bei Goethes "Faust" aber springt das Auge über Vordergrund und Mittelgrund jeden Augenblick weg, um sich in dieser unendlichen Aussicht zu verlieren ...' (quoted in Karl R. Mandelkow, *Goethe im Urteil seiner Kritiker*, vol. 2 [Munich, 1977], p. 180).

20. Goethe contradicts himself on the question whether *Faust II* was intended for the theater, at times speaking of the effectiveness of certain motives or scenes when imagined on the stage, at others seeming to dismiss the possibility of a performance of the play. ('Almost unthinkable,' to Eckermann, 20 December 1829.) He speaks directly of an 'audience' and of 'the performance' in his 'Ankündigung' to the *Helena*, which might more easily have been staged. On the question of performing the whole work, he says to Eckermann, 20 December 1829, 'Geht nur und laßt mir das Publikum, von dem ich nichts hören mag. Die Hauptsache ist, daß es geschrieben steht.' On the problems and challenges of staging a modern performance of *Faust II*, see, e.g., Jocelyn Powell, 'Reflections on Staging *Faust*, Part II' (*Publications of the English Goethe Society*, n.s., vol. 48 [1978], pp. 52–80).

21. It was also one of the reactions in the misunderstanding of the work when it first appeared: 'Für die Geschichte Fausts an sich, dramatisch genommen, könnten vielleicht die vier ersten Akte ganz wegfallen' (quoted in Mandelkow, *Goethe*, vol. 2, p. 68). This contention is repeated in effect by Heinrich Rickert in *Goethes Faust: Die dramatische Einheit der Dichtung* (Tübingen, 1932).

22. Manfred Wenzel makes this simple and most important point at the beginning of his extensively thorough study 'Goethe und Darwin: Goethes morphologische Schriften in ihrem naturwissenschaft-shistorischen Kontext' (Dissertation, Bochum, 1982).

23. In ch. V, 'Poetry Champions Evolution: Goethe,' Crum (*Scientific Thought*) looks for reflections of the new scientific view only in Goethe's didactic poems and not in the inner structure of his art. Since Thomas S. Kuhn's *The Structure of Scientific Revolutions* (Chicago, 1970) we have come to see the relation of science to its times in a new light.

24. The great world that Calderon opens up in his dramas is sometimes cited as a precedent for the 'große Welt' that Goethe creates in *Faust II*, but Calderon is drawing on a world and universe already preconceived in Catholic doctrine, as we noted earlier in the similar comparison with Dante, whereas Goethe was attempting to reflect a view only newly emerging and as yet to take established form either in thought or in art. On Calderon and Goethe see, e.g., Swana Hardy, *Goethe, Calderon und die Theorie des romantischen Dramas* (Heidelberg, 1965); also Stuart Atkins, 'Goethe, Calderon and *Faust II*,' *Germanic Review*, vol. 28 (1953), pp. 83–98.

25. As Goethe said of Act IV to Eckermann, 13 February 1831.

26. To Wilhelm von Humboldt, 1 December 1831; similarly in a conversation with his assistant Fr. Wilhelm Riemer, undated, 1830/31. Eckermann himself speaks of a 'set of small world circles [in *Faust*], which, enclosed within themselves, certainly affect, but have little do with, one another' (13 February 1831).

27. Quoted in Klaus F. Gille, *Wilhelm Meister im Urteil der Zeitgenossen* (Assem, 1971), p. 283.

28. From Part I: 'Was du ererbt von deinen Vätern hast, / Ewirb es, um es zu besitzen' (ll. 682–3).

TOBIN SIEBERS

# The Werther Effect:
# The Esthetics of Suicide

The "Werther effect" denotes within psychological literature the tendency of people to commit suicide under the compulsion of imitation rather than for individual motivations. In a 1974 essay, David Phillips uses the term to explore the idea that widely circulated stories of suicide cause a rise in national suicide rates. His idea is derived from the effect that Goethe's novel had on its reading public. *The Sorrows of Young Werther* was an esthetic failure, if esthetics is to be defined as a symbolic and essentially disinterested activity, for Goethe's readers were known to translate the novel into deadly practice. *Werther*, of course, was banned in Leipzig in January 1775 precisely because the theological faculty of the university believed that it would be successful in advocating suicide. The Werther effect, in short, stands as one of the great examples of the imitative effect of fiction on moral life.

We tend, however, not to recognize this same Werther effect within Goethe's life and work. Rather than emphasizing imitation, we focus on either the original feelings that made Goethe write the novel or the originality of the novel itself and its role in literary history. We tend to view the novel, then, as separated from the imitative effects that most concerned its first reading public and against which any concept of "originality" must be defined. As a result, we lose the means to view the events surrounding the book as an opportunity for creating a more interdisciplinary view of the

From *Mosaic* 26, no. 1. © 1993 by Mosaic.

reading experience in general. First, we stress Goethe's now famous explanation of the origins of *Werther* in which he attributes the novel to his feelings of depression and makes a special point of denying that he was imitating other books. There is, however, something strange about this explanation. Although Goethe was only twenty five when he wrote the novel, he never again produced a work with a tragic conclusion like that of *Werther*. Apparently, the writing of *Werther* purged Goethe forever of his unhealthy feelings. Second, we give *Werther* a unique position in literary history. According to some critics, the book is the first psychological novel, and it continues to be regarded as one of the great literary models in the tradition. The same argument has been extended to Goethe's hero. Werther has acquired a unique status in the history of literature because he represents an exemplary case of personal emotion being transferred to literature and because he became the model for the artist-suicide in the Romantic age.

I would argue, however, that we will never comprehend the great artistic achievement of *Werther* if we insist on linking it to real suffering, because the novel's triumph is ultimately esthetic rather than ethical—although I hasten to add that distinctions between esthetics and ethics are of limited value in the age of Romanticism. The fact that we are tempted to trace the novel's power to Goethe's ability to sublimate his own personal sufferings in fiction exposes the extent to which we remain under the domination of the same esthetic ideology that created *Werther*, namely the Romantic myth that suffering is necessary to cultivate artistic originality and to be recognized as a unique individual. In this essay, therefore, I would like to pursue an anti-Romantic reading of the novel. I want to insist that the Werther effect and its imitative patterns are as much a *cause* of the novel as its effect. If *Werther* is more imitative than original, if something like a Werther effect produced Goethe's novel, we must seek an explanation for the power of the novel not in Goethe's emotions but in literary history—or, at least, in the effect that this history had on Goethe.

What does it mean, however, to claim that *Werther* is imitative? I do not mean to suggest that the suicide of Carl Wilhelm Jerusalem, Goethe's melancholic student acquaintance at Leipzig, serves as a model for either the novel or Goethe's emotional state during its writing. Jerusalem's suicide did have an impact on Goethe, but only because the incident resonates with the dominant esthetic of the period. The knowledge of Jerusalem's death merely serves to mediate between Goethe's artistic aspirations and the Romantic tradition. It is a red herring because it allows Goethe the pretense of relating his artistic work to an unmediated experience of suffering, when in fact a precedent exists in literary history that makes it unnecessary for Goethe to experience suffering in order to write about it.

Jean-Jacques Rousseau created this precedent, for he was the first to establish in a major way the value of the suffering self for the production of literary works. He initiated the esthetic movement called Romanticism by constructing a double image of himself. As I have explained elsewhere, Rousseau exposes the cruelty and injustice of society by making an example of himself: "to make an example of oneself," to become the example and outcast of society, is to resolve a certain division between victim and victimizer as well as to achieve a uniqueness extremely beneficial to esthetic goals (72). Another way of elaborating this proposition is to state that Rousseau's early writings, whether essayistic or fictional, are deeply autobiographical, and that contemporary readers experienced them in precisely this way. Rousseau thus establishes himself as a series of personalities—as the victim of culture, as its paragon and as a character in a narrative—through which individuality may be represented. He embarks on an enterprise to create an idea of individuality for himself and his culture. He creates another Rousseau with whom he may converse. He feeds on his own substance and nourishes himself. As self-sufficient as God, he is at once savior and condemned.

Rousseau's genius was to have realized that he could be his own victim and victimizer, but his discovery did not necessarily have happy consequences for the Romantics. For a logical outcome of this attitude is suicide, and in this progression we find the potential for both a great novel of suicide and much genuine self-destruction. *Werther* is an esthetic expression of Rousseau's ethical system: Goethe's Romanticism defines itself by reproducing esthetically the basic elements belonging to the scenes of persecution that Rousseau describes in his writings. When Goethe disclaims any relation between his novel and the tradition, therefore, and names personal suffering as its sole origin, he both suppresses and imitates Rousseau.

The Romantic tradition views the suffering self as a work of art, but if we wish to understand Romanticism, we need to acknowledge that it distinguishes some forms of suffering as possessing greater esthetic potential than others. Rousseau discovers the idea that the forms of suffering with the greatest esthetic value portray the self as a victim of persecution. This achievement derives less from Rousseau's esthetic taste than from an ethical ability to describe the ways in which persecution relates to social life. In Rousseau's eyes, violence against the individual is at the heart of culture. For René Girard and his school, however, this insight acquires even greater import. As they see it, persecution is not merely an effect of culture but part of its founding order. Girard has made a strong case for the fact that persecutors represent their violence in a particular way: they depict their victims through a series of distorted images and ideas, making them into scapegoats of culture. Persecution produces a "text of persecution," a mythological language, in which the actions of the persecutors are concealed, all blame for violence is placed on victims, and a form of social hierarchy emerges (6–9). In Eric Gans's language, then, persecution creates "scenes of representation" (13–15). Persecution is "scenic"—in the same way that Freud defines the primal scene—both because it produces fabulous accounts of victims and victimizers and because it configures internal, mental scenes that permit social order to be imagined. Historically, these scenes contribute to social order, although today we recognize them increasingly as a form of mythology serving violence. It is our sympathy with the victim—a recognition of the centrality of victimization in such representations—that exposes the true nature of these mythological scenes.

Sympathy also provides the ethical thrust behind the modern alliance with the victim, of which Romanticism is the emergent form. Nevertheless, the ethical nature of our sympathies does not always escape the esthetic dimension of the scene of persecution—by which I mean its capacity to produce fabulous images of the victim—because we continue to misrepresent the victim, first, by creating the specific cult of the Romantic outcast or *poète maudit* and, then, by maintaining a cult of the victim in general. This is to say that the consequences for selfhood are similar in both esthetic and real experiences of persecution, even though they may differ in great respects. Both experiences depend on the relation between violence and selfhood, but the esthetic scene, which reaches a critical stage of development during Romanticism, risks paradox. First, it endangers the self, as Nietzsche says, by producing a mendacious egoism. Second, it creates a morally ambiguous view of literature, for the knowledge of the scenic power of persecution that artists appropriate for their writings overturns their esthetic system with its violence. The violence that artists produce in esthetic scenes of persecution has its own victims: those called victimizers for the sake of the esthetic system. Romantic artists almost always fail to extricate themselves from this powerful association with violence. When they are least successful, their art looks unsympathetic or vengeful. When they are most successful, they achieve, at best, the appearance of egotism or hypocrisy.

There are, of course, many differences between Rousseau's writings and *Werther*, despite their fundamental reliance on the representation of suf-fering. The greatest difference turns on the issue of autobiography. *Werther* is supposed to be a novel: its protagonist is not Goethe but Werther. In contrast, Rousseau's writings are inherently autobiographical, and they therefore succumb to all of the paradoxes currently plaguing debate about the genre. In modern critical parlance, autobiography is essentially self-contradictory. One camp contends that it is impossible to write auto-biography, so strong is the fictional nature of all representation. Any attempt to compose one's life results in a novel. Another camp, influenced by psychoanalysis, holds that all writing is involuntary autobiography. So powerful is the unconscious that any attempt to move outside the self produces a return of the repressed in fictional guise. All writing speaks the truth of the self, without, however, being able to name that truth very effectively. Depending on which theory we believe, either the novel or autobiography is the dominant form. It grows increasingly clear, however, that modern critics have no language to explain the real difference. What is an obvious distinction for most people becomes a thorny issue for literary criticism.

The question of where the autobiographical element lies always returns us to the interaction between victimization and literary form, or, in different words, to the connection between the ethical and esthetic versions of the scene of persecution. Indeed, the actual texts written by Rousseau and Goethe differ most significantly in the role played by the scene of persecution. Rousseau conceives of himself as a victim of society and situate's his suffering at the heart of his writings. After the scene of his persecution has been established, however, it may be appropriated by other authors, without their having had to live it in reality, and as the scene becomes increasingly part of the esthetic tradition, it acquires greater availability and accessibility. Yet it is crucial to realize that the esthetic scene continues to reproduce the character of a real event. The temptation remains when reading an esthetic work to return to an original scene, if one can be found, or if not, to compose one by imagining a secret relation between the experiences of the character and those of the author. The most common of reading experiences verges upon the experience of ethnography because the reader, like the anthropologist, always conceives of the relation between fictional representations and reality according to what Gans calls the "generative model." This means that we tend, even in esthetic situations, to view the gap between reality and fiction as an obstacle to be overcome, whether it requires us to identify authors with characters or to plumb deep social meanings in the most farfetched literary fantasies.

This tendency explains, for instance, why a confusion exists between Goethe and Werther in particular and between authors and characters in general. Goethe's contemporaries automatically assumed that he was expressing his own personal angst through Werther, and this was in some ways true. Goethe describes a battle with depression, although he does not admit anything equaling the despair found in *Werther*. He views the book as a success because he has managed to transform "reality into poetry"; but the reactions of his friends and of the public still catch him off his guard: he in no way expects them to turn "poetry into reality" (147). Far from enjoying a Wertherian pleasure in the public's interest in his apparent suffering, Goethe was horrified by its desire to see him enact the emotions of his unfortunate protagonist. In short, Goethe did not wish his readers either to impose his fiction on his reality or to take it as a model for their own reality, but, of course, they did both. After the publication of *Werther*, Goethe was forced to travel incognito, and a number of pale young men donned the yellow waistcoat and fired a bullet into their brain.

Readers are driven unavoidably to find genuine suffering behind the representation of suffering, and for all the attempts by modern critics to put a stop to this thinking, by the invention of the so-called "intentional fallacy" for example, it is unlikely that anyone will ever be able to repress this all-too-human desire. Nor, in fact, should we wish to repress it, for the defining feature of the reading experience consists of trying to identify with what other human beings think and feel. We would be foolish, then, to expect that readers would want to stop thinking that characters are human.

Nevertheless, we must understand that Goethe's relation to his public is infinitely different from Rousseau's, and that any correspondence between their experiences is the product of what one must call an esthetic device. To call *Werther* esthetic is to recognize that it is inherently imitative—and not participatory in the same way as Rousseau's writings: despite the public's desire to create the cult of Rousseau *à nouveau*, to place Goethe, and not Werther, at the center of the scene of persecution, Goethe did not need to live through the experience of suffering in real life, simply because it existed esthetically. The important differences and similarities may be summed up by comparing *Werther* to the work most like it in Rousseau's canon, *The Reveries of the Solitary Walker*, although it was published after Goethe's novel. Rousseau, of course, died before finishing the *Reveries*; and Werther, it seems, dies before Goethe can finish the novel. These deaths are as different as can be. Yet they are similar insofar as both writers offer a rather truncated model of the Romantic personality to their readership. This is precisely the point. The essence of the Romantic personality lies in this very impossibility, its flirtation with death, and it will never surpass these two instances. Its success can be described as a direct result of the fact that the readers of Romantic texts always have a better chance of living a Romantic life than any Romantic hero because they possess the model of the entire life: readers have the opportunity to stage their own suffering in ways that will allow them to experience the distinction that Romantic heroes win only after death. The model of the Romantic hero's reception remains Goethe's success at Werther's expense, for Werther's death makes Goethe's esthetic life possible. Goethe could not have created Werther if Goethe had been a Werther.

Imagine the grand effect it would have had, however, if Goethe had subsequently killed himself in a fashion after Werther. The possibility of achieving this effect did not escape other Romantics, Pushkin and Lermontov for example, whose tardy arrival on the scene made them more vulnerable to the poetics of suffering.

After Rousseau, the esthetic scene of persecution is sufficient to summon the narrative elements necessary to give coherence to a Romantic experience, and readers need not necessarily apply the character's "reality" to themselves. Nevertheless, I add quickly, this is not to say that the temptation to live the scene disappears. The esthetic scene takes its toll on artists by urging them to injure themselves or to represent themselves as injured, which explains in part the existence of the Romantic myth of the mad artist, the appearance of the Doubles as a literary theme, and the veritable explosion of artist-suicides and Romantic madmen in the nineteenth century.

Suicide is itself a highly individualistic action within social structure. Indeed, it risks being the most individual of actions. Nevertheless, if we are to comprehend how it relates to Romantic esthetics, that is if we are to see that some forms of it begin as an esthetic formula that goes awry, we have to examine how the act is embedded in social relations. Another way of framing this problem is to ask how suicide relates to the scene of persecution that we have been analyzing. Émile Durkheim's book on suicide, as might be expected, relates this apparently individual action to collective representations. It seems an irrepressible irony that the birth of sociology relies both on the poetics of suicide and on what may be called in some respects a literary analysis. Durkheim relies on accounts of real suicide and on representations of suicide in literature. He creates his methodology by transforming the act of suicide, a marginal and eccentric activity, into a model for collective representation, demonstrating that sociology owes a great debt to the Romantic ethic of the nineteenth century. Indeed, his description of the forms of suicide amounts to an analysis of how suicide may be used to represent oneself to society at large. Durkheim's typology of suicides is not unrelated to the esthetic devices found in Romantic literature, and it will be useful in interpreting both *Werther* and the larger Romantic mythology of the victimized artist.

Durkheim begins his study by arguing that the suicide rate drops during extended social crises, not at their beginning or end, and he attributes the phenomenon to the greater social cohesion made necessary by times of duress. For example, the suicide rate is low among Jews, according to Durkheim, because of the general social hostility that they experience. When society requires the sacrifice of individuality, fewer suicides occur. With the greater possibility of individuality, more suicides take place. Indeed, Durkheim predicted that the suicide rate would climb as society became more modern and a greater possibility of individual freedom evolved, and this is exactly what has happened.

Suicide, then, relates intimately to the representation of individuality, and according to Durkheim, these representations take three forms: egoistic, altruistic and anomic suicide. Each form measures the relation between the individual and the social at different degrees. "Egoistic suicide," Durkheim concludes, "results from man's no longer finding a basis for existence in life" (258). Egoistic suicides are so removed from the normal social justifications of existence that they reject society in a radical way. Altruistic suicide places the basis for existence beyond life. Finally, anomic suicide occurs when someone's existence lacks recognition and regulation by other people. Both anomic and egoistic suicides spring from what Durkheim calls society's insufficient presence in individuals, or their greater individuality. Altruistic suicide, on the contrary, springs from too much of society's presence in the individual, or the lack of individuality.

In fact, however, altruistic suicide often places its faith in some future tribute or memorialization. It is characterized by less individuality, to be sure, but people who give their life for their country, for example, frequently win great distinction and uniqueness after their death. We give great reverence to war heroes and martyrs. This reverence is not unlike the esthetic effect produced by the scene of persecution: we revere the altruistic suicide as both victim of the enemy-persecutors and hero of his or her people.

Indeed, altruistic suicide is easily perverted by the promise of glory. The amusing modern film, *The Americanization of Emily*, takes this problem as its theme. A public-relations minded admiral seizes upon the harebrained idea that an American sailor should be the first to die on the beaches of Normandy. He recruits one of his aides, who is treated to a premature monumentalization in the form of vast favors, much feasting and grand social distinction. They even commission a statue of him, to be erected later at the proper moment. When on the beach itself, the hero changes his mind, his fellow soldiers fire upon him and try to chase him into the enemy's grasp. Much modern military recruitment depends on this kind of confusion of altruistic and egoistic motives.

Similarly, egoistic suicide attempts to build ego by sacrificing it. It creates a cult of the self by translating negative into positive attention. The unfortunate individual who reasons, "I will kill myself, then they will be sorry," wishes to attain in the future by extreme measures the distinction that he or she believes is due in the present. In egoistic suicide, the "perfect moment" merges death and self-celebration, as when Narcissus's death rattle joins his last gasp of admiration for his own image. Like altruistic suicide in its perverse form, egoistic suicide stages the victim's death to win the pity and attention of the community. Egoistic suicide is more or less the Romantic system under another name, and its evidence lies everywhere during the nineteenth century. In almost every instance, it is associated with mysterious talents and magnificent self-sufficiency. The Romantic ironist is one of its most obvious examples, for the self-negation of irony serves to make the artist, Kierkegaard tells us, a mysterious hieroglyph for his or her contemporaries.

The third type of suicide identified by Durkheim is anomic suicide. Although anomic suicide would appear to be far removed from the Romantic quest for difference, it reveals in extreme forms of psychopathology the failure of egoistic motives, and it serves in its more theatrical forms as a kind of strategy for stimulating interest in those who desire uniqueness. Anomic suicides, as Durkheim describes them, destroy themselves in remorse over their abandonment by society, for they cannot support the loneliness of anonymity. Whether this form of suicide reveals a last ditch effort to gain significance for the self—and thus its similarity to egoistic suicide—or whether it genuinely marks the absolute desperation of someone who has fallen out of place is difficult to analyze; in any case, it is clear that the self knows that its own value lies in the attention of society and that it must convert this attention into self-esteem or lose itself entirely.

The anomic profile has great resources to place in the service of self-representation. Anomic suicide becomes productive, Durkheim explains, if it can translate suffering into a strong preoccupation with the self. Rousseau's "flight" from society, for example, was a strategic use of the anomic profile. This tactic worked for him because he was not anonymous, and he hardly risked being forgotten. Goethe also took advantage of this strategy by publishing *Werther* anonymously: the public's desire to discover Goethe's identity was fired beyond belief, and his reputation was established once and for all. Indeed, the "pose of anonymity" often sets into motion the reactions cultivated by Romanticism and present all around us. Beau Brummell, for instance, used to attend balls sponsored by high society in a peculiar way. He would arrive and station himself in the antechamber, never entering but positioning himself well in view of the room, and after a certain interval, he would quit the event, leaving everyone to gossip about his motives and to make expressions of regret. We can detect a similar strategy in the aspiring social butterfly who sulks in the corner at cocktail parties. Likewise, in the more intimate field of sexual relations, no Don Juan ever admits his success to women; he begins by bemoaning his failures with them and complaining about his suffering at their hands. He lays out his suffering like bait to attract the sympathy of his prey. In a Romantic universe, often the slightest show of suffering or isolation will bring down upon the "victim" a shower of concern and affection.

Durkheim, of course, takes suicide seriously, as well a sociologist should. Literary critics are in a somewhat different position. We are not concerned with the death of human beings but with literary representations. We should insist, at the least, on the difference between the esthetics and the ethics of the act or, at the most, on how the esthetics of suicide feed on the ethical meaning of the real act. *Werther* involves precisely this issue, but critics have by and large shown little of the required disinterestedness. They are perhaps too much like Werther's pale young imitators; they are gourmets of feeling. Caroline Wellberg, for example, usefully explains how eccentric *Werther* is in comparison to other sentimental novels, giving reason for us to suspect sentimental responses to the novel. The critical reception of the novel, however, has generally been too sentimental to understand its power to organize feelings. Even those who view the book as a curiosity, as an example of the *Zeitgeist* of the age of sentiment, fail to escape this trap, for they unwittingly insist that Werther is either a victim—of love or of bourgeois Culture—or some kind of victimizer—hypocritical, aggressive or spoiled. Although I will not be able to elaborate it here, the point to remember is that we cannot understand Werther in any fashion by relying on an "either/or." His forcefulness as a character evolves from Goethe's ability to make him always "both"—that is, Werther's autonomy and distinctiveness derive from his ability to embrace oppositions and to symbolize in miniature the conflicts found in large social processes.

Werther, most critics imply, does not use the ethical power of suicide as a means to represent himself as a poetical figure. His self-destructiveness is unrelated to his desires to attain social distinction and poetic luminosity. He is a victim, perhaps a little deranged and with excessive sensitivity, but a victim nevertheless. He suffers the misfortune of falling in love with a married woman, and in that lies his great tragedy. (In some variations, he is considered a victim of class structure as well, as, for example, in the reading of Carol Ames.) These sentimental readings fail on two counts. First, they

ignore the extent to which Werther uses the tragedy of love to make claims
for his inimitable nature. Werther begins by using Lotte's sympathy to
distinguish himself in the sphere of love relations: "She knows how I suffer.
Today her eyes looked deep into my heart." Next, he transforms his suffering
into a historic event: "Sometimes I tell myself my fate is unique. Consider all
other men fortunate, I tell myself; no one has ever suffered like you. Then I
read a poet of ancient times, and it is as though I were looking deep into my
own heart. I have to suffer much. Oh, has any human heart before me ever
been so wretched?" (95). Lotte's relation to Werther parallels his own view
of himself; the important thing is that someone look deep into his heart. The
text cracks open to reveal a schizophrenic discourse, in which Werther
scrutinizes and takes the pulse of his abused heart, as if it were someone
else's. His taking confidence in himself serves to separate him from society,
mimicking a god-like self-sufficiency and demonstrating once and for all that
his "fate is unique."

Second, the sentimental explanation of Werther's suicide fails to see
what adulterous love buys for the ambitious young man. The essence of the
sentimental interpretation may be derived from the following scene, in
which Werther meets Lotte and Albert in the garden. Werther waits for
them in an "enclosure that has a mysterious aura of loneliness" (67). He runs
to meet their footfalls and they retreat back to the "gloomy enclosure" just
as the moon rises above the wooded hills. They sit for a time in the profound
darkness, when suddenly Lotte begins to speak as if she were Werther: "'I
never walk in the moonlight, never, without being reminded of my dead. In
the moonlight I am always filled with a sense of death and of the hereafter.
We live on'—and now she spoke with glorious feeling—'but, Werther, do we
meet again? Shall we recognize each other? What do you feel? What do you
believe?' 'Lotte'." Werther responds with eyes full of tears, "'we shall meet
again. Here and there ... we shall meet again'" (67).

Demoralized by his love for a married woman, Werther takes the only
course open to him; he kills himself so that they will meet again. This is high
tragedy, apparently, for not only does the adulterous love destroy Werther's
life, it ruins his creative talents. "It is a tragedy," he tells William, his
correspondent: "My creative powers have been reduced to restless
indolence" (64). Yet our view of Werther before he meets Lotte offers the
same vision. In the opening letter of the novel, we discover a Werther who
is stricken with inertia and who cannot express on paper the wonders
surrounding him (24). Moreover, he already carries in his heart a "sweet
feeling of freedom" in the knowledge that he can leave the prison of his own
body whenever he likes (29). Werther's adulterous passion, then, does not

bring on his depression; he is a "tragic figure" from the beginning. His adulterous love, however, does permit him a constant source of injury. Werther is not a victim of love; he loves being the victim. He traps himself in an adulterous affair because suffering is essential to the self-image required by his artistic ambitions.

Adultery is rarely successful in Romantic novels, despite the fact that its incidence is overwhelming. This fact should tell us that the Romantic is more interested in a problematic of failure and self-pity than in love. Adultery in novels, next to suicide itself, represents the greatest act of self-definition because it almost always ends in isolation and injury, and it guarantees that its victim will be able to convert this injury into a position of privilege. The victim of love becomes the victim par excellence. The way that novels present adultery makes this conclusion inescapable.

To fall in love with another's spouse or betrothed is one of the surest means available in novels to rebel against society at large and to disappoint oneself. Before Werther meets Lotte, he is warned not to fall in love with her. "And why shouldn't I fall in love with her?" he asks. "Because," he is told, "she is engaged" (34–35). Later, in a moment of anger, Lotte will speak the truth of Werther's attachment to her: "Be more manly! Divert this tragic devotion from a human creature who can only pity you.... Don't you see that you are deceiving and ruining yourself on purpose?... Why me of all people, who belongs to another?... I fear that it is just the impossibility of possessing me that makes your desire for me so fascinating" (108).

Indeed, why should Werther be captivated by Lotte?—for there is nothing intrinsic to her that should invite this morbid fascination. Whether Lotte is a *femme fatale* or an innocent is therefore beside the point, for she can be blamed neither for failing to save Werther nor for drowning him in a well of fatal sexuality (*pace* Kathleen Warrick). Lotte merely holds a position necessary to Werther's self-injury. Whenever he diverges from his path to himself, she calls on him to put it straight. In one episode, he explodes in frustration and emotion at a party, and she scolds him. "I was, please, to think of myself," Werther paraphrases her. "Angel! For you I have to live!" (48). Her love fuels his egoism, and when he first suspects that she loves him, he enters into this love as if it were a cathedral in which to worship himself. She "loves me," Werther says, "and how precious I have become to myself, how I—I can say this to you, who have understanding for such emotions—how I worship at my own altar since I know that she loves me!" (50–51). Werther's stuttering "I" represents in microcosm the entire problematic of the novel. It is a lapse that reveals how "defect" allows him to remain focused on himself, and how other people provide merely the occasion for him to adore his own image. Lotte plays the role of mirror to Werther's soul, just as Nature and God are presented as mirrors. Everything surrounding Werther serves to reflect him and to demonstrate his uniqueness and awesome power. None of this power, however, is wasted on others; Werther, like Rousseau, feeds on himself. My "soul is the mirror of Infinite God," Werther confesses, "but I am ruined by it. I succumb to its magnificence" (25).

Notice, incidentally, that this passage is especially effective in revealing Werther's self-divisiveness. In the translation that I have been citing, Catherine Hutter renders Werther's words in the first person, but in reality Goethe has Werther refer to himself in the second person. A modified translation of the full passage would read: "when it grows light before my eyes and the world around me and the sky above come to rest wholly within my soul like a beloved, I am filled often with yearning and think, if only you could express it all on paper, everything that is housed so richly and warmly within you, so that it might be the mirror of your soul as your soul is the mirror of Infinite God ... ah, my dear friend ... but I am ruined by it. I succumb to its magnificence" (25). In effect, the "I" gives birth to an alien half, a second person within it, whose power and god-like qualities both belong to the self and defeat it. To be ruined by one's magnificence is to dramatize one's own genius. The force of this account did not escape the great admirer of Goethe, Gérard de Nerval, whose novella, *Aurélia*, features a man competing with his double for the affections of his beloved, and whose own self-image is best rendered by the fatal motto, "*Je suis l'autre.*"

Genius for the Romantic generation was, of course, always a species of fatality; but we need to question why Romantic genius must attract chaos and pain. *Werther* underscores the relation between genius and persecution by enacting the process by which a sense of victimization serves fame and intellectual difference. In fact, nearly every one of Werther's statements on genius follows a scene with suicidal or persecutory overtones. In one episode, Werther stumbles on a beautiful landscape and decides to sketch it. His hand mimics his vision perfectly but without any effort on his part, giving him reason to think that genius always surrenders itself to Nature. Indeed, to him, Nature and genius are raging and destructive forces. Would you like to know, Werther asks William, "why genius so rarely breaks its bonds, why it so seldom bursts upon us like a raging torrent to shatter our astounded souls? My friend, it is because of the sober gentlemen who reside on either side of the river, whose precious little summerhouses, tulip beds, and vegetable gardens would be ruined by it, and who know so well how to build dams and divert all such threatening danger in good time" (31). On another occasion, Werther tries to threaten Albert by pressing the mouth of a pistol against his own forehead. Albert lectures him, calling suicide foolishness and madness; "I simply cannot imagine," he explains, "how a man could be so foolish as to shoot himself." Werther, however, grows more incensed. "Oh you sensible people," he cries. "Passion. Inebriation. Madness. ... I have been drunk more than once, and my passion borders on madness, and I regret neither. Because, in my own way, I have learned to understand that all exceptional people who have created something great, something that seemed impossible, have been decried as drunkards or madmen" (58). In his own way, Werther has come to understand something about the relationship of genius to madness, suicide and the violence of sensible people. Marginality has become part of the representation of genius, and one cannot aspire to artistic uniqueness without playing the part, but this very aspiration means that one desires to be mad, suicidal or the victim of intolerance and hatred.

The central problem of *Werther*, then, turns on the affirmation of the self through its negation. The novel repeatedly plays out this process by placing an accent on metaphors of the self and its annihilation. These metaphors most often belong to culture at large, but Goethe systematically collects them with an eye to strengthening our vision of Werther's marginality. Usually they are tied in some way to violence, but there exist other marginal images that serve to distinguish the individuals associated with them.

Werther's body, we saw, is not a body but a shell to be discarded. Like the view of the self in Lacanian and some ego psychology, Werther's ego seems a prison or enclosure. This is the armored self found throughout Romanticism, in which the self takes on the character of a fortress, a wound or a scab, so burdened is it by injury and victimization. Goethe's own "machinations" on suicide in *Dichtung und Wahrheit* also use this metaphor. He insists that one kills a machine with a machine, which explains why the unnatural act of killing oneself always turns to "mechanical devices" to put the design into action. Falling on one's sword, as Ajax does, uses the dead weight of one's body as a weapon to meet the point; and the pistol, the most mechanical device of all, "assures quick action with no exertion." All these devices are "external aids," according to Goethe, "enemies with whom man forms an alliance against himself" (*Selected Writings* 145). The metaphor of the artificial or mechanical self is especially suggestive during a period when industrialization is coming into power; it marginalizes the self by allying it with inhuman devices, but it also appropriates their raw power and difference. Indeed, to ally one's body with the machine is a fantasy whose value for self-representation is demonstrated most successfully in that offshoot of the Romantic fantastic called science fiction, where we discover innumerable images of body and machine conjoined and always as a means to represent ultimate uniqueness, hyperbolic good or evil, and dreams of unchallengeable power.

Another use of metaphor found in *Werther* involves the association of difference and childhood. The metaphor of the child would seem at first glance to offer little to the Romantic self, but it generates, in fact, the required view of the self and its antithesis. Werther consistently allies himself with and compares himself to children because their marginal status in society offers him a way to achieve his aspirations. Children are surrounded in contradiction: they are naturally helpless, but they mirror the helplessness of adults. Little "children," Werther says, "do not know what they want, but no one likes to admit that grown men ... can be ruled, just like a child, by cookies, cake, and rod" (28). Moreover, children are selfish and wild in the extreme; yet Werther sees their self-assertiveness as "simple outbursts" (32). Finally, for Werther, children belong to the cult of feeling. We "should treat children as God treats us," Werther resolves, "when He lets us go our way in a transport of delightful illusions." Consequently, it means something when Werther exclaims to William, "we are children!" or "Oh William, what a child I am!" (49). Werther compares himself to children in order to appropriate their unique position in society.

The effect of this appropriation is nowhere more apparent than in the episode surrounding the children's game played by adults. Lotte instigates the game of "numbers," in which the players must anticipate their number as she pats them on the head. Whoever hesitates or says the wrong number gets a box on the ears. The adults form a circle and some purse their lips and wriggle in happy anticipation of a smacking. Werther is the best narrator in these matters: Lotte "walked the circle with her arms outstretched.... Then she began to move faster, and someone missed ... *ptch*! ... a box on the ears. That made the fellow sitting next to him laugh ... *ptch*! ... he got one, too. And faster and faster. I was boxed on the ears twice, and with secret delight felt that she had boxed my ears harder than any of the others" (40). The game for children is a good-natured display of discipline and punishment, and we should not make too much out of it. We should not fail to notice, however, that the episode provides a perfect model for Werther's adulterous strategies. His relationship to Lotte sets him apart, and whenever he transgresses the rules, he receives the great distinction of having his ears boxed the hardest. He rises out of the general crowd, winning this position through injury and transgression. In short, Werther's relationship to Lotte guarantees that he will have a way to distinguish himself from everyone else.

Rousseau came to understand that too much personal difference spells disaster, but his followers did not hesitate to embark on the fateful journey. Either they allied themselves with suffering to win distinction, or they discovered that their personal distinction cut them off from the rest of humanity. If consciousness individualizes itself beyond a certain point, it separates itself too radically from other people. It creates nothingness within by creating it without. Activity gives way to passivity, as artists stress their own inner life and melancholy. *Amour propre*, in Rousseau's terms, supersedes *amour de soi* or the desire for self-preservation. Likewise, the only meaningful object of reflection is lively melancholy and morbid joy, where death resembles a voluptuous lapse into the infinite. Spiritual isolation becomes a shroud, through which the artist-suicide no longer wishes to see human beings but Nature and God. This is "the disease of the infinite," of which Durkheim speaks in his analysis of Lamartine's *Raphaël* (278). Love of Nature apparently justifies suicide, for it enables the Romantic artist to release himself or herself into Nature and to mingle with it. If the self is mechanical, it appears, we must remake it by sacrificing ourselves to that anthropomorphic god called Nature. In fact, however, this action reveals nothing except a self objectified, and a Nature personified.

The transports of Nature prevalent during Romanticism, then, belong to the transports of delightful illusions. Natural supernaturalism reveals itself to be a game of voodoo in which objects are substituted for human beings in the mistaken belief that some magic will be the result. Modern criticism has, of course, attacked the undue association between Nature and human feeling under the name of the "pathetic fallacy," but this concept does not go far enough. Although critics understand that human beings see weather and Nature as symbols of their inner turmoil, they have not recognized the fact that most natural descriptions in the novels of this period enact the drama of Romantic agony. Natural description both sets the mood of isolation and self-injury for characters and becomes an active means of expressing the social landscape that the Romantic protagonist occupies. We like to believe that the realistic landscape painting of Romanticism expresses a love of Nature and the world, but these paintings often act out a desperate drama in which a solitary entity—a leafless tree, a stone, a church, or a minuscule figure—struggles to distinguish itself against a general background of natural formations. The resting point for the eye, the spot to which the viewer always returns in these paintings, expresses the aspiration of the solitary to attract again and again our attention and to stand out from his or her surroundings.

Goethe's use of Ossian may provide a case in point. It is somewhat remarkable that anyone ever believed in the literary hoax; so Romantic is the text that it could only have been a "modern" invention. As Werther's condition declines, Ossian takes Homer's place in his esteem, and the long readings of Ossian, of course, provide much of the atmosphere of the novel. Werther and Lotte cannot play out their emotions in any other way, and so Ossian comes to symbolize their intense feelings.

It is obvious why Werther adores Ossian: the text overflows with desolate images and outcries of suffering. It is not at all certain, however, why Lotte should find these descriptions so moving. Clearly, she is not entirely an "innocent" figure but as much a sphinx as a Madonna in Goethe's usage. Whatever the reason, her participation adds fuel to Werther's already excessive passions, while the readings themselves affect Werther because they so serve his self-representation. They also play his game, translating injury into personal distinction and general melodrama. The readings are too long to cite in their entirety, but if we keep in mind that they take up many pages in *Werther*, we will have some idea of the couple's as well as Goethe's devotion to Ossian. Here is a truncated version of Colma's solitary lament, which the couple reads before Werther's suicide:

> COLMA: Night has fallen. I am alone and lost on the storm-swept hill. The wind howls down the canyon; no hut protects me from the rain. I have been abandoned on this stormy hill.... But I must needs sit here on the rocky banks of the stream, alone. Stream and storm roar, and I cannot hear the voice of my beloved.... There is the rock, and there is the tree, and here is the rushing stream. Oh, where has my Salgar lost his way? ... I sit in my misery, bathed in my tears, and wait doggedly for the morn. Dig the grave of the dead, my friends, but do not cover it until I am come. Like a dream, my life leaves me—how can I remain behind? Here, beside the stream in the echoing rocks, I shall dwell with my friends.... (113–15)

Some parts of the passage read as if they were a description of a Romantic painting—by Caspar David Friedrich, for example. Unlike such paintings, however, this passage provides the narrative that viewers may only imagine—indeed, that they must imagine in order to have a satisfactory esthetic experience of the art work. The Ossian quotation tells us why we find a young woman, alone, set out from a background of natural objects, and it tells us what she desires. Moreover, her voice tells us that these objects also are solitary. She contests with them in a struggle for difference, in which she wishes to make her way through their interference to reach, in this case, her beloved. Yet she remains in isolation, set apart, until she can stand it no longer and begins to fantasize her own death as a way of joining someone whom she now presumes to be dead. Like Echo of the classical fable, she intends to be absorbed into the natural landscape and to dwell there with the spirit of Nature. How many Romantic heroines and heroes have expressed this same desire! We should not be surprised, then, that landscapes in Romantic art are haunted by human emotions and aspirations and that they serve so well to map out the desires of characters. These landscapes are charged with the desire for and loss of individual difference.

Goethe's use of various metaphors of marginality, of natural description, and of Ossian lends a moody and fatalistic atmosphere to his novel. These evocations act as scenarios for Werther's claims of persecution. Nevertheless, the scene that ends by having the most effect on readers is written by Werther himself. Werther is a *poète manqué*, of course, and his attempts demonstrate little artistic talent: his only real artistic achievements are a handful of sketches and his translation of Ossian. His diary, however, does include what must be called his "masterpiece," and, appropriately, this masterpiece is a suicide note addressed to Lotte. Several strange factors surrounding the farewell letter are worth remarking from the outset. First, Goethe intersperses the suicide note with other episodes—meetings with people and the readings of Ossian—so that its unveiling in the novel consumes many pages. It also takes Werther several days to compose the letter, and the dates are significant for his claims to uniqueness. The opening entry of the letter is dated December 21st, after which the dating of the entries breaks down; it is clear, however, that Werther's intention is to shoot himself as close to Christmas as possible. Some critics have interpreted this timing as an indication that Werther wishes to give his life to Lotte as a Christmas present. Christmas is a dramatic occasion for someone who wants to represent his or her status as victim. To choose to die on the day when Christ was born is to make a statement about one's relationship to the system called Christianity, and it reveals another attempt to appropriate the victimary status of a cultural figure. Moreover, it is probably no accident that Werther both shoots himself and dies at the meridian, thereby demonstrating once again his liminal status.

Second and more important, the suicide letter is read before the action takes place. We are allowed to "discover," so to speak, Werther's suicide note in advance, and this fact lends it even more power and suspense. We should not forget that this reversal is deliberate and quite necessary to the esthetics of the scene of persecution. It is no accident that the letter precedes the act in a novel that stresses at every moment that self-destruction is the product of esthetic aspirations; nor is it an accident that this device is used in a Romantic novel, for Romanticism takes its creative force from the estheticization of the victim's position. The situation is almost analogous to Goethe's relation to Rousseau. Rousseau's suffering precedes his representation of it and in some ways makes the representation possible. Goethe does not need to suffer in order to write his novel. The poetics of suffering in both Goethe's life and writing precedes and displaces the act of suffering, and only Werther must die.

The text of the suicide note itself, as one would expect, exists to record Werther's suffering. Yet there are suicide notes and there are suicide notes, and Werther's letter clearly strives to be a work of art. It is emblematic of the confusion between the ethical and the esthetic dimensions of suicide that one cannot decide whether the esthetic quality of the letter derives from some intrinsic aspect of Werther's writing or from the moral nature of the action that it forecasts. What is undebatable about the note, however, is Werther's consistent aligning of persecution and literary tropes. He will represent himself in any way that he can to justify his self-destructive action, and his note systematically collects images that serve this intention. The letter paints Werther as sacrificial lamb, as adulterous villain, as sinner, as Christ and as the victim of a jealous husband.

The opening entry of the note presents in litany form Werther's desire to die, thereby introducing the religious motif that will guide his self-representations. The phrase, "I want to die," tolls four times in the first paragraph. Ironically, Werther writes that he is composing the "note without any romantic exaggeration" (109), whereas it is precisely on a Romantic context that his representations depend for their affect and logic. He describes himself as the recipient of a thousand blows and as the place of a thousand perspectives. At first, he is to be sacrificed and then he expresses his desire to make himself a sacrifice: "I sacrifice myself for you" (110). The logic of sacrifice is indeed critical for Werther's act; it is not the pagan variety, in which a victim is killed by a priest but the Christian variety, in which the victim sacrifices himself or herself. In pagan sacrifice, the death of the victim attests to the existence of a powerful deity, whereas in Christian sacrifice the victim ends by being divine; and it is surely Werther's intention to achieve this god-like autonomy.

Sacrifices of this kind are crucial to the Romantic cult of self, for they muster all attention to the individual. Werther can at times call himself a villain and a sinner; he may say that his motivation for suicide is to seek forgiveness. These are, however, all means of attracting attention to himself. In the end, he expects to meet his maker and to be honored and comforted by him: "I go on ahead to my Father. To Him I will complain, and He will comfort me until you come, and I fly to meet you and enfold you and remain at your side in the sight of Infinite God in one eternal embrace" (121). Consequently, Werther does not hesitate to drink of the terrible cup; he is a Christ who does not suffer the Passion but gladly accepts to die: "Here, Lotte ... see, it does not make me shudder to grasp the cold and terrible cup from which I shall drink the transport of death." The point of this sacrifice is not to return him to a community of believers. Rather, he is destined to remain forever alone and marginal. Indeed, Werther requests that his body be buried in isolation from the other graves: "It would be too much to expect a faithful Christian to lie beside a poor unfortunate like me. Oh, how I wish you could bury me by the wayside or in a lonely valley, so that priest and Levite might bless themselves as they pass the stone marker and the Samaritan could shed a tear there" (126). We need to stress the importance of this request. Although it was extremely likely that his body would be set apart because of customs regarding suicides, Werther strives to bend custom to his will, thereby empowering himself and ensuring his own self-sufficiency.

The last entries display Werther's great generosity in death. He forgives those who have trespassed against him. He gains Christ-like power, and even forgives Albert. Perhaps this is because Albert lends him his pistols. Werther's note requesting the pistols arrives in the middle of an unpleasant scene between Lotte and her husband—who is in a foul mood, brought on by traveling too much, bad roads, unhappy tidings, and, no doubt, by Werther's constant pestering of Lotte. When Werther's request arrives, then, Albert casually surrenders the pistols, as Lotte's heart sinks. Albert is presented only once in a negative light in the novel, and it is crucial that it be in the scene in which he gives his pistols to the suicidal Werther. Werther has earlier launched a diatribe against the idea of "Husband," and now this husband apparently seeks "revenge" against the transgressor of his family. The scene obscures Werther's egotistical motives and presents him once more as a victim. Werther's generosity in death, therefore, attains its full meaning only as a counterpoint to Albert's "generosity" in surrendering his pistols. Werther plays the forgiving victim to Albert's unthinking and casual victimizer—and thus he dies.

As Werther's entry breaks off for the last time, the novel adopts the third-person form characteristic of the second part. Werther writes *The Sorrows of Young Werther*, it seems, with the help of an editor. Yet our glimpse of the editor is limited. It is only in the second part and at the conclusion that he surfaces. The editor continues the narrative and presents the details of Werther's death and burial as well as the reactions of his friends. Despite the arguments of Eric Blackall and Benjamin Bennett for the similarity between the perspectives of Werther and the editor, I would submit that the two perspectives present a stark contrast. The editor is almost Stendhalian in his economy and terseness. Goethe avoids any lengthy discussion of Werther's last moments, or rather his last moments have taken up the entire text, so that the end needs no elaboration. Indeed, as I have been suggesting, Goethe's representation of the suffering suicide does not really need this end because it takes its force from an esthetic system available to him. Thus, the editor writes, "At twelve noon, Werther died" (127).

Although supposedly an understanding friend—one who comprehends emotions such as Werther experiences—the editor produces a text that is surprisingly condensed and unemotional. His dry and critical prose contrasts sharply with Werther's letter to Lotte and implies, it seems, a criticism of suicide. What is the effect of this conclusion? Does it strive to salvage an optimistic world view and to condemn suicide as a desperate and insane act? Or do the editor's criticisms mirror Werther's own self-destructive urges? If the latter is true, the novel as a whole turns against itself and takes on the double aspect given to Werther's personality: *Werther*, the novel and the man, are both killed by themselves. "What is man made of," we may ask ourselves with Werther, "that he may reproach himself?" (23).

It would be necessary to introduce the issue of self-criticism to appreciate fully what the editor's remarks bring to Goethe's project. For the moment, it suffices to notice that the editor's comments bear witness to the success of Werther's self-representation. Werther's arrangements, the editor explains, silence those attending his funeral. Albert cannot walk behind the bier, and people fear for Lotte's life.

Werther is entombed apart, and no priest attends him. No one surrounds him who might interfere with his claim to difference. In short, *Werther*'s action (*Werther* now being a term that reveals our inability to distinguish between the novel and the character) has the desired effect: *Werther* attains uniqueness. Whereas those egoistic suicides who try to use self-destruction to monumentalize themselves in the real world almost always fail to attain their goal, *Werther* does achieve a monumental status in the world of letters. This success derives from the superior power of "esthetics" to organize our sentiments, and its ultimate effect is best judged within the past history of literature and in its future. The success or failure of *Werther* in the continuing history of literature will rely not on how

powerfully readers identify with Werther but on whether they can imagine a
position similar to Goethe's: Goethe identified with a character whose
beautiful individuality comes from imagining himself as a victim, but he
rejected this character as a model for himself. For the esthetics of the novel
as a genre—its affective power—will exist as a possibility only as long as there
are readers who both identify with characters and resist the temptation to
become them.

## WORKS CITED

Ames, Carol. "Competition, Class, and Structure in *Die Leiden des jungen
    Werther.*" *German Quarterly* 50.2 (1977): 138–49.

Bennett, Benjamin. "Goethe's *Werther*: Double Perspective and the Game of
    Life." *German Quarterly* 53.1 (1980): 64–81.

Blackall, Eric A. *Goethe and the Novel.* Ithaca: Cornell UP, 1976.

Durkheim, Émile. *Suicide: A Sociological Approach.* Trans. John A. Spaulding.
    New York: Free, 1951.

Gans, Eric. *The End of Culture: Toward a Generative Anthropology.* Berkeley: U
    of California P, 1985.

Girard, René. *The Scapegoat.* Trans. Yvonne Freccero. Baltimore: Johns
    Hopkins UP, 1986.

Goethe, Johann Wolfgang von. *The Sorrows of Young Werther and Selected
    Writings.* Trans. Catherine Hutter. New York: Signet, 1962.

Phillips, David P. "The Influence of Suggestion on Suicide: Substantive and
    Theoretical Implications of the Werther Effect." *American Sociological
    Review* 39 (1974): 340–54.

Siebers, Tobin. *The Ethics of Criticism.* Ithaca: Cornell UP, 1988.

Warrick, Kathleen E. "Lotte's Sexuality and Her Responsibility for
    Werther's Death." *Essays in Literature* 5.1 (1978): 129–35.

Wellberg, Caroline. "From Mirrors to Images: The Transformation of
    Sentimental Paradigms in Goethe's *The Sorrows of a Young Werther.*"
    *Studies in Romanticism* 25.2 (1986): 231–49.

SIGRID LANGE

# The "Other Subject" of History:
## Women in Goethe's Drama

"Enlightenment," understood in the eighteenth century as a category of
the philosophy of history, is oriented around three concepts: "the subject,"
the self-consciously acting human individual; the related notion of
"responsibility"; and "history" in its temporal dimension, structured as
"progress" with the possibility of a future utopia. As "character" and the
unfolding of a developing "plot," "subject" and "time" are simultaneously the
constitutive categories of the poetics of tragedy. The category of "guilt"
corresponds to "responsibility" and gives rise to the cathartic effect in the
audience. In this parallel of concepts the aesthetic debate since its origins in
antiquity transmits the semantic transformations that have arisen due to
philosophical reflections on reality. Especially in the eighteenth century we
can follow closely this connection between philosophy and aesthetics. I mean
the reformulation of the Aristotelian theory of tragedy in the aesthetics of
the Enlightenment and of the Storm-and-Stress period, using Shakespeare as
a model, in contrast to the French, classicist poetic of rules. Shakespeare was
viewed as a representative of modernity against antiquity because, in
Goethe's concise formulation, he reconceived in dramatic conflicts subjective
action and fate in the collision of our "pretended freedom of the will with the
necessary course of the whole."[1] This definition is already based on the
Copernican revolution in modern thought, whereby the individual human

From *Impure Reason: Dialectic of Enlightenment in Germany*. © 1993 by Wayne State University
Press.

141

subject, due to his native capacity for reason, was thrust into the center of the world. The adversary of this autonomous subject is "history," whose apparent fatality is to be recognized in its regularity and thus made subservient.

The turn to the classical does not mean a rejection of this fundamental understanding, but rather a problematization and deepening of it. With regard to drama the debates around the ancients and the moderns in both their theoretical and practical dimensions continue to focus on the concepts of history, the subject, and guilt, and define the difference in the way in which the human being exists in the world. The classical authors use the forms from the ancient world of high literature in order to legitimize their own worldview and aesthetics, which differ from those of antiquity. As Rudolf Brandmeyer expressed it in connection with Goethe, the classical dramas achieve—against the foil of the notions of "fate" and "heroes" of ancient tragedy—a modern version that favors individual over representative subjectivity and history over the repetitive circularity of a divinely determined world. Against the background of rapidly enriched, eventful, temporal experience at the end of the century, consensual fixations were absent. What is tragic, when history, like blind necessity, breaks in and still does not fulfill the former divine fate of a well ordered world? What is human about a subjectivity that is set free, that no longer exhibits moral exemplarity, and that for this very reason has become "natural" and unfree again? And what kind of an aesthetic system of values can be founded on such a subjectivity?

Such questions are explicitly raised in the theoretical discussions of tragedy in the works of Goethe and Schiller, of Hölderlin and Kleist, and of A. W. Schlegel and Hegel. I maintain—and I am not alone in this assertion[2]—that implicitly in Goethe, namely in the dramatic literature itself, the very phenomenon is elucidated that we have come to call the "Dialectic of Enlightenment." Moreover, I would contend that in his dramatic working out of this problematic he generally employed a descriptive model that drew on gender-specific typology of the previous history of the Occident, as well as its patterns of thought and expression. In terms of content, Goethe calls this history masculine and opposes it to a feminine utopia; in formal terms, this trope does not break with aesthetic tradition. To be sure, after his early romantic tragedies, and the two early historical tragedies he *de facto* abandons the tragic genre; but he trivializes the objective problem of form by conceiving it as a matter of taste: he believes that he simply had no affinity for the tragic. Actually, however, I believe that the ambivalent patriarchal self-criticism and the equally ambivalent use of the category of "femininity" expresses itself indirectly in the dramatic form.

I will demonstrate my thesis with three closely related dramatic texts: the play *Iphigenie at Tauris*, the tragedy *The Natural Daughter*, and the festival play *Pandora*, but begin with the prehistory in Goethe's earlier works. In his early poetic productions, Goethe did not proceed from abstract theoretical considerations but rather from the empirical and biographical realm in the romantic tragedies *Clavigo*, *Stella*—whose early conciliatory ending was replaced in 1806 by a morally and aesthetically "appropriate" tragic conclusion—and the Gretchen tragedy. In each case it is a question of a subjective guilt-conflict on the part of a young hero who uses his lover as a means to his own self-realization and who then, by abandoning her, sacrifices her for the sake of his ego. In comparison to other contemporary versions of the same subject, Goethe avoids a moralizing of the character constellations: the male and female protagonists are not dichotomized into good and evil, nor are they distinguished in a political fashion in terms of class with the inclusion of an aristocratic seducer and a middle-class victim. Instead, Goethe presents a youthful lover, a social climber in the middle-class sense, who is tragically torn between his responsibility to himself—the internal duty to exhaust fully his human potential—and his responsibility to others. Especially with the figures Clavigo and Faust, he avoids the kind of one-dimensional amorality that characterizes their satanic doubles, Carlos and Mephisto. In this way Goethe explores the romantic conflict on its own terms, problematizes in the conflict the limitless claim to autonomy in the bourgeois subject, and at the same time validates individual experience as something essential (see Brandt).

In these constellations I am concerned with significant gender-specific patterns of characters and actions. These can be derived from the opposition between motion and rest that appears as a leitmotif: the male protagonists are always "on their way somewhere" in accord with their roles as active and developing individuals. The motif of the wanderer, frequently found in lyric poetry, appears here in the figure of the traveler. In this group belong, besides Clavigo and Faust, Weislingen from *Götz*, Fernando from *Stella*, and even Egmont, all of whom contrast with their female partners (who remain in one place). At the same time this spatial tension repeats the social and psychic gender dispositions, according to which the male figures are active and the female figures are passive. The characters are so strictly drawn in terms of gender that their actions can turn into those of their counterparts: since the women fulfill their expected roles in their deep, immutable, and always forgiving love, in a moment of threatening catastrophe the ability to act can grow out of their absoluteness of their feeling. With Clavigo and Faust the initiative for action passes first—and with disastrous consequences—

to their mephistophelian representatives, but then later to the women. Weislingen's Marie rescues her unfaithful lover, who has failed in his attempt to climb the social ladder; Clavigo's Marie acts in a similar fashion; the most obvious inversions of the original model of action occur with Stella and Cäcilie in the recognition scene with Fernando and with Gretchen in the jail scene. Stella and Cäcilie turn the apparently unsolvable tragedy into the suggestion of a *ménage a trois*, while Gretchen decides—correctly, despite her insanity—against Faust's self-deceptive escape plans. This recurrent dramatic pattern assumes in the later work of Goethe—and this is the rationale for this brief digression about the early work—the function of a dramaturgical model.

I am speaking of *Iphigenie*. Essential for the exposition of the play is the mythological concreteness of the disposition of the woman for sacrifice: Iphigenie is selected by her father as a sacrificial victim in order to acquire the blessing of the gods for success in war. The goddess Diana intervenes to save her—a *dea ex machina* in the sense of ancient tragedy—and brings Iphigenie to Tauris. This exposition is critical for an understanding of Goethe's play. The same constellation is repeated in a drama conceived more than twenty years later, *The Natural Daughter*, except that the mythical abstraction is translated into the prose of contemporary political reality. The title character, Eugenie, is the victim of a modern intrigue, which is taken from the authentic memoirs of Princess Stephanie-Louise of Bourbon-Conti. The miraculous rescue of the heroine from the consequences of a deadly fall at the beginning of the play proves to be deceptive; similar to Iphigenie, Eugenie needs the full time of five acts of dramatic action to elude the planned sacrifice. Finally, Pandora, who is in a special sense the "heroine" of the festive play, is likewise a sacrificial figure. As a character symbolizing the feminine and love, she is sacrificed to the modern Promethean culture— which is another mythological symbol for the Faustian. Rejected by the "creative" Prometheus—and for Goethe in 1807, "creative" means forging weapons and ruling peoples—and driven by the person of deeds and days into the dark side of life, Pandora leaves the earthly world. In contrast to Goethe's earlier plays, the female victims become figures of redemption and in this double disposition transform these plays into parables that have implications for a philosophy of history.

Before I provide the evidence for this, I would like to call attention to the following phenomenon: in Goethe's oeuvre one finds, in addition to the early plays that are either comedies and musical plays or the romantic tragedies already mentioned, two tragedies: *Götz* and *Egmont*. Whereas the romantic tragedies with their private, individualistic conflicts place women figures in the very center of the action, in the historical plays they recede into the background and appear as part of a general ensemble of characters. For the chief conflict, the autonomous subject versus the historical course of the world, they play only a marginal role. After these early plays, Goethe abandons not only Shakespearean formal traditions, but also a content anchored in a historical milieu. With the turn to fables with historical and parabolic dimensions he again includes female protagonists. My thesis, which is based on these changes in his work, is that Goethe replaced the tragic constellation of his historical dramas and their unsuccessful male heroes with an abstractly historical and utopian project that explores in fiction the "other" subject of history, the feminine.

In the mythical context, Iphigenie's role as victim appears real from a contemporary standpoint as well: "I do not argue with the gods; however, the situation of women is lamentable."[3] This is true of any woman's dependent position at home as either daughter or wife, but she is even more defenseless in a foreign land. The long opening monologue intentionally makes this factor equal and parallel to the other central element of conflict: the curse of the race of Tantalus. Goethe himself later referred to this connection in his early writings: "Tantalus, Ixion, Sysiphus were my saints, ... and when I show them as members of an enormous opposition in the background of my *Iphigenie*, I am indebted to them for a portion of the effect that this play had the good fortune to produce."[4] The opposition of the autonomous subject, which is represented in the mythical story as human hybris in confrontation with the omnipotence of the gods, is conjured up in the drama essentially by the growing cycle of previous human history, which has countered violence with more violence. This concept of action, according to Goethe, allows a new power relationship to arise from the originally justified indignation against arbitrariness; this duplication of power relations involves an apparently unavoidable implication in guilt that leads to the extermination of the race of Tantalus, or by implication of the human race. Within the parameters of the play this concept of action is identified as masculine, as a male logic that demands the sacrifice of the woman, in this case Iphigenie. Thus both components of the previously described constellation, which originally referred to eighteenth-century reality, are carried over into the mythical projection.

At the same time, in the detachment from its ancient subtext, the modern play *Iphigenie* orients itself along the lines of gender-specific models of action. Essential elements of the ancient fable influence the plot from the exposition of the heroine's conflict to her forced decision under the greatest moral pressure, produced by the anagnoresis in the third act. The demand that Iphigenie reach a decision involves exclusively her sacrifice: either of her own moral identity or of the bodily existence of her brother and his friend—and the latter alternative is an unreasonable demand that would destroy Iphigenie psychologically and morally just as surely as would the first. The tragic model from antiquity would at this point call for the pernicious or salutary intervention of the gods, and with this we would come full circle back to the original situation, when the goddess Diana appeared at the last moment before the tragic outcome. In fact, from the very beginning, Iphigenie does direct her gaze hopefully to the gods above. Even the monologue before the song of the Parcae appeals to the unity of the human and the divine, with the implicit demand that the order of the world be affirmed. As long as this order appears just, it legitimizes the natural and lawful fate of divine arbitrariness. Opposition to it is hybris, and hybris is avenged mercilessly, as the song of the Parcae reminds us. The modern reinterpretation of the myth begins at precisely the point where human self-understanding comprehends divine rule as lawless despotism and mobilizes autonomous human reason against this "natural power." However, in the hybris of Goethe's Tantalus and its consequences we do not find a reflection of the provocation of suprahuman arbitrariness, but a human implication in guilt. Reason, although intended and just, cannot free itself from the fetters of the myth. It is well known that Adorno himself interpreted Goethe's *Iphigenie* in accord with this understanding of the dialectic of enlightenment.

With regard to this plot-model it seems to me important that even women figures—for example, Klytemnestra—can be integrated into the role of agents, of guilt-ridden victors, to the extent that they involve themselves in the reality of power relations. At least in her thoughts, Iphigenie carries this possibility through to its logical conclusion; symbolically she thereby returns to the origin of this tale, to the hybris of Tantalus. On the one hand, Goethe thus revises his earlier understanding of history by relegating the "adulthood" of the modern age to the realm of prehistorical barbarity,[5] including the two steps of the human process of civilization symbolized in Sythian and Greek.[6] On the other hand, at the point when Iphigenie undertakes an active initiative, the utopian anticipation of another type of modernity begins. I would describe the feminine concept of action that Goethe displays with Iphigenie as a refusal to choose between false alternatives.

One line of recent research has attempted to reinterpret *Iphigenie* as a drama about Orestes and thus to examine critically or overturn the analyses that traditionally praised the female protagonist. In this respect, Wolfdietrich Rasch's interpretation agrees with the feminist reading by Irmgard Wagner.

Rasch views the climax of this "drama of autonomy" within the context of a critique of religion, since Orestes *reinterprets* the oracle (rather than merely revising his earlier "misunderstanding," as the traditional interpretation has it) and concludes that it does not mean the divine sister of Apollo, but his own worldly sister. Wagner radicalizes this interpretation to the point of seeing a cooptation of Iphigenie by a sort of male fraternity. By contrast, Hans Robert Jauß follows the original line of *Iphigenie* commentary and comes to the conclusion that Goethe replaces the ancient myth of the gods with the myth of the feminine. I believe that this reading is in accord with the text insofar as the play constructs the idea of a pure, feminine morality, personifies it in Iphigenie, and ascribes to it a deed that redeems humanity. However, the "regression" to the ancient model is thwarted because Iphigenie is supposed to initiate a history that is connected to the real sacrifice of woman in the patriarchy; this history is socially as exact as the mythological parable permits. Iphigenie's moral greatness lies solely in her ability to avoid the sacrifice and with it corruption by the hegemonic culture of the perpetrators.

The play does not stop here. The historical non-specificity of time and space in the plot is made concrete by models of action that were decipherable for Goethe's contemporaries. This is accomplished by motifs and in structure. For the former, one could point to the song of the Parcae, in which the alternation of rebellion and fall conjures up the early Prometheus ode even in its language and thus demonstrates the reproduction of hierarchical social relations. The motifs thus reinforce the structure of the ensemble of characters and their actions, where we also find a clearly defined social hierarchy. If we were to construct a pyramid from the figures involved in the play, then Thoas would be placed at the top because of his social status. As the ruler of the island, he has all the other figures in his hands: on the one hand Iphigenie, his temple priestess, and Arkas, his servant; on the other hand his two prisoners and potential victims. Both pairs of figures would have to be seen in opposition to each other according to the original constellation. As long as Thoas as king possesses the initiative for action—from his wooing of Iphigenie until his punishment of her for refusing to continue with human sacrifices—this hierarchy remains in place. However, when Iphigenie finally gains the initiative for action at the beginning of the fifth act, which was anticipated earlier by her threefold rejection of her sacrificial role, she ascends to the top of the dramaturgical pyramid and at the same time dissolves it as a hierarchical constellation; the figures in the play become equal in status. They part from each other as brother, sister, or friend—the only human relationships that, according to the understanding of that era, are nonhierarchical and thus "purely human."

My conclusions are supported by the cult of friendship in the eighteenth century. For the important brother–sister relationship between Iphigenie and Orestes, in which Pylades and Thoas are then included as friends, one could cite Hegel, who sees in the family an embodiment of divine law, a "naturally moral community," and defines the relationships within the family by reference to the degree of morality between husband and wife, or parents and children. "But the unadulterated relationship occurs between brother and sister. They have the same blood, but in them it comes to *rest* and *equilibrium*. They therefore do not desire each other; and they have neither given nor received this being-for-itself. Rather, they are free individuals with one another. As a sister, the feminine therefore possesses the highest *premonition* of moral being" (336).

The immanent problematic of this mythically stylized theory of the family and society cannot be discussed here. Important for me is the high esteem shown for the brother–sister relationship: it is not infected with the sexual desire of the "natural" relationship between men and women and is therefore not unfree; nor is it structured in an obviously authoritarian fashion as the father–daughter relationship is. We should recall once again the relevant passages in Iphigenie's opening monologue as well as the relationship of Thoas to her, which is both paternal and charged with male sexual desire. From this perspective the final constellation of *Iphigenie* takes on the function of a symbolic model. We should not forget, of course, that it exists in the absence of "natural" relationships and is thus an obvious construction.

When Goethe sketched his trilogy *The Natural Daughter* (*Die natürliche Tochter*) at the start of the nineteenth century, it appeared that reality had become what *Iphigenie* only hinted it could be: chaos had become part of the times; the world order had been demolished. "O this time of fearful signs: / The lowly swells up, the heights sink downward."[7] The French Revolution forced Goethe to look back again at its prehistory in order to fathom it and perhaps—as *Pandora*, written a few years later, suggests—to correct it poetically with utopian intent. The anticipated eruption of the revolution is, however, as Hans Rudolf Vaget has persuasively argued, accompanied in the structure of motifs by a steady up-and-down movement. After *Iphigenie*, this play—conceived as a tragedy, but no longer based on the classical model of guilt and penance—endeavors to comprehend real historical processes symbolically.

The connections between the two plays have been dealt with many times, for example by Wagner and Böschenstein. The similarity is most obvious in the motif of the woman exiled on a barbaric island, in several aspects of the brother–sister–father relationship, and in the portrayal of the heroine as a figure of salvation. With regard to my analysis of *Iphigenie*, I could add, moreover, a significant structural analogy in the doubling of the constellation of characters. The five figures in *Iphigenie* all act on the level of royalty: king, king's daughter, king's son, king's friend, and king's servant. The corresponding group in *The Natural Daughter* is the king, the duke, his daughter Eugenie, the abbess, the governor, as well as the two minor figures, the surgeon and the count, whose roles do not further the action and who therefore can be discounted in the parallel. A second grouping of five persons consists of the secretary, his wife—the tutor of Eugenie—the lay priest, the monk, and the judge. Clearly these two groups are symbolically associated with class principles, which then oppose each other in the revolution as aristocracy and bourgeoisie. The first group contains persons that belong to the aristocratic party either because of their position and profession, or, as in the case of the king, the duke, and Eugenie, because of familial relationships. This emphasizes the principle of personal relationships in the feudal system in contradistinction to the reified system of objective relations in the ascending middle-class order. This order characterizes the second group, although the individuals are only partially members of the traditional bourgeois estate. To the traditional bourgeoisie belong the secretary, the tutor, and the judge as the potential leader of the rebellion, as the plan of the trilogy suggests. The two clergymen, who technically belong to the second estate, function nonetheless in the second, "bourgeois" group: the secular priest acts out of purely material motives, and the monk prophesies the approaching revolution and advises Eugenie to seek a new life somewhere outside of this uncertain and dangerous environment. Most decisive is that the figures in this group are connected with each other essentially by a variety of exchanges: founding a household, social climbing and profit. Both groups of characters are connected by the central figure in the background of the play: Eugenie's brother, the head of the intrigue. He is the perfect representative of the bourgeois principle in that he embodies the merciless competition for profit, though he never appears in the play as a person.

The plot of the play shows us Eugenie immediately before her planned social legitimation by the king. While this is happening, the brother initiates the intrigue by allowing their father to believe that Eugenie is dead and preparing her abduction and exile. She tries to obtain protection in vain from the governor and the abbess; she considers suicide, but then accepts her tutor's solution of a bourgeois marriage with the judge. Of course, this marriage is not without preconditions: "Can you promise me that you will receive me / As a brother with purity of affection, / Granting me, the loving sister, protection / And advice and the quiet joy of life?"[8] At the end of the first part, the brother–sister relationship—the prerequisite for her salvation—places Eugenie in the same position that Iphigenie had acquired earlier: expecting salvation no longer from outside, but from herself.

Because of the doubling of the character groups, the analogy between the two dramas has yet another dimension. Eugenie finds her bourgeois counterpart in the figure of the female tutor. None of the previous interpreters of *The Natural Daughter* have devoted enough attention to her, despite the fact that, aside from Eugenie, she has by far the greatest number of lines. She is far more than the typical trusted servant who betrays her mistress reluctantly and only under duress; she is also concerned with salvation: "Eugenie, if you could renounce / The lofty happiness that appears boundless...."[9] She introduces the bourgeois notion of renunciation. In Goethe's thought this notion played a significant role from the 1790s to *Wilhelm Meister's Travels* (*Wilhelm Meisters Wanderjahre*, 1821/1829), with its subtitle "Those Who Renounce" ("Die Entsagenden"). It was conceived by Goethe as the individual's compromise vis-à-vis the earlier concept of autonomy, which insisted on the total development of individuality. When Eugenie—with the identical notion of renunciation—repudiates her claim to class privileges at the close of the play, she does not simply become a member of the bourgeoisie. As a "sister" she acquires a personal freedom that goes beyond any class or hierarchical order. In this play, the "solution" of the conflict is thus located between the social and political compromise of inter-class marriages in the *Wilhelm Meister's Apprenticeship* (*Wilhelm Meisters Lehrjahre*, 1795–1796) and the concept of redemption in *Iphigenie*. In *The Natural Daughter*, however, Goethe goes to great lengths to accomplish a synthesis of the individual figure and the abstract ideal. Both functions are conceived for this single figure; she is the only person in the play with a proper name, and she is distinguished in the title with the designation of "natural daughter" with its threefold meaning of illegitimate child, of a person raised according to Rousseauist principle far from courtly society, and of someone representing the purely human beyond any social status. When brought back into the concrete history of the times, however, the symbolic intention fails: Goethe gives up on a continuation of the project.

With regard to dramatic tension, Peter Pütz defines plot as "successive re-presentations of anticipated futures and recovered pasts" (11). This definition makes most sense where the temporal structures are simultaneously covered by the historical notion of time. In *The Natural Daughter* a turning-point in history is the theme, and in accord with historical reality the initiative for action is always given to the bourgeois estate. When Eugenie in the first act is miraculously saved from her apparently fatal accident as the duke prepares her introduction at court, the opposing party has already taken action behind the scenes. When at the end of the first act the king, the duke, and Eugenie all dream of a new Golden Age in which a peaceful, patriarchal harmony exists among the classes, the plan for Eugenie's abduction has already been worked out to the last detail. When she opens the chest filled with ostentatious clothing and regalia in anticipation of her impending elevation into courtly circles, the secretary and the tutor are already prepared to take her into exile. A preoccupation with blinding diversions, imprisonment in a world of appearances, cripple the aristocratic party, and accordingly it is progressively removed from the play. The king does not appear after the first act; the duke disappears in the third act, after Eugenie's apparent death, into his fantasy world of the Eugenie mausoleum. Only at the end of the play does Eugenie acquire the initiative for action in her symbolic role as redeemer after she has been freed from the fetters of her social existence.

Goethe finally accomplished and thematized such a structure of meaning around historical time in his play *Pandora* (1810). It is suggested in the symbolism attached to the names of Prometheus and Epimetheus as the man of forethought and the man of afterthought and is introduced in the old Epimetheus' account of his life. With the opposition of youth and old age he opens the first, biographical dimension of the temporal problematic, which is expressed in the contrast between spontaneous action and reflection. This corresponds to the opposition between the youthful dreams in sleep, which drive out the presence of the day, and the nocturnal waking dreams of his old age, which recall the day in order to pose the question of human capacity for self-determination. In the confrontation of these two stages of life, the monologue reflects this opposition in the form of a contradiction between enjoyment of life and responsibility, and then gives it an additional dimension in the polarity of the active man of forethought, Prometheus, and the nocturnal man of afterthought, Epimetheus.

This anthropological reflection leads the drama into an artistic play of interwoven action and contemplation—in which the reflection posited in the exposition is carried out in an action. The play of thought and dramatic play are joined in a synthesis whose philosophical center is the potential of the play of thought for altering reality, as it results from the interpretation of the name Epimetheus: "For my progenitors named me Epimetheus / To reflect upon the past, with laborious plays of thought / To lead back that which has occurred quickly / To the murky realm of possibility for combining forms."[10]

Thus the "festival play" would consist of tracing back the regretted deed to alternative possibilities and playing it through again.

The initially abstract profundity of this reflective exposition is revealed gradually in the play. It takes up the theme of generations and begins with the youth Phileros, who is hurrying to a romantic rendezvous and reminds Epimetheus of his own past romantic bliss, causing him to utter envious blessings as well as concerned prophesies of disaster. This apparently banal occurrence takes on symbolic significance through the repetition of the intimated past experience of Epimetheus: the new generation, which here frivolously risks catastrophe in the pursuit of romance, appears not to have the chance to begin again with new possibilities. At the same time, the drastic result—Phileros almost murders his lover out of jealously and then wants to commit suicide—points to a more profound level of meaning than the mere misunderstanding that apparently occurs. This meaning is suggested by the related genre of the pastoral romance—Goethe himself had composed pastoral romances with this motif in his youth. The abrupt end of the envisioned idyll signals in an extremely parabolic abbreviation the transition from the Golden Age to a present of mistrust, guilt, and violence.

Thus, biographical time is constructed in a second dimension to elucidate differences in human epochs. The interpretive framework for the scene is given by the familial relationship between Phileros, the son of Prometheus, and Epimeleia, the daughter of Epimetheus. The social semantic of these symbolic relationships is disclosed only at the climax of the play, when these four persons are brought together. At the intersection of these levels of meaning and of the lines of dialogue and action, however, stands Pandora, or more accurately, an image of Pandora which determines the actions of the male characters in this drama. "Speak, is it Pandora? You saw her once, / Ruinous for fathers, a torture for sons,"[11] asks Phileros at the moment of the violent ending of his love affair. The projected image of Pandora in Epimeleia that he refers to encompasses both the goal and the content of the drama at the same time: Pandora, symbol of love, whose return is the implicit telos of the play, is present in clashing perceptions. Absence and contradictory images mutually reinforce each other and make the present time symbolically one of absent love combined with the image of love as happiness and peril, threat and promise. Epimetheus' fantasy of Pandora's return finds its polar opposite in Prometheus' anxiety about her; this had caused him to reject the female messenger of the gods, from whom he had emancipated himself. This constellation characterizes Promethean culture's ambivalence, arising from human self-creativity in isolation.

Phileros' tragedy is caused by the perseverance of his father's image of Pandora, which is characterized by the negative attributes of deceptive appearance and infidelity, while, for his part, Epimetheus lives with a threefold longing for Pandora. She is present for him in the waking dream that recalls their shared intimacy, in the sleeping dream of her daughter Elpore promising to return, and in the likeness of his daughter Epimeleia. The positive image is arrested in contemplation; the negative image motivates the actions of Prometheus and Phileros. Thus the dominance of the "demonic" Pandora appears to affirm the pessimistic account of life and history and to bolster Promethean culture. On the other hand, this image acts as a decisive factor in unleashing the catastrophe. This involves more than the individual relationship between Phileros and Epimeleia, in that Prometheus' son kills the shepherd who approaches with loving desires and thus provokes the rebellion of the pastoral folk. For them, Prometheus' prediction comes true: "Wander away peacefully! You do not go to find peace."[12]

At the same time, this scene of the strife between the lovers exhibits a countervailing tendency by bringing together Prometheus and Epimetheus. While Pandora had formerly separated them, as her image separates Phileros and Epimeleia, now, with the reunion of the fathers, the progressive line of Promethean culture is thwarted and led back to another possibility in the course of the dialogue. This interweaving of plays of thought with the dramatic play is realized in the temporal structure of the entire drama in that the realm of the deed is preceded by the realm of reflection, which thus calls into question the finality of the action: Epimetheus' narration of his meeting with Prometheus comes before the first scene with Prometheus, and Epimetheus' dream of the return of Pandora occurs before the scene depicting Phileros' jealousy. In this manner the chronology of factual happenings that is defined in terms of a Promethean line—according to which the rejection of Pandora coincides with the act of creating culture—is hypothetically cancelled. Similarly, the repetition of this rejection in the Phileros–Epimeleia episode precedes the possibility of understanding. A reversal seems to be possible.

A spatial symbolism corresponds to this temporal structure, and it is introduced in the scenic configuration of the surroundings of Prometheus and Epimetheus. One side suggests repose, peace, the permanence of human settlements that face the open sea. With its crude and unfinished buildings, the other side represents the restlessness of beginning, grounded on the craggy cliffs and mountain ranges. This cliff symbolism is drawn from the fragment of "Prometheus Unbound," where it designates the powerful hierarchy of the rule of the gods. It always carries within it the danger of overthrow, as the rebellion of the shepherds shows. Promethean culture, which is itself grounded on rebellion, reproduces the social hierarchy of master and slave, as well as the patriarchal relationship of father and son—"A good son honors the absence of the father."[13] Violence is an integral part of this social hierarchy, which has long since left behind the vision of the peaceful patriarchal realm from Goethe's early "Prometheus" fragment, replacing the building of huts with the forging of weapons (see Borchmeyer).

The symbolic spaces of cliffs and sea are repeatedly evoked at the end of the play and integrated into the temporal structure. The punishing father Prometheus sends his disobedient son to the cliffs at the sea so that he can condemn himself and plunge to his death. The fate of Phileros, who follows these directions just as he had followed his father's image of Pandora, represents the third sequence in the chronology of the Promethean line of the drama. Again it is preceded—in the dialogue of Prometheus and Epimetheus—by a reflective scene that aims at a reconciliation of both under Pandora's sign. The rising pathos from Pandora's rejection of Epimetheus to the bloody repudiation of Epimeleia achieves in Phileros' attempted suicide a climax and possible turning point which are condensed in the action and in the symbolism of space and time. In terms of space, the cliffs and the sea move closer together. The fall from the cliffs into the sea marks the transgression of the spatial boundary between life, death, and rebirth.

Rebirth is eventually granted to Phileros, but it does not happen because of him, just as in general the reconciliation of the strife-ridden cultures does not take place. Work, property, domination and servitude remain separated from the world of dreams, of beauty, and of love—on the border of their times of day. During the first appearance of the nocturnal Epimetheus, Phileros embarks on his romantic rendezvous under the sign of the morning star; his rescue occurs under the rising morning sun.

The dramatic conception of *Pandora* can be summarized in the following formula: not the solution of the conflict, but the redemption from the conflict. In the parabolic abstraction of the festival play, one line of the great historical process of the genesis of modern society is thematized and parried by one that runs contrary to it. This other line may be interpreted by its origins in the Olympian realm above as a utopian projection of a possible future.

Goethe's dramas with female protagonists, written over a period of thirty years, have various implications for a philosophy of history. In *Iphigenie*, with its parabolically abbreviated form, this message shows the previous development of humanity to be determined by self-destructive relations of power; *The Natural Daughter* relates the development of bourgeois modernity to the French Revolution; in *Pandora*, again fully abstracted from any concrete political reality, the theme is human cultural development as a connection between the unfolding of productivity and social relations of domination. This history is always described as masculine and one that demands sacrifice: the sacrifice of the woman. It is only logical, therefore, that the removal of the sacrifice of the woman means the entry into a new, human history, in other words, into a utopian dimension. The dramatic conflict, which in each case stages the immanent and pernicious self-propelled dynamics of this (hi)story—the dialectic of Enlightenment—is never resolved, however, through its own structure. It is "redeemed" insofar as the former victims become figures of redemption.

It is possible to read Goethe's early dramas, taking as representative the first part of *Faust*, as critical of a male morality that can then be expanded to include a bourgeois-male model of emancipation. In this way, this aspect of these three plays takes on a historical significance. *Iphigenie* is a parable of male history that is identified as barbaric: the myth of the rise and fall of Tantalus and the resulting curse on his descendants, who will destroy themselves in a chain of violence, is a metaphor for human history. Independence, autonomy of mankind is shown to be regression into a natural matrix of history in the sense that these rebellious human beings, these men, are insulated from the consequences of their actions. With Adorno, who interpreted *Iphigenie* in this sense, we can say that Enlightenment returns to myth.

*The Natural Daughter* refers to concrete history, namely to the French Revolution, and in so doing postulates rebellion, individual autonomy instead of collective responsibility as the metaphor of the age. An order crumbles, and in its place arises the chaos of competing subjective interests—bourgeois society, which for Goethe initially appears as the disintegration of original values. The Revolution, present in this play only as premonition, is the extreme expression of this process.

Finally, *Pandora* abstracts from the concrete political situation and takes as its theme the cultural expression of bourgeois society. Unlike the early dramatic fragment *Prometheus* (1774), *Pandora* is not concerned with the creative aspect of mankind's emancipation from divine domination, but rather with the destructive component of this culture, which threatens humane ideals. Goethe's new Prometheus no longer builds huts, symbols of human dwelling and protectedness, but rather has his servants make weapons in caves. In the play this production of weapons leads to arson and war. The pastoral age of human innocence is left behind; modernity makes way for itself with murder and death. Violence is directly connected to an exploitative, destructive relationship of humankind to nature; nowhere else has Goethe so clearly described the domination of humankind over nature as the destruction of the foundations of human life, a destruction that is expressed in social relations. Alienation, distrust, and violence are symbolically synthesized in the inability to love. Rejecting the misogynist tradition of the myth of "Pandora's box," Goethe portrays Pandora as the embodiment of love, but she is excluded from this culture.

To simplify matters, it could be said that at the end of all three plays an "unrealistic" conflict resolution replaces a "realistic" view of history and a resulting configuration of conflict. In a utopian way, male history is freed from its inextricable contradictions by a female character. Iphigenie cuts through the Gordian knot of violence that breeds violence when she makes the ethical decision to refuse the false alternatives of male history, that is, to sacrifice either oneself or another; in so doing, she opens the way to a new history (or herstory). This play can thus be read as an attempt to insert the woman—the "other sex," in Simone de Beauvoir's sense—as the "other subject" of failed male history, though in a poetic-utopian play. *The Natural Daughter* aims at the same goal; it was originally planned as a trilogy, of which only the first part was completed. The return of Pandora, promised at the end of the play, also promises resolution.

The re-introduction of the ancient deus ex machina as a modern dea ex machina in these plays uses the then-modern image of woman as a collection of ideal characteristics, an image that is abstracted more and more from the real existence of woman. Real woman is the victim of the new bourgeois age, as Goethe's early dramas show. But male guilt, which is connected to this age, can no longer be dependent on the morality of individual characters, if it is to represent the character of the age, and the elimination of this guilt cannot be tied to an individual female character. Beginning with Iphigenie, who merges individual character and utopian projection, Goethe's female characters become more and more abstract. They tend toward an image of the feminine. A male fantasy becomes evident, which functions as a vehicle of a worldview that is no longer cohesive. The image of redemption by the feminine takes the place of a historical telos that is no longer recognizable but only hoped for, a telos that resolves the contradictions of the modern age. Drama, which portrays these contradictions, cannot resolve them, but only furnish rescues from them. In this way we take leave of a conception of tragedy that elevates, confirms, sublimely raises up the male hero through his tragic defeat by reality. In this sense, Goethe's plays end very appropriately with the "festival play," *Pandora*. Nevertheless, classical drama finds meaning in the dramatic due to the category of the female.

## NOTES

1. "prätendierte Freiheit unseres Wollens mit dem notwendigen Gang des Ganzen" (12: 226).

2. See, for example, Adorno or Borchmeyer.

3. "Ich rechte mit den Göttern nicht; allein / Der Frauen Zustand ist beklagenswert" (5: 8).

4. "Tantalus, Ixion, Sysiphus waren meine Heiligen, ... und wenn sie als Glieder einer ungeheuren Opposition im Hintergrund meiner 'Iphigenie' zeige, so bin ich ihnen wohl einen Teil der Wirkung schuldig, welche dieses Süick hervorzubringen das Glück hätte" (10: 277).

5. This thesis is also implicit in Reed, who follows the maturation ('Mündigkeit') of Iphigenie during the course of the play and thus locates the real enlightenment with the integration of the women.

6. Adorno places an emphasis on this distinction although it is canceled by his own interpretation.

7. "O diese Zeit hat fürchterliche Zeichen: / Das Niedere schwillt, das Hohe senkt sich nieder" (5: 226).

8. "Vermagst du zu versprechen, mich als Brüder / Mit reiner Neigung zu empfangen? mir, / Der liebevollen Schwester, Schutz und Rat / Und stille Lebensfreude zu gewähren?" (5: 298).

9. "Eugenie, wenn du entsagen könntest / Dem hohen Glück das unermeßlich scheint ..." (5: 240).

10. "Denn Epimetheus nannten mich die Zeugenden, / Vergangenem nachzusinnen, Raschgeschehenes / Zurückzuführen mühsam Gedankenspiels / Zum trüben Reich gestaltenmischender Möglichkeit" (5: 333).

11. "Sag, ist es Pandora? Du sabst sie einmal, / Den Vätern verderblich, den Söhnen zur Qual" (5: 347).

12. "Entwandelt friedlich! Friede findend gebet ihr nicht" (5: 341).

13. "Abwesenheit des Vaters ehrt ein guter Sohn" (5: 346).

## WORKS CITED

Adorno, Theodor W. "Zum Klassizismus von Goethes 'Iphigenie.'" *Noten zur Literatur*. Ed. Rolf Tiedemann. Frankfurt: Suhrkamp, 1981. 495–514

Borchmeyer, Dieter. "Goethes 'Pandora' und der Preis des Fortschritts." *Etudes germaniques* 1 (1983): 17–31.

Böschenstein, Bernhard. "Antike und moderne Tragödie um 1800 in dreifacher Kontroverse: Goethes 'Natürliche Tochter', Kleists 'Penthesilea' und Hölderlins 'Antigone.'" *Kontroversen, alte und neue: Akten des VII. Germanistenkongresses Göttingen, 1985*. Vol. 8. Tübingen: Niemeyer, 1986. 204–15.

Brandmeyer, Rudolf. *Heroik und Gegenwart: Goethes klassische Dramen*. Frankfurt: Lang, 1987.

Brandt, Helmut. "Der widersprüchliche Held: Goethes 'Faust' im Lichte der Gretchentragödie." *Ansichten der deutschen Klassik*. Ed. Helmut Brandt and Manfred Beyer. Berlin: Aufbau, 1981. 119–47.

Goethe, Johann Wolfgang. *Werke*. ["Hamburger Ausgabe."] Ed. Erich Trunz et al. 14 vols. Rev. ed. Munich: Beck 1981.

Hegel, Georg Friedrich Wilhelm. *Phänomenologie des Geistes*. Frankfurt/M.: Suhrkamp, 1986.

Jauß, Hans Robert. "Racines and Goethes 'Iphigenie.'" *Rezeptionsasthetik*. Ed. Rainer Warning. München: Fink, 1975. 352–98.

Pütz, Peter. *Die Zeit in Drama: Zur Technik der dramatischen Spannung*. Göttingen: Vandenhoeck & Ruprecht, 1970.

Rasch, Wolfdietrich. *Goethe's "Iphigenie auf Tauris" als Drama der Autonomie*. München: Beck, 1979.

Reed, Terence James. "Iphigenies Unmündigkeit." *Germanistik: Forschungsstand und Perspektiven: Vorträge des deutschen Germanistenverbands 1984*. Ed. Georg Stötzel. Vol. 2. Berlin: de Gruyter, 1985. 505–24.

Vaget, Hans Rudolf. "Die natürliche Tochter." *Goethes Dramen: Neue Interpretationen*. Ed. Walter Hinderer. Stuttgart: Reclam, 1980.

Wagner, Irmgard. "Vom Mythos zum Fetisch: Die Frau als Erlöserin in Goethes klassischen Dramen." *Weiblichkeit in geschichtlicher Perspektive*. Ed. Ursula A. J. Becher and Jörn Rüsen. Frankfurt: Suhrkamp, 1988. 234–58.

HARALD WEINRICH

# *Faust's Forgetting*

The learned professor and doctor of philosophy Heinrich Faust, Goethe's Faust, has professional and existential problems. At first glance, the conditions of his scholarly work seem reasonable. He has a study (*Studierzimmer*) with a substantial library (*Bücherhauf*), as well as a laboratory (*Laboratorium*) equipped in generous, if somewhat outmoded, fashion (*mit Instrumenten vollgepfropft*). The staffing can also be considered satisfactory, even by today's standards. Faust has a research assistant, the famulus Wagner, who will succeed him. He is also surrounded by students (*meine Schüller*), one of whom—a rather hapless fellow—appears later in the *Schülerszene*. Faust himself, who must be about sixty—the same age as Goethe when he published part I—has many talents suitable for extraordinary scholarship: he is intelligent (*klug, gescheit*), diligent (*mit saurem Schweiß*), even a workaholic (*so manche Mitternacht*), interdisciplinary (*habe nun, ach! Philosophie*), experienced (*schon an die zehen Jahr'*), idealistic (*die Menschen zu bessern und zu bekehren*), and unselfish (*weder Gut noch Geld*). He is a celebrity at the height of his career (*großer Mann*).

And yet Professor Faust is profoundly dissatisfied with himself and his mental efforts. He characterizes his knowledge as "learned obfuscation" (*Wissensqualm* [396]), his attempts at understanding as word-shuffling (*und*

From *Modern Language Quarterly* 55, no. 3. © 1994 by University of Washington.

*tu' nicht mehr in Worten kramen* [385]), and his laboratory as an "accursed, musty hole of stone" (*verfluchtes dumpfes Mauerloch* [399]).[1]

> Nature's doors are closed against me.
> The thread of thought is torn asunder,
> and I am surfeited with knowledge still.
>
> [Vor mir verschließt sich die Natur.
> Des Denkens Faden ist zerrissen,
> Mir ekelt lange vor allem Wissen.] (1747–9)

Like many scholars he is suffering from a serious creativity crisis; in Faust's case it extends into the deepest levels of his existence and threatens to drive him to suicide.

The Easter bells and resurrection chorus save him. More precisely, since he has no faith in the Easter message, it is the memories they arouse of his innocent childhood and youth:

> And yet these sounds, familiar since my youth,
> summon me now again to life.
> ....................................................
> the memory of childlike feelings now
> keeps me from taking the last, solemn step.
>
> [Und doch, an diesen Klang von jugend auf gewöhnt,
> Ruft er auch jetzt zurück mich in das Leben.
> ....................................................
> Erinnrung hält mich nun mit kindlichem Gefühle
> Vom letzten, ernsten Schritt zurück.] (769–70, 781–2)

Of all the intellectual talents available to this great scholar, apparently only memory still offers some connection to life.

So life goes on. Yet I have not mentioned that during his scholarly career Professor Faust not only has pursued his research conscientiously but, by his own confession, also has employed problematic scholarly methods: "That is why I've turned to magic" (*Drum hab' ich mich der Magie ergeben* [377]). But even this desperate attempt fails, and the Earth Spirit brusquely rejects Faust. He collapses (*stürzt zusammen*). After this painful experience with magic will he keep his distance from similar "alternative" methodologies?

Enter Mephistopheles. He and Faust agree on the famous bet. It is scaled with blood, which means, says Mephisto, "Consider well your words, we'll not forget them" (*Bedenk es wohl, wir werden's nicht vergessen* [1707]). Evidently the devil has a good memory. What does Faust gain? An enormous, undreamed field of research opens before him, otherwise known as life; with the devil's help, he can now explore it up and down, in and out, and experience it in ceaseless striving (*immer strebend*). The bet guarantees that this striving will never end. And what does Mephistopheles hope for? The devil always wants only one thing, the soul. He calculates that this goal is attainable if he, who never forgets anything, drags Faust through a tumult of events from one forgetting to the next, until Faust at last—perhaps— forgets himself. At stake is memory.

Auerbach's Cellar: for a professor the worse for scholarly wear an ideal place for forgetting, thinks Mephistopheles. Perhaps he has read Vives: *vinum memoriae mors*. But here he has underestimated Faust, who remains sulky and monosyllabic: "I wish we could go on our way" (*Ich hätte Lust, nun abzufahren* [2296]). This first experience of life is never mentioned again.

Now Mephistopheles changes the strategy and cooks up a different distraction for his victim. The setting is the witch's kitchen: the sixty year old is rejuvenated by some thirty years, a generation, as various details suggest. A change in status accompanies the rejuvenation: the scholar becomes a man of the world, a nobleman (*Junker*). Now Faust's forgetting leaps forward: along with the canceled years he forgets his previous circumstances. Even when the drama jumps back to the high-vaulted Gothic room (*hochgewölbtes gotisches Zimmer*) and the laboratory after some ten years, as one can calculate from the text, there is no recollecting: Faust sleeps through this scene and we learn nothing of his memory. When he awakes he is thinking about Helena, whose image appeared to him in a dream. His environment, however, has an excellent memory for everything that has happened. Thus Wagner, who has succeeded Faust and who now continues the latter's research program, has piously changed nothing in Faust's study; it has been preserved as a monument. Even the erstwhile student, now a baccalaureate and more intolerable than ever, still remembers exactly all the circumstances of his previous advising session with the famous Professor Faust (as he still thinks; it was in fact Mephistopheles). So everyone remembers, as does Mephistopheles, since he is directing the show and would otherwise not have had to choose this spot. He is also driven to reassure himself about the quality of his memory:

Nothing, no matter where I look,
has changed or suffered harm; perhaps
the colored window-panes are more opaque,
the cobwebs certainly have multiplied;
the ink has thickened and the paper yellowed,
but everything is where it was before;
even the pen's still lying here
with which Faust signed his contract with the devil.
In fact, down here inside the quill there's stuck
a drop of blood like that I wheedled out of him.

[Blick' ich hinauf, hierher, hinüber,
Allunverändert ist es, unversehrt;
Die bunten Scheiben sind, so dünkt mich, trüber,
Die Spinneweben haben sich vermehrt;
Die Tinte starrt, vergilbt ist das Papier;
Doch alles ist am Platz geblieben;
Sogar die Feder liegt noch hier,
Mit welcher Faust dem Teufel sich verschrieben.
Ja! tiefer in dem Rohre stockt
Ein Tröpflein Blut, wie ich's ihm abgelockt.] (6570–9),

Thus is the criminal drawn back to the scene of his misdeeds. Faust, by contrast, notices nothing. Along with his other senses sleep also erases here his memory.

Whether the Gretchen Tragedy constitutes the center of Faust's tragedy I will leave an open question; but it undoubtedly occupies the center of Faust's drama of memory. Young Margarete has a good natural memory embedded in the collective memory of her environment. What then does it mean when her lover swears "eternal faith" to her, as is the custom among lovers? Faust avers, "I always will be near her, even far away, / and never can forget or bear to lose her" (Ich bin ihr nah, und wär' ich noch so fern, Ich kann sie nie vergessen, nie verlieren. [3332–31]).

Like every other girl of her class Margarete knows that however much in love she may be, it can rapidly end in forgetting: "Yes, out of sight and out of mind!" (*Ja, aus den Augen, aus dem Sinn!* [3096]). Proverbs often express the social knowledge stored in the collective memory. Of course, Margarete did not heed the wisdom. She "forgot herself," though only once, as the saints interceding for her at the end say in her favor (criticized by Adorno as "petty condescension"):[2]

Grant unto this good soul also—
one who lost her head but once,
unaware that she did wrong—
as is fitting, your forgiveness!

[Gönn auch dieser guten Seele,
Die sich einmal nur vergessen,
Die nicht ante, daß sie fehle,
Dein Verzeihen angemessen!] (12065–8)

Faust has forgotten Margarete rapidly. "Two nights from now" (*übermorgen* [3662]) is already Walpurgis Night. Departure, distractions, new amusements: these are the tried and true *remedia amoris*, conducive to forgetting. And Mephistopheles, who helps mightily in forgetting, is always ready to take his master in tow: "I'll drag him through a life of riot, / through meaningless inanities" (Den schlepp' ich durch das wilde Leben, Durch flache Unbedeutenheit [1860–1]). Here, the professor, distracted by Mephistopheles with devilish skill, has his witches' sabbatical: an orgy of forgetting. He is ravished (*hingerissen* [4021]). But there, suddenly, unexpected for both travelers through the Harz, a memory surfaces before Faust's eyes:

Mephisto, do you see
off there, alone, dead-pale, a lovely girl?
Now she is slowly moving away,
dragging her feet as if they were in fetters.
I have to say I can't help thinking
that she looks like my own dear Gretchen.

[Mephisto, siehst du dort
Ein blasses, schönes Kind allein und ferne stehen?
Sie schiebt sich langsam nur vom Ort,
Sie scheint mit geschloßnen Füßen zu gehen.
Ich muß bekennen, daß mir deucht,
Daß sie dem guten Gretchen gleicht.] (4183–8)

The stiffly circuitous last two lines show how hard it is for the professor caught up in the dancing to remember even vaguely his recent affair with so modestly circumstanced a girl. This memory is also uncomfortable for his companion, since it doesn't suit the plans. And so Mephistopheles tries to interpret the recollection away:

Leave that alone—it only can do harm!
It is a magic image, a phantom without life.
It's dangerous to meet up with;
its stare congeals a person's blood
and almost turns him into stone—
you've surely heard about Medusa!

[Laß das nur stehn! dabei wird's niemand wohl.
Es ist ein Zauberbild, ist leblos, ein Idol.
Ihm zu begegnen, ist nicht gut;
Vorn starren Blick erstarrt des Menschen Blut,
Und er wird fast in Stein verkehrt,
Von der Meduse hast duja gehört.] (4189–94)

But the vision won't go away; in anticipation of the death sentence, it takes growing possession of Faust's consciousness. (Here, a temporal leap of nine or ten months is built into the scene.)

What ecstasy, and yet what pain!
I cannot bear to let this vision go.
How strange that on that lovely neck
there is as ornament a single scarlet thread
no thicker than a knife!

[Welch eine Wonne! welch ein Leiden!
Ich kann von diesem Blick nicht scheiden.
Wie sonderbar muß diesen schönen Hals
Ein einzig rotes Schnürchen schmücken,
Nicht breiter als ein Messerrücken!] (4201–5)

On the Blocksberg Faust is not yet the virtuoso of forgetting that Mephistopheles wants to make of him. And so he reproaches Mephisto (in prose no less!): "And all this while you lull me with inane diversions" (*Und mich wiegst du indes in abgeschmackten Zerstreuungen* [An Expanse of Open Country]). Mephistopheles replies: "She is not the first" (*Sie ist die erste nicht*). In his memory, cases of this kind pile up.

In "Night, Open Field," Faust, together with Mephistopheles, storming ahead on black horses (*auf schwarzen Pferden daherbrausend*), hurries to Margarete's aid. The Rabenstein, along which they ride, portends the place of execution: an oppressive forward-memory. It too is wiped away by

Mephistopheles: "Vorbei! Vorbei!" That is his motto of forgetting. The dungeon scene follows. Once again, the dialogue between Faust and Margarete revolves around remembering and forgetting. Faust implores her: "Let what is past, be past, / or you will be the death of me" (Laß das Vergangne vergangen sein, Du bringst mich um [4518–9]). Even in this situation Faust stakes all on forgetting. So, there is no escape from the dungeon, though the doors stand open. Faust's forgetting is Margarete's tragedy.

Part 2 begins in a charming landscape (*anmutige Gegend*). Faust, exhausted, seeks sleep. Fairies help him to obtain it. Ariel sings, accompanied by aeolian harps:

> You who are circling in the air above this head,
> now demonstrate your elfin worth—
> compose the angry strife within his heart,
> remove the burning barbs of his remorse,
> and purge him of all sense of horror!
> The watches of the night are four;
> start now to make each one agreeable.
> First rest his head on cushioning coolness,
> then bathe him in the dew of Lethe's waters;
> his body will recover quickly from its numbness
> if sleep gives him the strength to face the coming day;
> perform your noblest elfin duty
> and grant him restoration to its sacred light!
>
> [Die ihr dies Haupt umschwebt im luft'gen Kreise,
> Erzeigt euch hier nach edler Elfen Weise,
> Besänftiget des Herzens grimmen Strauß,
> Entfernt des Vorwurfs glühend bittre Pfeile,
> Sein Innres reinigt von erlebtem Graus.
> *Vier* sind die Pausen nächtiger Weile,
> Nun ohne Säumen füllt sie freundlich aus.
> Erst senkt sein Haupt aufs kühle Polster nieder,
> Dann badet ihn im Tau aus Lethes Flut;
> Gelenk sind bald die krampferstarrten Glieder,
> Wenn er gestärkt dem Tag entgegenruht;
> Vollbringt der Elfen schönste Pflicht,
> Gebt ihn zurück dem heiligen Licht.] (4621–33)

Lethe, the river of forgetting, flows through this charming landscape, and the fairies, spurred by Ariel, will sprinkle Faust with its waters.[3] At the same time, this forgetting-cure is a "lethargic" healing sleep. Notably, Mephistopheles no longer needs to bestir himself to promote the forgetting. He has found mild, gentle (or should I say, inoffensive, unsuspecting?) helpers, who perform this work on Faust unaided. Forgetting no longer seems so strenuous; a pleasant feeling of alleviation spreads:

> Hours are obliterated,
> pain and joy have vanished now;
> be assured, you will recover—
> take hope from this day's first gleaming!

> [Schon verloschen sind die Stunden,
> Hingeschwunden Schmerz und Glück;
> Fühl es vor! Du wirst gesunden;
> Traue neuem Tagesblick.] (4650–3)

Here, all depends on the word *neu*, because forgetting opens the way for the new. The spirit chorus had already promised the professor this in his study: "start a new life" (*Neuen Lebenslauf / Beginne* [1622–31]) Novelty, however, is above all Mephisto's temptation:

> Will it be long before you've had enough of this?
> How can this life continue to amuse you?
> No doubt it's good to try it once;
> but then go on again to something else!

> [Habt Ihr nun bald das Leben gnug geführt?
> Wie kann's Euch in die Länge freuen?
> Es ist wohl gut, daß man's einmal probiert;
> Dann aber wieder zu was Neuen!] (3251–4)

And on Walpurgis Night he urges the Huckstress-Witch (*Trödelhexe*), "You should go in for novelties, / that's all that customers now want" (*Verleg' Sie sich auf Neuigkeiten! Nur Neuigkeiten ziehn uns an* [4112–3]). Even at the end of his life Faust lets himself be dazzled by the fascination for the new in his land reclamation. He remains a scientist, who swears by innovations, and the devil well knows what profit he may elicit from that.

Goethe clearly envisioned the second part of *Faust* as being distinct from the first (*von dem ersten durchaus verschieden*) and self-contained (*von jenem sich völlig absondert*) (letter to Stapfer, 4 April 1827).[4] And so it is; not only does a structural boundary divide the two parts but also sharp divisions separate the episodes within each part. Rapid and disorienting changes of place are especially evident in part 2: from the imperial palace to the Mothers, back to Faust's study, then the classical Walpurgis Night in Thessaly, followed by Peloponnesus, and returning to the north with mountain and coastal landscapes. In the third act and elsewhere the stage directions could read: "The setting changes utterly" (*Der Schauplatz verwandelt sich durchaus*). So likewise Mephistopheles had already promised in part 1:

> We'll simply lay my cloak out flat;
> it will carry us through the air.
> But just be sure, since there's a certain risk,
> that you don't carry too much luggage.

> [Wir breiten nur den Mantel aus,
> Der soll uns durch die Lüfte tragen.
> Du nimmst bei diesem kühnen Schritt
> Nur keinen großen Bündel mit.] (2065–8)

Does "Bündel" mean only the material luggage or perhaps also the burden of memory, which at such a traveling tempo can only be a hindrance? Whichever, the numerous masks and disguises of Faust (as Plutus, as a knight) and Mephisto (as avarice, as Phorcyas, as foreman) also suit this whirl (*Taumel* [1766]) and add the irritation of metamorphosis (*wechselnden Gestalten* [11588]) to the accelerated travel. The law of tempo governs all:

> I've never tarried anywhere;
> I snatched from fortune what I wanted,
> what did not please me I let go,
> and disregarded what eluded me.

> [Ich bin nur durch die Welt gerannt;
> Ein jed' Gelüst ergriff ich bei den Haaren,
> Was nicht genügte, ließ ich fahren,
> Was mir entwischte, ließ ich ziehn.] (11433–6)

Memory constantly faces quick extinction in connection with abrupt changes: "Let what is past, be past forever!" (*Vergangenheit sei hinter uns getan!* [9563]). One expects such a thing from Mephistopheles, but it is Faust himself who says, as he paints yet another new existence in imagination, "Our happiness be Arcadian and free!" (*Arkadisch frei sei unser Glück!* [9573]).

Is Mme de Staël then correct when she calls Faust an inconstant character (*un caractère inconstant*)?[5] (For the classically schooled Frenchwoman that is a marked rebuke, since consistency of character is a fundamental dramatic quality in Aristotelian poetics.) Where in Faust, as the title of a well-known Goethe poem has it, is the permanence in change? What is the goal of this course? With what joy, what profit will Faust take the seminar for free (*den Cursum durchschmarutzen* [2054])? It is often said and can be read plainly in many lines that Faust's striving is itself the goal. Posited as an absolute, testing itself on ever new objects, striving by definition cannot deliver peace and rest; a "tarry awhile" (*Verweile doch*) is to be expected neither from the young gallant nor from the sturdy man (*wackrer Mann*) of advanced years, neither from gloomy nor gay mood, neither from the northern nor the southern hemisphere. Or is it perhaps? But then the bet is lost. Or perhaps not?

The judgment is passed in the last scenes. Is Faust, now a hundred years old by authority of the eighty-year-old Goethe, still the hero of the deed who, grasping at new shores, storms ever onward at the price of forgetting and now, finally, wants to crown his diffuse exploits with a last great act of service to humanity? When Faust actually utters his "tarry awhile" in this scene, he is a poor, old, and blind man, whose striving, as he had occasionally feared at some moments, now definitively misses its aim (*ins Leere* [6251]). Have better conditions been established for memory? That can't be said. Faust remains to the end the man he has made himself with Mephisto's help. He is the fugitive from memory. Possibly, as Adorno ingeniously conjectured, having arrived at the edge of the grave, he has even repressed the bet out of his memory "along with all the crimes that Faust in his entanglement perpetrated or permitted" (119). Adorno adds a legal inference that shuttles between the juridical concepts of limitation (*Verjährung*) and culpability (*Schuldfähigkeit*) and amounts to exoneration. "Perhaps the epic form of the work, which calls itself a tragedy, is that of form in the process of falling under the statute of limitations. Perhaps Faust is saved because he is no longer the same person who signed the pact" (119). In the same connection: "The power of life, as a power of continued life, is equated with forgetting. It is only in being forgotten and thereby transformed that anything survives at all.... Hope is not memory held fast but the return of what has been forgotten."[6]

Adorno surely also had Nietzsche in mind, for in the second *Untimely Meditation*, "On the Use and Abuse of History," Nietzsche singled out forgetting as a useful and hygienic faculty because it frees us from the burden of history. Can this new, modern forgetting in Nietzsche be dated back to Faust? That is worth careful consideration.

First, it is a truism of literary criticism that the author should not invariably be equated with the creation, especially not—echoing a famous phrase of Goethe's—to a "fragment" of autobiographical confession. Without losing sight of Faust, I must raise the question of Goethe's own position on memory, in his life and in his work. Apparently contradicting my own reflections, Helmut Schanze has made an impressive attempt to read *Faust* not as a drama of forgetting but as a work of memory, with explicit reference to Frances A. Yates's classic study, *The Art of Memory* (1966). Schanze relies chiefly on the "Dedication" to *Faust*, but also connects it with several other passages in which the themes of this "paratext" (as Genette would say) reappear in the text itself. In particular, he regards the "schwankende Gestalten" as mnemonic pictures (*phantasmata, imagines*) in the manner of the old art of memory, or mnemotechnics; the poet's task is to bring these shadow images into the light and to fix them in poetic memory. He concludes that Goethe's "*Memoria* is the basis of his poetry."[7]

Nevertheless, I see no unbridgeable opposition to my position thus far, but rather a dialectic between Goethe, the poetic man of memory, and his dramatic creature Faust, the unhappy but finally saved hero of forgetting. (And behind, naturally, stands Mephistopheles, his powerful assistant in forgetting, who is ultimately cheated of his booty.) But this dialectic—if I can assume one without encroaching on Hegel—was surely typical of Goethe the man, as we know from many documents, including his often-cited maxim, "Let memory fade, so long as judgment is present when needed" (*Das Gedächtnis mag immer schwinden, wenn das Urteil im Augenblick nicht fehlt*).[8] Clearly, the dismissal of long memory in favor of the short moment—which links Goethe to the large chorus of modern, enlightened critics of memory— is not ill-suited to Faust's esteem for the unique poetic moment, with its existential potency. In a letter of 1830 to his friend Zeller we read a statement that sounds almost like Nietzsche, in a striking formula remarkable for a man so advanced in age: "That with each breath an ethereal Lethean stream penetrates our entire life, so that we remember our joys but moderately, our woes hardly at all. I have always had the sense to value, exploit, and enhance this great gift of the gods" (*Daß mit jedem Atemzug ein ätherischer Lethestrom unser ganzes Leben durchdringt, so daß wir uns der Freuden nur mäßig, der Leiden kaum erinnern. Diese hohe Gottesgabe habe ich von jeher zu schätzen, zu nützen und zu steigern gewußt* [15 February]). This etherealization of Lethe fits well with some equally sublimated passages in *Faust*: "Then bathe him in the dew [!] of Lethe's waters" (*Dann badet ihn im Tau aus Lethes Flut* [4629]). Finally, Goethe has drawn the notice of the friends of historical memory for according historiography a modest epistemological value: "All history is doubtful and uncertain" (*Alle Geschichte ist mißlich und schwankend*). "World" history, unlike "world" literature, seemed to him "the silliest thing in the world" (*das Absurdeste, was es gibt*), so that contemporary historians have called him a historical skeptic or even a "structuralist."[9] Is that the way to talk about a great man of memory?

Wavering between pious remembrance and restorative forgetting, Goethe may be confronted with an argument that is entirely based on memory and history and hence perhaps helpful in clarifying the foundations of the modern culture of forgetting. First, Goethe and Faust are both scholars, or more precisely natural scientists, though neither one is merely that. Goethe's professional interest in science covers extensive studies of botany, zoology, and anthropology, along with his optics, which was partly written at the same time as *Faust*. The same is true—with different local and temporal coloring—for Faust; it is not accidental that he is repeatedly invoked in this essay with his academic titles.[10] The words of the introductory monologue, however, may perhaps leave us in doubt whether the doctor and professor Faust (to put it somehow anachronistically) is more a natural scientist or a humanist, since in one room he busies himself with both folios and vials. But the Earth Spirit, who appears forthwith, makes no mistake about Faust's home department. He understands that Faust, as a scientist, endangers his realm.

Since Galileo, Descartes, and Bacon the natural sciences character-istically grant memory only a limited role in acquiring knowledge and disseminating truth.[11] For them the Aristotelians and scholastics impede scientific progress by dallying far too long with "words," rather than proceeding as quickly as possible to "things."[12] Even Doctor Faust takes up the Bible only, after some failed attempts, to replace "word" with "deed," as he translates the prologue to the Gospel of John. As a result, in a *déformation professionnelle*, his stance leads him away from cultural memory, even if it isn't directly opposed. For professional reasons forgetting "suits him." This weakness—if it is such—does not escape the devil, who for his part understands forgetting as well as remembering. Exploiting Faust's weakness without restraint, he turns the scientist—who by profession must always strive and consequently must easily forget—into a "striver" (in the nonpejorative sense) and, if such an eighteenth-century coinage may be allowed, into a "forgetter"—a curriculum with relevance for world history, though highly problematic in its inevitable corollaries.

Here is the "Faustian" side of modern science: in its boundless striving for innovations, which belongs to its innermost ethos, it accepts—almost without reservation—the other side of this striving, forgetting, and thus legitimates a culture to which we modern academics have delivered ourselves, with or without Mephistopheles, for weal or woe. To the great citizen of Weimar—to Goethe the poet and scientist—we owe this remarkable literary paradigm of the Western culture of forgetting, from which, at the end of the drama, we can perhaps draw the consolation that the irresistible striving for novelty and the quickest forgetting of the old do not necessarily exclude a salvation *in extremis*.

## NOTES

Translated from the German by John Crosetto, Jane K. Brown, and Marshall Brown.

1. German quotations are from *Goethe's Faust*, ed. Erich Trunz (Hamburg: Wegner, 1962). English translations are from Johann Wolfgang von Goethe, *Faust 1 & 2*, vol. 2 of *Goethe's Collected Works*, ed. and trans. Stuart Atkins (Boston: Suhrkamp/Insel, 1984).

2. Theodor W. Adorno, "On the Final Scene of *Faust*," in *Notes on Literature*, trans. Sherry Weber Nicholsen, vol. I (New York: Columbia University Press, 1991), 116.

3. Here, as the terza rima also indicates, the influence of Dante is clearly evident. In Dante the stream of Lethe flows through the Earthly Paradise (*Purgatorio* 29). See Peter Michelsen, "Fausts Schlaf und Erwachen: Zur Eingangsszene von 'Faust II' ('Anmutige Gegend')," *Jahrbuch des Freien Deutschen Hochstifts* (1983): 21–61, esp. 25, 50.

4. See Victor Lange, *Bilder—Ideen—Begriffe: Goethe Studien* (Würzburg: Königshausen und Neumann, 1991), 172–3; and Jane K. Brown, *Faust: Theater of the World* (New York: Twayne, 1992), 68.

5. Germaine de Staël, *De l'Allemagne*, ed. Simone Balayé (1813; rpt. Paris: Garnier-Flammarion, 1968), 1:348 (*Germany*, ed. O. W. Wight [1814; rpt. Boston: Houghton, Mifflin and Company, 1887], 1:369). Mme de Staël refers here to Aristotle's *Poetics*, 1454a.

6. Adorno, 120; see also the symposium "Der Schluß von Goethes 'Faust': Die Szene 'Bergschluchten,'" in *Sprachkunst: Beiträge zur Literaturwissenschaft* 21.1 (1990).

7. Helmut Schanze, "Szenen, Schema, Schwammfamilie: Goethes Arbeitsweise und die Frage der Struktureinheit von 'Faust I und II,'" *Euphorion* 78 (1984): 383–400. The quote is found on p. 395

8. *Maximen und Reflexionen*, no. 111.

9. As to the remarks on history concerning Chancellor Willer see Lange, 116–7. On Goethe as "structuralist" see Reinhart Koselleck, "Goethes unzeitgemäße Geschichte" (MS, 1993), 21

10. "Without a doubt, the problem of the university occupied Goethe for his entire life. Faust is the passion of a German for whom the university became too confined" [Das Universitätsproblem hat Goethe, man darf wohl sagen: zeitlebens beschäftigt. Der 'Faust' ist die Passion eines deutschen Menschen, dem die Universität zu eng wurde] (Ernst Robert Curtius, *Deutscher Geist in Gefahr*, 2d ed. [Stuttgart: Deutsche Verlags-Anstalt, 1932], 58).

11. Historically, the Royal Society of London for the Improvement of Natural Knowledge (founded 1662) considers remembering primarily in the form of "impertinent quotations." See Richard F. Jones, "Science and English Prose Style in the Third Quarter of the Seventeenth Century," *PMLA* 45 (1930): 977–1009, esp. 988; and Uwe Pörksèn, *Deutsche Naturwissenschaftssprachen* (Tübingen: Narr, 1986).

12. For a more detailed account see Harald Weinrich, "La Mémoire linguistique de l'Europe," *Francofonia: Studi e ricerche sulle letterature di lingua francese* 20 (1991): 3–20.

DAVID CONSTANTINE

# *Rights and Wrongs in Goethe's*
# Die Wahlverwandtschaften

$G$oethe's *Die Wahlverwandtschaften*, a novel, began life as a Novelle, and
was to have been inserted into Wilhelm *Meisters Wanderjahre*. Goethe first
mentioned it in April 1808, declared it finished on 30 July (already speaking
of it as a novel suitable for publication in two small volumes), but took it up
again the following spring and began the expansion into the work we have
now. He put himself under pressure by allowing printing to begin before the
last chapters were written; and brought the whole thing out in October 1809.
For years he had been in the habit of dictating his works (and not just his
literary works—his letters and diaries too), and *Die Wahlverwandtschaften* was
composed aloud and taken down by Goethe's secretary Riemer. Indeed, on a
coach journey between Jena and Weimar in May 1808, before dictation
began, Goethe recounted a large part of the (then) Novelle to his friend
Heinrich Meyer, and did so almost as though it were already complete in his
mind. The novel is told by a narrating voice and contains a Novelle told as
an evening's entertainment, but it does not read in the least like the spoken
word. The discrepancy is an intriguing one, one of many.

Goethe was sixty when he published *Die Wahlverwandtschaften*. He had
been in Weimar, employed at the Court, since 1775. Behind him already
were enormous literary achievements, as well as serious work in most
branches of the contemporary sciences. He was famous in Europe. Napoleon

From *German Life and Letters* XLVII, no. 4. © 1994 by Basil Blackwell Ltd.

received him in 1808, and decorated him with the Cross of the Legion of Honour the following year. In the pay of the Duke of Weimar, ennobled by him in 1788, given the title Excellency in 1804, he became the alternative eminence of the place, and at his house in the centre of the little town he received and entertained on a large scale. Weimar would have been very little without Goethe and the many talented men and women drawn there by him; he was not only part of the Establishment, in large measure he constituted it; and was for all that a difficult and scandalous person to have around. Wieland called him 'unser *beliebter*, aber doch noch mehr *gefürchteter National-* Schriftsteller'.[1]

In 1786, having served ten years at the Court and ten years also in a relationship with the severe and married Charlotte von Stein, Goethe broke away and, travelling incognito and telling nobody at home until he could present them with a *fait accompli*, he went to Italy—to Rome, Naples and Sicily—for nearly two years. That interlude was decisive. It confirmed or re-confirmed him in his vocation as a poet, and he resolved to live thenceforth in such a way as to serve that vocation best, which caused many contemporaries to think him inconsiderate and selfish. Italy itself put him at odds with Weimar society when he came home; he had shifted, they had not. Then he affronted them more emphatically by taking a girl from the local artificial-flower factory, Christiane Vulpius, to live with him in his 'Gartenhaus', as his mistress. For her, but with Rome in mind, he composed the *Römische Elegien*, circulated them first among friends, and published them in 1795 as the scandalous manifesto of a classicism whose central tenets were enjoyment, happiness, the life of the senses.

Christiane, as Goethe's mistress and because of her class, was not presentable. She withdrew when guests came. Schiller in his scores of letters to Goethe mentions her only thrice: once as Mlle Vulpius, once as 'jemand aus Ihrem Hause' and once, on the occasion of her fifth confinement, as 'die Kleine'. Goethe, in his letters to Schiller, mentions her just as evasively and scarcely more often.[2] But in his published correspondence with her the tone on both sides is warmly and ordinarily human—domestic, tender, chatty, amusing. She lived with him until her death in 1816, bore him five children, only one of whom survived. In 1806, when French troops passing through Weimar after their victory at Jena disrupted Goethe's household and threatened his life, Christiane behaved with great bravery and presence of mind, and in acknowledgement of that and to give her more protection in dangerous times, Goethe married her, on 19 October, their son August being present as a witness. Goethe did not think this official sanction itself important—'Sie ist immer meine Frau gewesen', he used to say[3]—but after it at least Christiane could be taken out and introduced. No more a lady married than unmarried, however, she was gossiped about hatefully by the real ladies.

It is worth mentioning Christiane Vulpius in this context since *Die Wahlverwandtschaften*, obviously, has to do with marriage. Goethe lived with her for eighteen years before they married, and 'though his relationship with her was not only the longest-lasting but also the fullest in his life, still he never felt obliged to forsake all others on her account, and between 1788 and 1816 was in love elsewhere, more or less passionately, more or less intimately, half a dozen times at least. Goethe loved women, the love of women is the chief inspiration of his poetry. Really, he was almost always in love. In 1824, then seventy-four and in love with an eighteen-year-old, he wrote a poem for the jubilee re-issue of *Werther* lamenting the condition he was in as being no better than it had been when he wrote that novel of unhappy passion half a century before. Though bound and then also married to Christiane he was frequently away from home—three months in 1797, four in 1808, five in 1815, six in 1810, seven in 1790, for example,[4] and in her letters to him, and more so in the published gossip of contemporaries, there are allusions to his infidelities. Goethe himself edited their correspondence before his death, and none of the letters written by Christiane in the years 1804-09 survived. Perhaps they contained too many recriminations. And there is other contemporary testimony that in that period, at the end of which *Die Wahlverwandtschaften* was written, Goethe's life with Christiane was more than usually troubled. Scarcely a year after marrying her, Goethe, withdrawing as he often did to Jena, met Minna Herzlieb there and soon began to feel for her 'mehr wie billig', as he put it.[5] She was only eighteen. Goethe wrote a sequence of sonnets for her; and it has very often been said that she moved him to write *Die Wahlverwandtschaften* much as Charlotte Buff had moved him to write *Werther*, and that she appears in it as Ottilie. But it has also been said that, if you are looking for the woman, the one most likely is Sylvie von Ziegesar whom Goethe was seeing frequently during his usual summer stay in Karlsbad in 1808. Goethe in Rome, whenever his incognito failed to protect him, was pestered by people wanting to know whether *Werther* were true or not, true in the sense of having really happened. He found this very tiresome. There was similar speculation, and confident assertion, as soon as *Die Wahlverwandtschaften* came out. Wilhelm Grimm: wrote to Arnim on 3 January 1810:

> Wer die Personen in den *Wahlverwandtschaften*, hat man längst
> heraus, der Architect ist natürlich der Engelhard, in welchen die

Vulpius verliebt gewesen, die Luciane ist nicht die Jagemann sondern ein Fräulein Reizenstein, welche in Weimar ist und alle Herzen erobem soll. (Härtl, 110 and cf. 34, 35, 72, 80, 171)

And Goethe's own later remarks on the novel seemed to confirm the supposition that his own passionate life had gone into the writing of it. He said: 'Niemand verkennt an diesem Roman eine tief leidenschaftliche Wunde, die im Heilen sich zu schließen scheut, ein Herz, das zu genesen fürchtet' (Härtl, 285). In conversation with Eckermann, at the end of his life, he reiterated this emphasis: 'Es ist in den *Wahlverwandtschaften* überhaupt keine Zeile, die ich nicht selber erlebt hätte' (Härtl, 333). He was in no way distinguishing the novel by saying that. He had said the same about *Wilhelm Meister*, the felt truth of *Werther* and of his lyric poetry was manifest to everyone, indeed all his works were, as he said himself, 'Bruchstücke einer großen Konfession'. Still, the nearness and the livingness of the inspiration of *Die Wahlverwandtschaften* needs to be borne in mind, the more so as its tone is often remote and cold, and its subject is the denial of life and a sort of freezing to death. *Die Wahlverwandtschaften* is a lived book, then, in its different mode and tone as lived as *Werther*. But a further remark of Goethe's should deter us from reading it as autobiography and from seeking to establish real-life models for its characters. Eckermann reports: 'Von seinen *Wahlverwandtschaften* sagte er, daß darin kein Strich enthalten, der nicht erlebt, aber kein Strich so, *wie* er erlebt worden' (Härtl, 340). He has given us a novel, not an autobiography; which is to say that his life-experience occurs in it always and only as the novel itself requires. The novelist is released from matter-of-fact, from what was biographically or autobiographically so, and produces the kind of truth which it is peculiarly his business to produce. Had he not had the real experiences he would not have been equipped to produce that truth; but the truth he produces is other and more than those experiences. He conducts a sort of experiment with the material of his real experience, to see what is in it, what outcome it *might* have. In *Werther* he pushed the experiment consequentially through to destruction; and doing so he believed he saved himself from his hero's end. A cooler, crueller experiment seems to be underway in *Die Wahlverwandtschaften*.

When *Die Wahlverwandtschaften* appeared it sold like hot cakes and was swiftly pirated. It was read, re-read, read again, and passionately discussed. Many people felt it to be a very immoral book. Mothers forbade it their daughters. Wieland's correspondent, Elisabeth Gräffin von Solms-Laubach, thought no woman under fifty should be allowed to read it (Härtl, 158).

Friederike Helene Unger, writing to August Wilhelm Schlegel, referred to it as Goethe's 'lezten Stuhlgang' which he ought not, she said, to have forced upon the public (Härtl, 154). The characters were condemned, Eduard especially, but also Ottilie for going behind Charlotte's back; and Goethe, their creator, was condemned for not being harder on them. A Berlin pastor was still trying to protect his flock from the book as late as 1831. He reviewed it in the *Evangelische Kirchen-Zeitung*, and began by recounting the plot, or as much of the plot as he could bring himself to recount. At the point where Eduard visits Charlotte in her bedroom the pastor wrote: 'Wir müssen hier [...], aus Achtung für unsere Leser, Scenen der Schlüpfrigkeit übergehen, die der Dichter mit großer Behaglichkeit ausmalt, und die wahrscheinlich schon manche Unschuld grausam gemordet haben'. And at the Captain's kiss, which Charlotte *almost* returns: 'Wir eilen auch von dieser Scene mit Ekel und Abscheu hinweg' (Härtl, 351). 'Ekel und Abscheu' were what many people felt, or in public and in letters to one another said they felt. Jacobi and his sisters simply could not get over how *Die Wahlverwandtschaften* disgusted them.

Other people thought it a very moral book. Bernhard Rudolf Abeken, in a review which Goethe liked so much he had it privately printed and distributed as counter-propaganda, praised Charlotte and Ottilie, and Goethe their creator, as proof of what reason, moderation and moral strength can do against the blind (immoral) forces of Nature. He called *Die Wahlverwandtschaften* 'ein Compendium der Moral' (Härtl, 210). And it was said in Goethe's favour that if his characters sinned, at least they were well punished for doing so.

Really, the division in opinion was according to whether readers thought Goethe upheld the institution of marriage or undermined it. Those who thought he did uphold it (a surprising number) pointed particularly to Mittler's oration in Chapter Nine: 'meisterhaft ist die Lobrede auf den Ehestand', 'was Mittler [...] über die Ehe sagt, ist eben so wahr, als schön' (Härtl, 130, 325). They supposed in a very straightforward fashion that Mittler and Goethe were of one mind (Härtl, 292). Karl August Böttiger, in his review of the novel, quoted Mittler on marriage entire, and commented:

> Wie herrlich! Wie tief eingehend! Und welch ein Wort zur rechten Zeit! Wahrlich, es war hohe Weisheit, die Ehe unter rohen Menschen für ein Sakrament zu erklären, denn sie wandelt ja eine thierische Handlung in eine moralische um, und ist der Kitt des Bürgervereins, daher dieser locker wird, wenn der Staat Ehescheidungen begünstigt, und, wie im *Preußischen Landrecht*,

die Ehe für einen bloßen bürgerlichen Contrakt erklärt. (Härtl,
181)

Others noticed that Mittler achieves nothing, only meddles, interferes, and
makes himself ridiculous, and thought that Goethe must be being ironic,
which is to say immoral, to put such correct views into the mouth of such a
man (Härtl, 349).

Whether Goethe was for or against the institution of marriage is not, in
itself, in discussing this novel, a question anyone need bother to try to decide.
*Die Wahlverwandtschaften* is no more a tract for or against marriage than it is
an autobiography; it is a novel and is moral in the way that all great literature
is moral: it quickens, through its art, an awareness of issues which we may
call moral, if by that we mean having to do with better and worse ways of
living. There is never any easy passage from a literary work, not even from a
novel in which moral issues, issues of human life, are depicted and rendered
palpable, into practical life itself; and opinions as to what the 'message' of *Die
Wahlverwandtschaften* is, what it teaches, have been and always will be wildly
divergent. The most honest among its first readers admitted that their
feelings were painfully mixed. Humboldt noted: 'Endlich ist eine Tendenz im
Ganzen, die zerreißt...' (Härtl, 88; cf. 89 and 287–8). Goethe was aware and
proud of the complexity of this work. 'Ich habe viel hineingelegt,' he said,
'manches hinein versteckt' (Härtl, 41), and at least in any attempt to
understand it and have it affect our lives as novels can and should,[6] we must
avoid being monolithic and reductive.

Just before the novel came out Goethe put an advertisement for it in the
*Morgenblatt für gebildete Stände*. Writing in the third person he surmises that
the author must have been led to his strange title by his continuing work in
the physical sciences where, he says, we often make use of comparisons
drawn from the world of human behaviour ('ethische Gleichnisse') so that
things which are essentially remote from us may be brought a little nearer;
and in the novel, he continues, in a case concerning morality ('ein sittlicher
Fall'), doubtless the author was seeking to trace an expression used as an
analogy in chemistry back to its origin in the life of the human spirit.
'Elective affinities' then, belonging properly in the world of chemistry but
deriving from a human world of choice and inclination, is returned to that
world as a note on, or as a means of understanding, the novel's human events.
The advertisement concludes with a general remark, the essence of which is
this: that there is after all only one Nature, and that even in our human zone
of it, the cheerful zone of reason and freedom of choice, still there are traces,
in the passions, of bleak and irresistible Necessity. That question, whether

we, or the characters in Goethe's novel, have any choice or not, is central, of course; and it disturbed the first readers perhaps even more profoundly than the question of marriage, which, so to speak, it preexists and underlies. Thus some thought *Die Wahlverwandtschaften* immoral because in it Goethe seemed to be siding with 'die Herren Materialisten' (Härtl, 84), and erasing, with his chemical analogy, all distinction between us and mechanical Nature. Charlotte, when the Captain and Eduard explain the technical term to her, insists, very characteristically, that we cannot properly speak of choice or election in the case of helplessly parting and combining chemical substances and that choice, the ability to choose a better course over a worse, is what uniquely characterises human beings. That discussion takes place before the arrival of Ottilie. Some fifteen months later, on the brink of the final catastrophe, both women believe they are being hounded by a fate which quite overrides their volition and their own codes of right and wrong. Charlotte says:

> Es sind gewisse Dinge, die sich das Schicksal hartnäckig vornimmt. Vergebens, daß Vernunft und Tugend, Pflicht und alles Heilige sich ihm in den Weg stellen: es soll etwas geschehen, was ihm recht ist, was uns nicht recht scheint; und so greift es zuletzt durch, wir mögen uns gebärden, wie wir wollen.[7]

Ottilie writes (by then she has ceased speaking):

> Ich bin aus meiner Bahn geschritten, und ich soll nicht wieder hinein. Ein feindseliger Dämon, der Macht über mich gewonnen, scheint mich von außen zu hindern, hätte ich mich auch mit mir selbst wieder zur Einigkeit gefunden. (*HA* VI, 476–7)

And in a passage of great pathos as the account nears its end, we are shown the physical inability of Ottilie and Eduard to stay away from one another when they are living in the same house. They are drawn into proximity irresistibly.

But that is only one demonstration, perhaps the most poignant, of a compulsion all the characters have been under, to a greater or lesser extent, throughout; or we may say more precisely that they suffer a continual restriction, contradiction or reversal, often cruelly ironic, of individual volition. This thwarting is the negative revelation of the characters' own compulsive drive to determine, control, order and choose. And how often (it is part of the same compulsion) they utter prophecies and hopes that come to nothing! All the characters are driven in this way, not just the four of the equation. Mittler, the Assistant, Luciane, the Architect, all more or less significantly in their subordinated roles, are impelled to impose and shape things, at the very least by wishing, and most often by an active intervention; and almost always they are thwarted or achieve an unhappy opposite. The Assistant prophesies that Ottilie will be a source of happiness to herself and to others. His confident bid to marry her founders irrelevantly. Luciane bosses and interferes wherever she can, catastrophically in the case of the girl whose mind has been disturbed by a domestic accident. Renovating the chapel, and at the same time falling in love with Ottilie, the Architect is in fact preparing her tomb. And Mittler, most notoriously, belies his name and wreaks nothing but havoc whenever he intervenes. Intentions, hopes and predictions proliferate, and scarcely one of them is happily fulfilled.

Events correctly predicted would be easier to manage. That is the commonest impulse: to forestall, control, and sanitise. The Captain subjugates the estate, on a map (which Eduard, falling in love, disfigures). The Captain is a lover of card-indexes and system; rigorously he separates business from what he calls 'life'. At his instigation the stream and the road through the village are tidied up, as are the villagers; begging is restricted and regulated. The people are either kept at a distance—neither Eduard nor the Captain wants any relationship with them except that of command—or so arranged, in 'informal' family groups, that they do not offend the eye. Charlotte, having prettified the churchyard, which Eduard dislikes crossing and Mittler categorically refuses to enter, seeks to render her own household safe, learns about verdigris and lead glazes, and in alliance with the Captain appoints, all in vain as far as her own child, Ottilie and Eduard are concerned, a surgeon to minister in the case of accidents. Again and again, in little things and in large, the characters struggle to shape life to their liking, and are all the while drifting towards catastrophe as inexorably as leaves on a mill race. In a place the Revolution has not touched—'Alles eigentlich gemeinsame Gute muß durch das unumschränkte Majestätsrecht gefördert werden', says the Captain (*HA* VI, 286)—where all they do is footle and converse, they exercise the old forms of their class to shape a manageable life, and are overwhelmed.

Of the four it is Charlotte who most, and most pathetically, embodies the continually thwarted drive to make life safe. She is renowned for her aplomb in 'difficult' social situations; she defuses conflict, smoothes over unpleasantnesses. She shows most openly what characterises them all, even Eduard, though he frees himself somewhat, and that is fearfulness in the face of life. She is, like Mittler, a great fixer, and has no more success than he does.

She plans or has planned marriage for Ottilie with Eduard, the Captain, the Assistant. She speaks readily in aphorisms, as if she hoped or even believed that life could be reduced to them. In one extraordinary passage, climbing the hill to the new house and accompanied by Ottilie carrying the unlucky child, she rattles off truisms and wise old sayings like a desperate mantra:

> Auch auf dem festen Lande gibt es wohl Schiffbruch; sich davon auf das schnellste zu erholen und herzustellen, ist schön und preiswürdig. Ist doch das Leben nur auf Gewinn und Verlust berechnet! Wer macht nicht irgendeine Anlage und wird darin gestört! Wie oft schlägt man einen Weg ein und wird davon abgeleitet! Wie oft werden wir von einem scharf ins Auge gefaßten Ziel abgelenkt, um ein höheres zu erreichen! (*HA* VI, 428)

Ottilie in her diary is even worse. Charlotte's caution when Eduard first suggests having the Captain to stay exceeds the real situation. 'Nur daß wir nichts [...] Fremdes hereinbringen!' she says, 'Nicht immer was Neues [...] heranziehen' (*HA* VI, 247, 251). Her leading words in discussing the proposal are 'wagen', 'Gefahr', 'Wagestück' (*HA* VI, 252, 256). Really she is expressing something of the large reservoir of fearfulness which is in her, just below the surface, all the time. Again and again, long after the drift towards catastrophe has begun, she seeks pathetically to reverse the process, to return, to get back out of boundlessness into a safer enclosure: 'sie [bestärkte] sich nur immer mehr in dem Wahn: in einen frühern, beschränktern Zustand könne man zurückkehren, ein gewaltsam Entbundenes lasse sich wieder ins Enge bringen' (*HA* VI, 329). Her motive is always the same: fear; and as her aphorisms fail her she resorts to wishful thinking. She aims at prevention, she lives off *not*-wanting. Her realisation at the end, that by resisting she has caused the death of her child, is a poignant moment, but still not an acknowledgement of her fundamental state, which is rather the absolute fear and denial of life.

As their lives slip out of control the characters refer repeatedly to Fate or to a fate which they feel to be directing or compelling them, and the Narrator uses such language too. Eduard, obeying an instinct which at the very outset Charlotte criticised in him, wagers his life in a war, and, when he survives, thinks Fate has saved him for happiness with Ottilie; he views the inscribed glass which did not shatter when expected to as a corroborating sign. But Charlotte and Ottilie, after the drowning of the child, view this determination, as it seems by an outside force, in a blacker aspect. To them it is something monstrous, the word ('ungeheuer') becomes a leitmotif, one of several. They feel they are being overridden by something quite inhuman, by something to which their little human categories of right and wrong and all their efforts at personal volition are entirely irrelevant. But we need a nearer definition of this monstrous Fate, and rather than believe, or suppose Goethe to have believed, in the existence of exterior malignant forces, let us say instead that what threatens the characters in *Die Wahlverwandtschaften* is life itself, they are being threatened by the demands of a real life, and their own denial of life, their attempts to repress, reduce and prevent it, cause its demands to appear monstrous. In the end, indeed, by denying and resisting life, they conjure up death, and succumb to it.

Goethe's novel is steeped in death. The second book is fixated on it, but in the first also, in the fear of the graveyard, the fear of poisoning, the fear of drowning, death nudges into prominence. Occasions which should be joyous, the laying of the foundation stone, the fireworks on Ottilie's birthday, are shadowed by death, and the christening in the second book meets death full on when Mittler's intervention gives the aged parson the coup *de grâce*. The Architect, who will stand and watch one night over Ottilie's corpse, spends his time robbing tombs and showing his finds in society as though they were little fashionable commodities. This socialising, trivialising, aestheticising of death no more reduces its real power than does Charlotte's prettification of the graveyard. And in his work, dilettante work, as a painter, all the Architect does is decorate a tomb and encourage in Ottilie, when she sits and dreams under the finished ceiling, a willingness to side with death and duck the demands of life.

Art altogether, if landscape-gardening, *poses plastiques* and *tableaux vivants* are to be called art, not only does not increase the sense of life, which true art does, but rather reduces it and joins in the drift towards death. The gardening, though with the arrival of the Captain it becomes less cramped, is still only a pastime as, with the arrival of the Count, the Captain realises himself. And though the style aimed at is English and so, by comparison with the French, informal, this is still only the studied informality achieved also in the village when the villagers, spruced up for Sundays, gather before their cottages in 'natural' family groups. The principal impulse in the garden is still to control, arrange and tame. They take a walk to the mill, it is a walk into unexplored territory, and during it a profound advance is made in the new relationships, especially in that between Eduard and Ottilie. Their impulse immediately afterwards is to tame that walk, lay it out comfortably, so that it may be done and done again without fatigue or risk. The view from the new house, whose situation was chosen by Ottilie in the first upsurge of her love for Eduard, promises a good deal, since the Hall is excluded from it; but like the new house itself, which is never properly lived in, but receives instead the corpse of the drowned child, that promise of novelty, openness, extension of life, is not fulfilled. The greatest scheme, the merging of the three ponds, threatens catastrophe at its inception when the boy nearly drowns, and provides the scene of it when Charlotte's child is drowned. Ironically, by merging the ponds they were returning them to their former and, in that sense, more natural state; for they were once, as the Captain has found out, a mountain lake. Nature, especially water, 'das schwankende Element' (*HA* VI, 324), constitutes a threat throughout the novel; or, we might say, it is present as an alternative to the rigidity of the estate. That alternative, the way of greater naturalness, appears as a threat, and in the end as a deadly threat, to people afraid to embrace it. So life itself, the fate which is hounding them, must appear monstrous; indeed, must appear at last in the form of death.

The Architect is an adjutant of death. He turns the little boys, already marshalled in uniform in a corps, into a frieze for a summer house. He assists Luciane by drawing her a pedantically detailed mausoleum. Her notorious liveliness consumes itself in the merely social; her tongue is so sharp that, as the Narrator says, it is a wonder anything is left alive for fifteen miles around. In her party pieces, in her *poses plastiques*, her roles as a living statue, she prefigures the final freezing of Ottilie. The Count, assisted by the Architect, entertains the company with *tableaux vivants*, in which living people strike and hold an unnatural immobility. At Christmas then, in the nativity he induces Ottilie to star in, the Architect fixes a picture full of chilling ironies: her virginity, the borrowed baby, the child she will never bear. Ottilie freezes, stiffens: she is 'festgehalten und erstarrt', 'ein starres Bild' (*HA* VI, 404, 405), and that will be her fate. Already the Narrator has said of her that with the departure of Eduard 'das Leben ihrer Seele war getötet' (*HA* VI, 422). When she presses the drowned child to her uncovered breasts it freezes her to the heart: 'die kalten Glieder des unglücklichen Geschöpfs verkälten ihren Busen bis ins innerste Herz' (*HA* VI, 457). Frozen herself, Ottilie kills the life in Eduard. Far from becoming a saint she becomes a vampire: leaches the life from him and, having done so, and having resolutely sided with death in herself, she speaks at last and says—it is one of this chilling book's most chilling and sadistic utterances: 'Versprich mir zu leben!' (*HA* VI, 484). In her abstention from food she perfects the life of denial. She is its priestess. Her most characteristic gesture, which none who loves her has the heart to contradict, is a gesture of refusal and denial.

The form and tone of the novel itself, its symmetry and careful fixing of the scenes, the formality, often the stiltedness, of the dialogue, especially between husband and wife, its often difficult syntax, its narrator's remoteness, irony and sententiousness, all this contributes to the oppressive rigidity and unnaturalness which is the world itself on that bizarre estate. And the strange child born of a double adultery, who resembles the Captain and Ottilie, by its very unnaturalness, even by its manifest artificiality as a literary device, puts a seal on the whole. Life wears that mark when it is perverted and repressed. Learning of its conception Eduard was 'turned to stone' (*HA* VI, 358). Viewing it dead the Captain saw 'sein erstarrtes Ebenbild' (*HA* VI, 459).

I began this reading of *Die Wahlverwandtschaften* by mentioning morality. Clearly, the moral issue of the novel is not whether the institution of marriage should be upheld or not. Mittler, unmarried himself and fatally ham-fisted, cannot be listened to as if he were the unassailable spokesman (Goethe's mouthpiece!) on the subject of marriage. He is far too frequently ironised, criticised and countered. But nor does his opponent, the Count, deserve any more unqualified respect. The issue is elsewhere. The issue is whether life should be lived or not.

Goethe asked his publisher Cotta not to publish excerpts from the novel as an advertisement in advance. He wrote: 'Es ist dergestalt in einander gearbeitet, daß ich nichts davon abgelöst wünschte' (Härtl, 47). Rather like *Tasso*, the text is sewn together with repeated words. 'Ungeheuer' I have mentioned; 'erstarren' is another; their repetition insists on the crucial issue. The words 'Recht' and 'Rechte' make up another such nexus. Charlotte, beginning to lose her husband, cries: 'Kannst du mir zumuten, daß ich auf [...] die schönsten Rechte [...] Verzicht leisten soll?' (*HA* VI, 342–3). Those are her rights as his legal wife. Set against them, quite brutally, in the antithesis 'lebhafte Wünsche/gesetzlicher Bund' (*HA* VI, 455), are the rights of love: 'So ist die Liebe beschaffen, daß sie allein recht zu haben glaubt und alle anderen Rechte vor ihr verschwinden' (*HA* VI, 322).

Then are the characters wrong to live the way they do? Charlotte, at the end, acknowledges that it was wrong to marry Eduard when, not having fought to do so the first time, a second chance was given them years later. He likewise realises that was a mistake, though he pushed hardest to commit it. The question is should they abide by their mistake. In love with Ottilie, he thinks they should not, and Charlotte herself comes to that conclusion. Not that his marriage with Charlotte is worthless, but his love for Ottilie is better, in the sense that more of the person is engaged, and more deeply. There is ample demonstration of this, and Eduard himself is certain that, having been an amateur and a dilettante all his life, he has finally, in loving Ottilie, found something in which his personality is wholly taken up (*HA* VI, 355). There is much that is dislikeable about Eduard (as about all the characters in this, as it seems, designedly unsympathetic book) but he has this in his favour, as Goethe himself pointed out (Härtl, 139): that meeting Ottilie he loves unconditionally. His going to war, at least as he views it once he is there, is more a deliberate ordeal in the name of love than capitulation to a death-wish. He makes a trial of himself and his life. Having come through, he feels he has a right to claim what his life, a real life now, most needs: Ottilie. By the lake he begins to claim her—'er wollte seine alten Rechte geltend machen' (*HA* VI, 454–5)—the words echo those used to describe his seduction of his wife, and he halts when he is shown the child, the product of that occasion.

Eduard is the only one who breaks out. (The Captain, though he comes and goes, gets ever more shadowy.) He seeks by force of a lover's persuasion to animate the frozen Ottilie, and when he fails and she is dead he finds, to his credit, that he cannot follow after her by starving himself, because that way is false, as he says, 'ein falsches Bemühen' (*HA* VI, 489), and against his nature. He has at least the makings of salvation in him.

Marriage is not the issue, but by abiding in a marriage which is false Eduard and Charlotte extend at best a shallowness and at worst a fundamental falsity over all they undertake. Thus although in real life there may be nothing particularly wrong—at least, nothing deserving of death—in landscape gardening, speaking in aphorisms, or even in teaching children the way the Assistant does, in the novel, cumulatively, these things and many more like them typify a society which is set against any change or expansion of its members' lives. The Assistant's exercise of tight control over his pupils' wayward imaginations and his uneasiness at even the thought of life among 'Affen, Papageien und Mohren' (*HA* VI, 416) in foreign parts, are akin to Charlotte's anxiety at any opportunity—or threat—of opening up. The novel has a social interest, which was recognised at once, in that it depicts a class whose forms, already anachronistic in 1809, seem to be signalling their own desperate need for renewal. Incapable of that, they excite a sort of vengefulness instead. Love in that context, as so often in Goethe's work, arrives as an animating and revolutionary force; it turns destructive, indeed deadly, when the characters, stuck in dead forms, prove unable to accommodate it. Charlotte and Eduard are husband and wife, but both are in love elsewhere. Eduard reanimates his marital passion by lasciviously remembering the past; and sustains it, and Charlotte responds, by thinking of somebody else. In her darkened bedroom 'sogleich behauptete die innre

Neigung, behauptete die Einbildungskraft ihre Rechte über das Wirkliche'
(*HA* VI, 321). Having slept together they feel they have done wrong. As the
Narrator says: 'Doch läßt sich die Gegenwart ihr ungeheures Recht nicht
rauben' (*HA* VI, 321). The present, in this case, is the love each feels for a
person outside their marriage, a love which has in it, at least potentially, the
beginnings of a real life. That life demands its rights, and denied them it
brings forth a monstrous recrimination.

The Novelle told by the English lord's companion to entertain the
ladies offers a radical alternative to the novel's fatal trend. There the girl,
drifting into a marriage which would be only nominal, liberates herself
violently, throws herself upon the mercy of the river and in so doing makes
a provocative trial of herself to the man she loves. He responds instinctively,
they are carried away out of the sphere of the merely social, and land in a
place apart where, naked and nearly drowned, she is recovered, reanimated
by her lover. That scene is remarkable for its drastic confrontation of death
and sexual passion, and for the triumph of the latter: 'Nichts ward versäumt,
den schönen, halbstarren, nackten Körper wieder ins Leben zu rufen. Es
gelang. Sie schlug die Augen auf, sie erblickte den Freund...' (*HA* VI, 440).
Sure of themselves, reborn into certainty, they face their families in bridal
clothes, and force the issue in favour of love and life.

Eduard tries—'Es war, als wenn er, so gut durch Fröhlichkeit als durch
Gefühl, Ottiliens Erstarren wieder beleben, ihr Schweigen wieder auflösen
wollte' (*HA* VI, 479)—and fails. Ottilie, allying herself with death, triumphs.
'Nun feiert erst das Sittliche seinen Triumph', as Goethe said (Härtl, 211)—
a bitter victory.

The endings of most of Goethe's major works, of *Iphigenie*, *Tasso*,
*Wilhelm Meister*, *Faust*, are notoriously problematic, not to say evasive.
Perhaps only in *Werther* was he truly consequential to the end. The ending
of *Die Wahlverwandtschaften* is Goethe at his shiftiest. Ottilie's saintliness is
no such thing. She starves herself and kills the will to live in Eduard. Or was
she still wavering when Mittler settled the issue with his usual aplomb?
Eduard had hopes, and the others too thought she might begin speaking
again on his birthday. She looked, the Narrator says, like a person carrying a
happy intention towards her friends. Were the clothes she laid out really her
bridal wear? Were the asters for a wedding? At least we can say that any
impulse in her towards love and life was being countered all the while by her
refusing food. She was as ready for death, perversely, being young, as was the
old parson when Mittler dispatched him at the christening. Shifting then
through apparent miracles emphatically towards an after-life, Goethe offers
us nothing we can believe in. The lovers may be buried together, now dead

being permitted to lie side by side, but in there with them is the monstrous child, as a devilish irony in their unbelievable heaven. Transcendence of that kind is a poor compensation, and no redemption either from a life unlived. 'Ich heidnisch?' Goethe once expostulated; 'Nun, ich habe doch Gretchen hinrichten und Ottilien verhungern lassen, ist denn das den Leuten nicht christlich genug? was wollen sie noch Christlicheres?' (Härtl, 171).

Goethe was not an easy member of Weimar society, and he is no easier now. His book confronts us, as he said it would, 'als ein unveränderliches Factum'. 'Das Gedichtete behauptet sein Recht' (Härtl, 100). Nothing in the least bit cosy can be deduced out of *Die Wahlverwandtschaften*. The indictment of wrong living is quite merciless. It is a chilling, in some ways a repellent book, and would be nihilistic, the characters drifting helplessly to ruin, did it not through the passion of Eduard and Ottilie and through their braver equivalents in the Novelle, call for its own wholehearted contradiction.

## NOTES

1. *'Die Wahlverwandtschaften'. Eine Dokumentation der Wirkung von Goethes Roman 1808–1832*, ed. Heinz Härtl, Berlin 1983, p. 158. All further references to this invaluable book are included (as Härtl) in the text.

2. Schiller to Goethe: 31 October 1796; 9 May 1800; 16 December 1802. Goethe to Schiller: 13 July 1796 ('mein Ehestand'); 7 August 1799 ('die Meinigen'); 16 December 1802 ('die Kleine'). 'Mein Ehestand' is, of course, significant. See Note 3.

3. *Goethes Gespricke*, ed. Wolfgang Herwig, Zürich 1969, II, p. 146. Charlotte Schiller recalls Goethe saying, probably in 1790: 'Ich bin verheiratet, nur nicht mit Zeremonie' (quoted by Hans Gerhard Grüf in *Goethes Briefwechsel mit seiner Frau*, ed. Gräf, Frankfurt a.M. 1989, I, p. 18). See also Goethe's letter to Schiller of 13 July 1796: 'Mein Ehstand ist eben 8 Jahre und die Französische Revolution 7 Jahre alt.'

4. See Grif, p. 33.

5. In a letter to Zelter of 15 January 1813.

6. Zacharias Werner, Goethe's rival for the love of Minna Herzlieb, became a Catholic on reading *Die Wahlverwandtschaften*; and a Prussian General Bardeleben divorced his 'brave und kluge, wenn such nicht

anmutige Frau [...], um eine unbedeutende Demoiselle zu heiraten, von der er behauptete, nicht lassen zu können' (Härtl, 212, 216).

7.   *Goethes Werke*, ed. Erich Trunz, Hamburg 1948–60, VI, p. 460. *Die Wahlverwandtschaften* is referred to throughout in this edition, and all further references are included in the text, e.g. *HA* VI, 123.

ILONA KLEIN

# *Goethe's* Die Leiden des jungen Werthers:
# *An Epistolary Novel, Or A Stage Drama in Disguise?*

Photography of the late 1920s generated repercussions in other fields of the arts. It sparked an interdisciplinary interest in critics who balked at viewing the frozen images as merely one moment's reality, and who wanted, instead, to recompose and integrate underlying cultural, literary, or political discourse within the photographic frame. This fertile interdisciplinary backing guaranteed an in-depth interpretative dissection of artistic expression which had not been previously possible. The small photograph, a still visual image, became connected to the larger visual images of stage sets—these, a series of visual, immobile backgrounds which framed the characters acting within.

Within this scope, August Langen investigated the connections between the principles of the original, less sophisticated, *camera obscura* and eighteenth-century German literature. Analyzing correlations and interrelations between artistic and literary systems, he discussed how the former had come to serve literary purposes. Langen showed that a clear diachronic development was traceable from pre-Romantic literature (with its still rather fixed literary genres) to the structurally more elaborate and supple literary boundaries found in later eighteenth-century works. His treatments of blending of genres ("Verschmelzung der Gattungen" 85), and of the slight overstepping of boundaries in the novel ("leichte Grenzüberschreitung im

From *European Romantic Review* 7, no. 2. © 1997 by European Romantic Review.

Roman" 82) became seminal in his quest for artistic creations capable of connecting novel, drama and etching together in early romantic manifestations. Langen wrote that "novel, theatrical pieces, and series of etchings ... embody the principle of image-framing and the structure of image-sequencing" ("Roman, Schauspiel und Kupferfolge ... verkörpern das Prinzip der Rahmenschau, und die Struktur der Bilderkette" 83).[1] All three artistic media represent creative expressions and interpretations of sequential images. They were finally connected through the workings of a *lanterna magica*.

Niel Flax's studies on *Faust II* (1979) and on *Faust* (1983) furthered these ideas more than just tangentially while also applying some of their concepts directly to Goethe's works. In the former essay, Flax treated, among others, popular usage of *lanternae magicae* and the lasting impact of these slide-projector prototypes upon dramatic entertainment in general (romantic, fantastic, phantasmagoric effects), and upon the literary structure of *Faust II* more specifically. Flax's latter study analyzed the use of semiotic and non-semiotic signs as means to transcend "arbitrary and motivated representation" (185) and discussed the general problem of allegory vs. symbol.

Both Langen and Flax, although for different reasons, treated the seminal importance of *logos* and of logocentricity: Langen regarded conversation (*Gespräch*) as the connecting factor between drama and novel; Flax pointed to metalinguistic signs as the necessary bridge between Goethe's theory of poetry and the use of language itself.

Through an analysis of the textual language, I will show in this study how Goethe's *Die Leiden des jungen Werthers* (*Werther*, henceforth) contains *and* surpasses the common structure of coeval epistolary novels, for it carries innumerable theatrical elements within its pages, hence bridging traditional literary genres. Expanding upon Langen's theoretical observations on the interdisciplinary relations between stage performance and other visual artistic expressions, and applying some of Flax's parameters to a close structural reading of *Werther*, I propose that Goethe—who was already thinking "dramatically" anyhow (Goethe's puppet theater comes to mind)—consciously embedded in this work dramatic elements, for he was influenced by the powerful imagery of fashionable contemporary raree-shows, or show-boxes. This study will highlight evidence of theatrical elements (stage effects, settings, scenes) embedded within the text, and of dramatic plot (sub)divisions which Goethe incorporated into his "script."[2]

Technically speaking, *lanterna magica*, *Guckkasten* (peep-show), *Zauberlaterne* (magic lantern), and *Zauberlampe* (magic lamp) are not identical objects. However, here they are treated synonymously because their creative principle is strikingly similar, and because this textual analysis of *Werther* is not affected by whether the artistic image is projected on a wall (as per prototypes of slide projectors) or is formed within the rotating device itself (as per a raree-show to be viewed through a peep-hole of a show-box). At any rate, the common underlying principle of these objects consists in showing the decodification of a narrative text through a sequence of visual images mechanically set in motion. In fact, any perceived void between the reader and a plot would be filled by the visual (de)signs representing the text.

Langen postulated that similarly in theater, the physical space which encapsulates a stage represents an enlarged show-box whose characters perform in the middle and whose sets exemplify the changing images of a *lanterna magica* on a much larger scale. Langen's references connected plots and scripts with sequential images, as he theorized striking resemblances between stage sets and fixed images of *camerae obscurae*.[3] He concluded that "often, especially in novels, directors' annotations are added in parentheses or in small print and correspond to the stage directions of a stage play" ("Oft, besonders im Roman, sind Regiebemerkungen beigefügt, die den Bühnenanweisungen des Theaterstücks entsprechen und eingeklammert oder auch in kleinerem Druck geboten werden" 83). That stage directions and acting suggestions often may be hidden between the lines of a novel is a concept seminal to my study.

Infinite different styles and *topoi* are employed in writing literature and the spectrum of genres does not span only from drama to novel. However, let us speculate for one moment that in the case of Goethe's *Werther*, drama and novel indeed stand at the antipodes of an imaginary literary scale: drama, a script whose traditional nature and intrinsic monologic or dialogue form requires an audience and a stage to come alive; and novel, whose linguistic canon and codes are varied and whose pages call for a reader asked to penetrate not only the words and actions of the characters but to unravel their silent thoughts as well.

In his autobiographical *Dichtung und Wahrheit* (*Poetry and Truth*) written several decades after *Werther*, Goethe discussed the genesis of poetry, drama and novel at great length, together with the employment of different possible linguistic registers for traditional literary genres.[4] Referring back to the development of *Werther*, Goethe wrote

> that drama had not been its author's sole occupation, for while it was being conceived, written, rewritten, printed and distributed many other images and ideas were stirring in his mind. Those

meant for dramatic treatment had the advantage of being thought through most often and nearly completed, but simultaneously a transition developed to a different kind of presentation, which is not ordinarily considered dramatic and yet has a great relationship to drama. This transition was brought about mainly by the author's peculiar habit of recasting even soliloquy as drama (transl. Heitner 424).[5]

During the creative process, thus, an author first chooses a literary form suitable to the theme of the composition, then selects style(s) of speech (monologue, dialogue, third-person narration, etc.), and finally writes the actual plot including characters' discourse. As Goethe successfully argued, for each literary creation which materializes, there exists also a myriad of other plots, characters and ideas which remain unexplored to a certain degree in the writer's mind. Assuming a literary polarization between drama and novel, then, the argument could be made that Goethe's *Werther* bridges these two genres, for even though formally his work conforms to the codes of an epistolary novel, it carries structurally within characteristics of a stage drama. Did Goethe intentionally disguise a theater "script" in *Werther*?

Again in *Dichtung und Wahrheit*, Goethe unveils the key for a close connection between dramatic monologue and epistolary novel:

> It is quite clear that such thought-conversations are closely related to correspondence, except that the latter responds to an established familiarity, while the former creates a new, ever-changing familiarity for itself, with no reply. Thus, when the author had to depict that ennui with life..., it immediately occurred to him to portray his sentiments in letters.... Other people's enjoyment of life is a painful reproach to him and so the very thing that ought to draw him out actually turns him back upon his innermost self. If he cares to discuss this at all, it will be through letters (transl. Heitner 424–5).[6]

Even though these two passages by Goethe in *Dichtung und Wahrheit* did not directly address the composing phases of his *Werther*, such observations are certainly applicable to this work. As other critics have noticed, Goethe may have disclosed here his conscious effort to bridge drama and novel.[7]

Traditionally, *Die Leiden des jungen Werthers* has been treated as an epistolary novel. However, it is a peculiar kind of epistolary novel, for it contains no exchange of letters. *Werther* represents the earliest widely-recognized example of this type, and is contrary to coeval models represented by Richardson's and Rousseau's epistolary novels where the reader is privy to both ends of the correspondence. In *Werther*, the reader only imagines Wilhelm's words and actions, as no words are ever written by Wilhelm in reply to his friend Werther's letters.[8]

Other aspects of *Werther*'s uniqueness become evident at a closer examination of the text. When looking at the capacity which this epistolary novel assigns to Wilhelm, a few dramatic elements in *Werther* come to light.[9] Even though the reader can assume that Wilhelm responds to Werther, and he interacts with his friend, we do not "hear" him. In fact, his character (a silent addressee of Werther's correspondence) mirrors the role of a likewise passive/silent theater audience watching this drama unfold on stage. In other words, notwithstanding the readers' imagination to fill in the blanks, effectively Wilhelm maintains his silence vis-à-vis Werther throughout the book, similar to the way in which a spectator normally would only observe a traditional performance, by not interacting with the actors on stage. And while in a few passages of the novel Werther describes his own emotional reactions to Wilhelm's suggestions, it is also true that Goethe's readers can only *imagine* how Wilhelm may be carrying out his role, for *Werther* never shifts the focus away from its homonymous character's self-centeredness. In fact, *Werther* contains no "first-hand" dialogues at all. Words relating to others are reproduced without exclusion through the filter of the protagonist's sole memory. It is Werther alone who "narrates" others' words in his own monologues.

Monologues recited on stage connect characters and their innermost thoughts immediately, passionately and intimately to an audience. In other words, in *Werther* the use of long monologues (disguised in prose passages) reveal the presence of a work which avails itself of stage elements within its text. A monologue also accentuates egocentricity (Werther's, in this case), for when it is recited, the stage's focus is narrowed solely onto the character who is speaking.

By postulating that *Werther* may be a stage drama in disguise, or—more reasonably—that it contains numerous dramatic performing elements in its structure, we recognize that this "play" is the performance of a long monologue in a one-man show.

Besides its monologic form, other clues to theatrical elements, stage imagery and drama are embedded in the text. These literary strategies can confirm Goethe's creation of a work in which the boundaries between drama and novel withered.

Werther's imaginary letter of 20 January 1772—which, chronologically and structurally speaking, appears at the exact center of the novel—contains a statement clearly referring to the importance of theatrical elements within the text: "I am amused by these puppets, or rather, I am myself one of them; I sometimes grasp my neighbor's wooden hand, and withdraw with a shrudder" (transl. Lange 45).[10] In yet other passages of *Werther*, a stage curtain is mentioned: "To lift the curtain, to step behind it" (transl. Lange 71) ["Den Vorhang aufzuheben und dahinter zu treten!" (*WA* I, 19: 153)], and also a stage: "A curtain has been drawn before my soul, and the stage of never-ending life has transformed itself into an ever-open grave before me" ["Es hat sich vor meiner Seele wie ein Vorhang wegezogen, und der Schauplatz des unendlichen Lebens verwandelt sich vor mir in den Abgrund des ewig offnen Grabs" (*WA* I, 19: 75)]. Werther regards himself as a puppet on a stage, being made to act out in a play about his own life, and feeling alternately empowered and powerless.

Goethe's creation of Werther as a character who knowingly acts out the story of his own life on stage was not a particularly new conception: to mention two examples among the most obvious, both Calderón de la Barca and Shakespeare recovered the classical Latin motif of "life as a play," of life on stage. However, Goethe's original touch was to include the *topos* in a new setting. In other words, in *Werther* Goethe experimented with a traditionally established genre (drama) by setting it within a relatively new frame (epistolary novel). He approached the epistolary novel within the proven literary pattern of a dramatic work. When considering the dramatic, theatrical core of *Werther*'s epistolary novel in this context, then young Werther can be regarded not only as protagonist of a novel, but also as a main character (actually, *the* only character) reciting on stage his life story through a long monologue.

The story in *Werther* is totally subjective.[11] The homonymous protagonist filters all external contingencies before revealing them to the (epistolary novel's) reader/(drama's) spectator/(fictional) addressee. With the exception of the two-paragraph "introduction" and of the concluding section in the novel "the Editor to the Reader" ("der Herausgeber an den Leser") where a few letters carry fictional editorial glosses, as readers we can safely assume that most of what is recounted by Werther does not necessarily depict reality, but merely reflects *his* perception of reality.

Given the monological form of the novel/drama and the focus on the protagonist Werther, it follows that the other "characters" are relegated to secondary and background positions. Lotte, Albert and the other figures do not seem to be entitled to an independent existence, for it is Werther alone who stands in the middle of the stage, acting out his one-man show. Through his ego-centered self-consciousness, he absorbs and re-elaborates narratives of events as though they were shadows projected on a wall, as if images of a *lanterna magica*. Werther analyzes, interprets and relates the story created by these projections in his own subjective way for the reader/spectator.

To a certain extent, then, the images temporarily told the story before Werther could elaborate logocentrically upon their meaning. Images were important during the eighteenth century, both when projected and when drawn on paper. As far as the illustrations go, Langen studied the artistic role of Chodowiecki's engravings for *Werther—Kupferstichfolge*, a sequence of images embodying the metalinguistic narration of a text.[12] In *Werther*, Lotte, Albert and other characters are corollary shadows for Werther's act; they are the puppets who play for his own *Guckkasten* and imagination. They represent the foundation of Werther's ego-filtered narration: "I stand before a puppet show and see the little puppets move, and I ask myself whether it isn't an optical illusion" (transl. Lange, 45) ["Ich stehe vor einem Raritätenkasten und sehe die Männchen und Gäulchen vor mir herumrücken und frage mich oft, ob es nicht optischer Betrug ist" (*WA* I, 19: 96)]. It is of course no coincidence that Werther should express doubts about reality, describing it as an optical illusion. This uncertainty is revealed again in that same letter of 20 January 1772 in which he compares his life to a puppet's. But such clues are not the only ones which Goethe expects his readers to decode.

There is yet an earlier passage in *Werther* where lack of love in the world is compared to a spent *lanterna magica* whose functional core is missing. Again, Werther laments his isolation, for he can relate his life only to a "plot" which materializes when others' images become visible to him, like visions projected on a wall:

> Wilhelm, what is the world to our hearts without love? A magic lantern without light. You have but to set up the light within and the brightest pictures are thrown on the white screen. And if that is all there is, fleeting shadows, we are still happy, when, like children, we behold them and are transported with the wonderful sight (transl. Lange 27).[13]

Later in this essay, I will propose and justify a division of Goethe's *Werther* in acts and scenes. For the moment, however, suffice it to consider "erstes Buch" as "Act I" of this "play." Structurally so far, the two passages in which metaphors of *lanterna magica* appear, surface in the middle of the novel (letter of 20 January) or, so to speak, in the "center" of "Act I." This pivotal positioning emphasizes their symbolic importance.

Werther stands in front of his *lanterna magica*, delighted like a youngster by the images in front of him, and invents his own story, told in his own words, to go along with the illustrations. The characters projected (Lotte, Albert, etc.) do not have, in turn, their own story to tell: their actions, intentions and words are all filtered by the protagonist's mind before being shared with the reader/audience of this epistolary novel/play. Sometimes Werther appears to realize the total subjectivness of his interpretation:

> If only I were a moody person, I might blame the weather, or an acquaintance, or disappointment, for my discontented mind; then at least this insupportable load of trouble would not rest entirely upon me. But ah! I feel all too clearly that I alone am to blame for my woe. To blame? No, my own heart contains the source of all my sorrow, as it previously contained the source of all my bliss (transl. Lange 59–60).[14]

Unsuccessfully, Werther tries to overcome the inner conflicts stemming from his dichotomous view of imagination vs. reality. Ultimately, Werther is doomed to succumb to this schism between subjectivity vs. objectiveness, and between what Friedrich Schlegel would define "Romanticism" vs. "Classicism."[15]

Show-boxes were so popular during the eighteenth century that the principle of image-framing" ("Prinzip der Rahmenschau"), and the miniature images" ("kleinformatigen Bildchen") became what we would regard today as household objects: "often, the engravings would be observed through the show-box, this most important psychological symbol of the time" and "in this period of geniality, the young Goethe was foremost in recapturing an artistic value in the raree-box".[16]

When a *lanterna magica* casts shadows upon the wall, the images are flat. Likewise, when secondary characters play a role only corollary to the protagonist's, their psychological development remains superficial and peripheral, that is, "flat." Langen explained thus:

> The mini-situations in question differ little from a contemporary stage image. In both cases, it is that which is cut from view, the frame around the situation which is decisive and didactically of value.[17]

Engravings (illustrations of books) or shadows (artistic projection on a wall) alone are incapable of portraying the complexity of life's nuances. However, as in the case of story-telling, when images and words come together, joined they have much more to offer.

Besides some of the stage references indicated above, Goethe's Werther presents other allusions pertaining to drama. First, let us consider the structure of the text. It is similar, in fact, to a traditional play. The literary *corpus* is divided into three main sections preceded by a brief fictional editorial introduction. Goethe does not actually label the "introduction" as such, but he identifies the other sections as "first book," "second book," "the editor to the reader" ("Erstes Buch," "Zweites Buch," and "Der Herausgeber an den Leser"). The sections are consistent with the traditional divisions found in dramatic tragedies, where their counterparts would be labeled: Prologue (for the short preface, which in this case is *a posteriori*), Act I, Act II and Act III—the latter operating simultaneously as Epilogue (again, *a posteriori*). Each of these sections ("acts") can be subdivided further into shorter segments ("scenes"), reflecting the text's natural partition, according to the dates of Werther's letters and/or following the different settings he describes. When viewed in this way, a reading of *Werther* as stage script could be justified.

To clarify further:

The *Prologue*: a brief, two-paragraph introduction (*a posteriori*) which precedes Werther's first letter of 4 May 1771.

*Act I* (or, *erstes Buch* in Goethe's words), subdivided into three scenes:

Scene 1: 4 May–30 May 1771. Werther's time spent in serenity before meeting Lotte.

Scene 2: 16 June–26 July 1771. Time spent together with Lotte until Albert's arrival.

Scene 3: 30 July–10 September 1771. Werther, with Lotte and Albert.

*Act II* (or, *zweites Buch* in Goethe's words), also subdivided into three scenes:

Scene 1: 20 October 1771–5 May 1772. At the Ambassador's service (Am Hofe).

Scene 2: 9 May–18 June 1772. Werther visits his home town and decides to return to Lotte.

Scene 3: 29 July–6 December 1772. With Lotte again.

*Act III* (or, *Der Herausgeber an den Leser* in Goethe's words): an Epilogue of sorts (also *a posteriori*) which concludes the story of Werther's life. There is one scene to this act:

Scene 1: 12 December 1772–until Werther's death.

It would appear that Goethe adopted classical literary means to delineate and separate the sections of this novel/play, while experimenting with new theatrical strategies.

Not only structurally, but also linguistically and syntactically, the text reveals peculiarities which reconfirm its subdivisions into "acts" and "scenes." For instance, both the *Prologue* and the *Epilogue* are written from an omniscient author's point of view. In them, the (fictional) editor details past facts now concluded, and all main verbs in these two sections appear in the past tense (except, of course, for when the editor reports direct speeches). The reader notices how Wilhelm, the narrator/editor, benefits in his cathartic, temporal and spatial distance from the events, so that his narrative can follow a linear pattern, based on logic and chronology, rather than reacting to the circumstances themselves.

It becomes apparent that in *Werther*, the *Epilogue* mirrors the traditional role of a "Greek Chorus." In classical drama, the Chorus represented a *vox populi*—the conservative *animus* of the play expressing popular wisdom and conventional tradition, for it opposed the passionate texture of a dialogue or a monologue. Here, the narrative voice of the editor may fulfill the same role of the traditional Chorus, in that it seeks to balance the protagonist's impulse with the *Epilogue's* grounded voice in the background.

By contrast, the main body of *Werther* sharply contrasts against the *Prologue* and the *Epilogue*. The plot of the "play" develops while the images of Werther's *lanterna magica* are projected onto the wall/stage and his thoughts are expressed through present-tense verbs only. In *Werther*, the *Prologue* and *Epilogue* (structurally, the peripheral/external sections of text) reflect a classical dramatic model and employ a peripheral/external voice to present narratives. Instead, the central "acts" (or, *erstes Buch* and *zweites Buch*) focus on the main character and on his egocentric narrative voice. In essence, the past tenses of the *Prologue* and *Epilogue* have transformed into "historical present" tenses in the central sections of the text.

It is at the end of what I have here defined as "Act II, Scene 3," that Goethe shows yet another classical dramatic strategy: by now, readers'/ audience's identification with the protagonist's tragedy is almost complete. So, Goethe applies the principles of Aristotle's catharsis by rapidly converting Werther's passionate narration into a detached omniscient author's voice, suddenly shifting from present-tense *pathos* to past tense verbs. Of course, this kind of proto-Brechtian *Verfremdungstechnik* serves to caution the readers/spectators about the fictional nature of the novel/drama which is absorbing their attention.[18]

If one carefully observes the internal structure of the play, both "Act I" and "Act II" reveal circular patterns, in contrast to the straightforward narrative structures of the "*Prologue*" and of the "*Epilogue*." To be more specific, "Act I" and "Act II" begin with the protagonist's arrival (at Wahlheim and at the residence of the Ambassador, respectively) after running away from his authoritarian mother at the beginning of the novel, and leaving Lotte and Albert behind—at the end of "Act I."[19] The theme of Werther's escape from his surroundings has been recently studied by scholars who emphasize the parallels between Werther's need for physical freedom and his breaking away from hierarchical social constraints (Furst 147).

Besides showing parallel beginnings, "Act I" and "Act II" also both end with similar scenes: as Fetzer pointed out, *erstes Buch* terminates with an "empty hug" in the darkness, *zweites Buch* finishes with Werther's desire of annihilation.[20] More specifically, at the end of "Act I," Albert and Lotte *exeunt* the scene, disappearing into the darkness, as the protagonist is left behind, helpless and alone, watching the couple vanish in the Ossianic landscape of moonlight and lengthening shadows.[21] "Act II" ends comparably, but here what vanishes are not the images of Lotte and Albert, rather the very foundation of the protagonist himself: it is Werther's consciousness which evaporates as he longs for self-annihilation into the darkness of infinity:

> What is man—that much praised demigod? Do not his powers fail when he most requires their use? And whether he soar in joy or sink in sorrow, is he not inevitably arrested? And while he fondly dreams that he is grasping at infinity, is he not at that moment made doubly aware of the dull monotony of his existence? (transl. Lange 65).[22]

Thus, "Act I" and "Act II"—the *lanterna magica*'s projections s(t)imulating Werther's interpretation of the shadows—have circular patterns with recurring motifs. This rotation and repetition of themes mirrors the same circular movement of images projected in sequence onto the wall to create a story of shadows through a *Zauberlampe*.

Narratively and structurally speaking, these circular motions lead nowhere. To give a conclusion to *Werther*, Goethe had to break away from the rotary pattern and carry his narrative into a linear conclusion. There is, earlier in "Act II," one unsuccessful attempt to do just this. *Zweites Buch* begins on 20 October 1771 *in medias res* at the Ambassador's service, but the reader/audience knows that Werther has not seen Lotte since September 1771. He will see her again in July 1772, when he returns to her after nine months, a long hiatus. This nine-month period (a gestation of sorts) should have allowed Werther to "deliver" the strength needed to break away from his circular pattern and launch himself into a linear structure which could bring a resolution to his life. Metaphorically speaking, however, his "gestation" is fruitless as he cannot create a new life for himself. Thus, as Werther returns to Lotte, he does not modify his monologic code, and he continues to stare at the shadows and interpret them in his own isolation, concluding "Act II" with yet another empty embrace.

Instead, the tragedy comes to an end through the abrupt change in narrative voice (from Werther's to the editor's), the abandonment of the *lanterna magica* devices, and the substitution of verb tenses from present to past, all pointing to the linear structure of the "Epilogue."

In addition to analyzing the structural patterns in this novel/script when considering dramatic elements in *Werther*, the reader will also look for other theatrical codes. For instance, the exaggerated ("theatrical") gestures which actors would adopt in a stage performance and which Goethe emphasized in his characters. "Theatrical" are the somewhat extravagant and overstated emotional mo(ve)ments found in the text. *Werther* abounds with such mo(ve)ments which substitute for a more traditional stage blocking:

> ... when Charlotte asked the coachman to stop and told her brothers to get down. They insisted upon kissing her hand once more, which the eldest did with all the delicacy of a youth of fifteen, but the other in a lighter and more impetuous manner. She asked them again to give her love to the children, and we drove off (transl. Lange 15);

and

> One wisely sat down in a corner with her back to the window, and held her hands over her ears; a second knelt down and hid her

face in the other's lap; a third pushed herself between them, and embraced her sisters with a thousand tears (transl. Lange 18);

and

I put my handkerchief to my face and left the room; I was recalled to my senses only by Charlotte's voice, reminding me that it was time to go home (transl. Lange 24);

and

They walked down the avenue. I stood gazing after them in the moonlight, then threw myself on the ground, and wept, sprang up, and ran out on the terrace, and there below me in the shade of the linden trees I saw her white frock gleaming as she disappeared near the garden gate. I stretched out my arms, and she vanished (transl. Lange 41);

Moreover, of course, the "kiss-scene":

Werther's eyes and lips burned on Charlotte's arm; she trembled, she wanted to go, but grief and pity lay like a leaden weight upon her. She took a deep breath, recovered herself, and begged Werther, sobbing, to continue—implored him with the very voice of heaven! He trembled, his heart ready to burst; then taking up the sheets again, he read in a broken voice (transl. Lange 80).[23]

Exaggerated and "theatrical" (albeit movingly tragic) is the scene of Werther's death, in which his groaning and suffering continue for twelve hours until his demise (a long stage scene it would be indeed!). Included, for the same reasons, are the overstated emotional reactions of Lotte's father and of her siblings:

At six in the morning, the servant enters Werther's room with a candle. He finds his master stretched on the floor, blood about him, and the pistol at his side. He calls to him, takes him in his arms, but there is no answer, only a rattling in the throat ... The bullet had entered the forehead over the right eye; his brains were protruding ... The old judge hastened to the house upon hearing the news; he kissed his dying friend amid a flood of tears. His eldest boys soon followed him on foot. In speechless sorrow they threw themselves on their knees by the bedside, and kissed his hands and face. The eldest, who was his favorite, clung to his lips till he was gone; even then the boy had to be taken away by force (transl. Lange 86–87).[24]

Moreover, the employment of a dramatic *topos* or *deus-ex-machina* in the "play" must be considered "theatrical" too. In fact, nature represents an important *topos*/metaphor, as exemplified in the case of the storm in "Act I" (on this topic, more in Ryder and, especially, in Ricks). Rather predictably, the tempestuous weather mirrors Werther's feelings of confused anticipation before he and Lotte get to know one another better. Indeed, the function of nature in *Werther* conforms to this *topos*' traditional role in Renaissance plays, when it can represent either a locus *amoenus* or a *selva obscura*. *Loci amoeni* and *selvae obscurae* were heavily borrowed in Germany following the tradition of late fifteenth- and sixteenth-century Italian pastoral plays and chivalric poems. These models, in turn, stem from Latin classical dramatic production. To take again Shakespeare's theater and Italian Renaissance epic poetry as two examples, the themes of both *A Midsummer Night's Dream* and of Ariosto's *Orlando Furioso* are heavily influenced by *selvae obscurae* metaphors. In both cases, the protagonists are so confused by the labyrinths of woods (i.e., by the confusion of their own minds) that they lose their discrimination. Eventually, they fail to see any other point of view but their own, and their focusing on themselves, their central position on the "stage of life," their madness become the very obstacle to the overcoming of their unsalvageable serenity. In their madness, a reasonable perception of the external world is lost.

Goethe employed the *topoi* successfully: the *selva obscura* reflects the confusion of the protagonist's mind, love as a crisis of the mind in neo-Platonic terms (for example, the storm at the end of 16 June 1771 the episode ending with the well-known reference to Klopstock). In his labyrinthine confusion, Werther experiences reality only through extremes and opposites; thus he is unable to conceive, let alone reach, an *aurea mediocritas* either in his private life or in his interactions with other characters. Already in his first three letters to Wilhelm, Werther presents his view of the world as bipolar: *past vs. present, city vs. country, worms/small vs. Allmighty/big, deceptive spirits vs. benign spirits*; more generally, *Werther vs. Albert*, and the *Ossianic conception vs. the Homeric tradition*.[25]

It comes as no surprise that the only instance in which Werther is temporarily able to establish some sort of *aurea mediocritas* for himself and overcome dichotomies is when he temporarily establishes his residence at Wahlheim (where else?, the *Heim* of his *Wahl*, the place and *home* of his choosing).[26] Appropriately and not coincidentally, Wahlheim is located about half-way between the unbearable city (civilization) and the edge of the forest (nature) where Lotte lives. Apart from this exception, however, Werther generally views reality through polarities.

In Goethe's novel, Werther loses his mind and loses himself, quite literally, through suicide. He kills himself by blowing his brains out, his very center of thought, thus disintegrating his egocentrical narration. Werther shoots himself because his brain/center cannot be free from its fixation on Lotte, on her image, on her shadow.

Also from a structural point of view, Goethe clues his readers about Werther's obsession for Lotte. In fact, all of the protagonist's letters are addressed to Wilhelm except one—the very central one—which is sent to Lotte. And it is exactly again in this central letter of 20 January 1771 that Werther writes how his very essence of life is missing, that "the leaven which set my life in motion is missing" ["der Sauerteig, der mein Leben in Bewegung setzte, fehlt" (*WA* I, 19: 97)]. Midway through the drama, Werther is already lost in his confusion, in the rotating labyrinth of his own *selva obscura* which forces him to move in circles between his egocentric possessiveness and his desire to obtain the unobtainable.

The protagonist's greatest need is to love Lotte, but in the sense of possessing her.[27] More specifically, Werther views her like a shadow projected on the stage's wall from his *lanterna magica*, hence he can manipulate her image and essence, and deny her a personality and life of her own. As a shadow, she can never develop into a woman for Werther, who will ultimately lose her *because* he coerces her into being no more than a silhouette.

Character Albert, on the other hand, represents Werther's alter ego from several standpoints: even though the reader/spectator of *Werther* knows nothing about Albert's own life previous to his entrance on "scene" in the "play," he has given up his own sense of possessiveness vis-à-vis Lotte in order to accept and love her more dispassionately. In literary tradition, the "happy medium" was reached by those people capable of finding their way out of the *selva obscura* without losing their fortitude (Aeneas and Dante, for instance, but not Orpheus). Or, mankind's peace might be found in the benevolent influence of nature as set in idyllic pastoral landscapes (*loci amoeni*—typical of plays in Arcadia). That which Werther perceives as

Albert's coldness and detachment in his relationship with Lotte is merely Werther's own interpretation of Albert's actions. We might assume, instead, that Albert has achieved a psychological balance, that he has reached his own *aurea mediocritas*. Whatever the reason for Albert's inner balance, it is clear— after readers'/audience's filtering of Werther's point of view—that he deeply cares for both Werther and Lotte. Albert is well aware of the awkward emotional triangle in which the threesome is caught. Yet, Albert respects Lotte profoundly, he does not directly interfere with her life, he does not manipulate her as a shadow when he expresses his desire that the encounters with Werther be less frequent. Albert appears to be immune to jealousy, perhaps because he is himself immune to possessiveness. His *aurea mediocritas*, dignity, and moderation are that which Werther will never attain, as Werther's view is too narrow and the perception of himself too ephemeral. Werther turns hopelessly in circles, while Albert's path is straightforward.

The purpose of this study has been to point out that there are numerous theatrical elements in *Die leiden des jungen Werthers*. The unveiling of such metatextual dimention in Goethe's epistolary novel reveals the possibility of a new or amended reading that further enriches *Werther*'s text. While at first glance, Goethe's work appears to be an epistolary novel, its internal structure reveals close resemblances to a stage drama. The book's division in sections could be interpreted as acts and scenes of a play. Linguistically, its contrasting narrative techniques (omniscient author's point of view *vs.* the voice of an "I-narrator") create the frame for the final catharsis of *Werther*'s "audience." To this effect, Wilhelm's (the fictional editor) strategy mirrors one of the functions of the classical Greek choir. Stage direction and dramatic effects such as chiaroscuro, curtain falls, scene changes, actors' exaggerated gestures and monologues are embedded within the text/script. The psychological traits of Werther and of Albert are partially based in the dramatic canon. Within the frame of an epistolary narration, Goethe created a dramatic structure as core for the narration. Overall, *Die Leiden des jungen Werthers* shows an intriguing and balanced mixture of novel and drama.

Why, then, did not many coeval epistolary novels savor the same kind of literary success that *Werther* enjoyed? Perhaps the intricacies and novelty of Goethe's creation can reveal some of the reasons for which *Werther* survived as a masterpiece for over two-hundred years. Goethe's work is still valid today because *Werther* is a carefully structured novel which contains just as many traditional literary devices as it holds innovative ones.

If *Werther* really were to be performed on stage divided into the three "acts" suggested in this study, some of the subdivisions into "scenes" might be technically difficult to accomplish due to the variety of scenographic effects required in each segment. This holds especially true when considering the brief interval of real-time allowed on stage for changes of scenes within an act. When treated only as a novel, instead, certain time fractures within the text (for instance, the two weeks preceding the June 16 letter in *erstes Buch*) do not disturb the flow of narration: actually, the lack of letters for weeks or even months enhances the work's structure, in that it engages readers' sensitivity and intuition. If performed on stage, temporal *lacunae* would probably interfere with the cohesiveness of the "script." In essence, the stage execution might suffer from a plot divided too rigidly. And it certainly would take an exceptional stage direction to manage such innovative work filled with shadows and fleeting images in the background. To perform *Werther* on stage would entail technical stage effects which would be very complicated to achieve, coupled with a script which would have been deemed too experimental to be performed at the time. Or, even if performed as a one-man show, the lengthy monologue with *laterna magica* projections in the background would have put to test the endurance of any eighteenth-century audience. Goethe must have realized the more advantageous flexibility of an epistolary form.

In conclusion, while Goethe must have consciously embedded numerous dramatic elements in his *Werther*, he gave his work the literary form of an epistolary novel, emphasizing its theatrical kernel. Goethe's *Werther* is, formally speaking, an epistolary novel; however, scholars should not dismiss the benefits of a different critical approach when studying *Werther*.

In light of this stage analysis, the character Werther is no longer seen as only a poor, desperate, hapless *poseur* who manipulates himself and others into self-deceptive depression leading to suicide. Instead, the tremendous amount of control which the protagonist exercises upon himself and upon Goethe's text, and the fact that Werther effectively thwarts and impedes any effort of self-existence in any of the other characters show to the reader/audience that Werther is in fact a strong, egocentric, egoistic, centripetal force in the text. A "black hole" of sorts, all elements rotate around him and his vicissitudes, and eventually are captured and sucked into his "gravitational" literary field. Werther is not a weak victim as postulated by many critics, rather he is so imbued of himself and sees nothing beyond his own world, that he can only color the other characters with his own words. Since the whole novel/play is nothing but a Werther-monologue, no character other than Werther has a chance to survive the text itself. Werther does so by monopolizing the narration, and he is, in the end, terminated by his own power within the text. He is effectively killed by his own monologue: the "black hole" has sucked itself up.

The obvious hints to theatre, to acting and to stage direction hidden within its text/script, enhance our understanding of the incredibly rich texture of this work.

## NOTES

1. My gratitude goes to Sante Matteo of Miami University (Oxford, OH), Valters Nollendorfs, (University of Wisconsin–Madison), and to the staff of Scholarly Publications at Brigham Young University for their insights and suggestions on an earlier version of this manuscript. All translations are mine, unless otherwise noted.

2. Ernst Feise also noticed possible dramatic elements in *Werther*. In one paragraph of his study, he went so far as to call the traditional divisions of the epistolary novel "Akte" (22). However insightful his reading, he failed to recognize the whole theatrical texture and dramatic elements present in Goethe's work.

3. Langen writes that "the stage is nothing more than the natural form of an unframed cut-out image, a show-box on an enlarged scale ... Drama ... basically offers only a sequence of images ... which equate the theater stage with the principle of image-framing" ("Die Schaubühne ist nichts anderes als die natürliche Form des unrahmten Ausschnittbildes, ein Guckkasten in vergrößertem Maßstabe ... Das Drama ... bietet im Grunde nur eine Bilderkette ... diese [ist die] Gleichsetzung von Schaubühne und Prinzip der Rahmenschau" 83).

4. Abbott points out correctly that *Dichtung und Wahrheit* "concentrates most heavily on the period in which *Werther* was written" (42).

5. Goethe's works are quoted in German from the Weimarer Edition, henceforth WA, followed by volume number, and page(s). "Jenes Schauspiel ... beschäftigte bisher den Verfasser nicht allein, sondern, während es ersonnen, geschrieben, umgeschrieben, gedruckt und verbreitet wurde, bewegten sich noch viele andere Bilder und Vorschläge in seinem Geiste. Diejenigen welche dramatisch zu behandeln waren erhielten den Vorzug, am öftersten durchgedacht und der Vollendung angenähert zu werden; allein zu gleicher Zeit entwickelte sich ein Übergang zu einer andern Darstellungsart, welche nicht zu den dramatischen gerechnet zu werden pflegt und doch mit ihnen große Verwandtschaft hat. Dieser Übergang geschah hauptsächlich durch eine Eigenheit des Verfassers, die sogar das Selbstgespräch zum Zwiegespräch umbildete" (*WA* I, 28: 206–7).

6. "Wie nahe ein solches Gespräch im Geiste mit dem Briefwechsel verwandt sei, ist klar genug, nur daß man hier ein hergebrachtes Vertrauen erwidert sieht, und dort ein neues, immer wechselndes, unerwidertes sich selbst zu schaffen weiß. Als daher jener Überdruß zu schildern war, ... mußte der Verfasser sogleich darauf fallen, seine Gesinnung in Briefen darzustellen: ... Der Lebensgenuß anderer ist ihm ein peinlicher Vorwurf, und so wird er durch das, was ihn aus sich selbst herauslocken sollte, in sein Innerstes zurückgewiesen. Mag er sich allenfalls darüber äußern, so wird es durch Briefe geschehn" (*WA* I, 28: 208–9).

7. Critic Buch wrote that "Goethe alluded to the relationship between this narrative technique and drama in *Dichtung und Wahrheit*. The technique is expressed in the illustrations of Chodowiecki—they themselves reminiscent of stage images. In the beginning he has a dramatic treatment of the material in mind ... Today we would speak of discourse based on experience or inner monologue. The modern montage technique is also anticipated in *Werther*. Just as he did in the *Lehrjahren*, Goethe joins together heterogeneous material, which arises from a completely different context" ("Goethe hat, wiederum in 'Dichtung und Wahrheit', auf die Verwandtschaft dieser Erzählweise mit dem Drama hingedeutet, wie sie in den an Bühnenbilder erinnernden Illustrationen von Chodowiecki zum Ausdruck kommt; anfangs schwebte ihm selbst eine dramatische Behandlung des Stoffes vor.... wir würden heute von erlebter Rede oder innerem Monolog sprechen. Auch die moderne Montagetechnik ist im 'Werther' vorweggenommen; ähnlich wie die eingeschalteten Novellen un Maximen in den 'Lehrjahren'... hat Goethe auch heterogenes Material zusammengefügt, das einem ganz anderen Kontext entstammt" Buch 37–38).

And critic Graham notices "What a fascinating transition from the most objective of all literary genres, the drama, to the monologue of the letter, and from Goethe's own inclinations of life to those of the 'pupil of loneliness,' which have fallen prey to *taedium vitae* and to Werther especially.... Werther's letters written in this vein enjoy such a manifold charm, remarks Goethe in conclusion, because their varied content had been discussed in such ideal dialogues with several individuals, but in their composed form appear finally to only one friend and participant" ("Welch ein faszinierender Übergang von dem objektivsten aller literarischen Genres, dem Drama, zu dem Briefmonolog, und von Goethes eigener Lebenszugewandtheit zu jenen 'Zöglingen der Einsamkeit', die dem taedium vitae anheimgefallen sind, und zu *Werther* im besondern! ... 'Jene in diesem Sinne geschriebenen Wertherischen Briefe haben nun wohl deshalb einen so mannigfaltigen Reiz', bemerkte Goethe abschließend, 'weil ihr verschiedener Inhalt erst in solchen ideellen Dialogen mit mehreren

Individuen durchgesprochen worden, sie sodann aber, in der Komposition selbst, nur an *einen* Freund und Teilnehmer gerichtet erscheinen'," Graham 291).

8.  See studies by Kowohl, Müller-Salget and Wellbery on the role of traditional epistolary novels in *Werther*.

9.  See also Doke 22.

10. "Ich spiele mit, vielmehr, ich werde gespielt wie eine Marionette und fasse manchmal meinen Nachbar an der hölzeren Hand und schaudere zurück" (*WA* I, 19: 96–7).

11. For an excellent, intelligent analysis of Werther's self-centeredness in Lacanian terms, see Kuzniar.

12. Chodowiecki and Berger created the portraits of Lotte and Werther for Himburg's editions of 1775 and 1776.

13. "Wilhelm, was ist unserem Herzen die Welt ohne Liebe! Was eine Zauberlaterne ist ohne Licht! Kaum bringst du das Lämpchen hinein, so scheinen dir die buntesten Bilder an deine weiße Wand! Und wenn's nichts wäre als das, als vorübergehende Phantome, so macht's doch immer unser Glück, wenn wir wie frische Jungen davor stehen und uns über die Wundererscheinungen entzücken." (*WA* I, 19: 55).

14. "O daß ich launisch sein könnte, könnte die Schuld auf's Wetter, auf einen Dritten, auf eine fehlgeschlagene Unternehmung schieben, so würde die unerträgliche Last des Unwillens doch nur halb auf mir ruhen. Wehe mir! Ich fühle zu wahr, daß an mir allein alle Schuld liegt—nicht Schuld! Genug daß in mir die Quelle alles Elendes verborgen ist wie ehemals die Quelle aller Seligkeiten." (*WA* I, 19: 127–8).

15. Moreover, as Doke pointed out, the very structure of *Werther* is based upon the subjectiveness and ego-centeredness of the main character (12). Without these, the novel as is would not exist.

16. "Oft werden die Stiche durch den Guckkasten, dieses psychologisch wichtigste Symbol der Zeit, betrachtet," Langen 87; and "erst der junge Goethe und die Geniezeit sieht in ihm. [dem Guckkasten] wieder einen künstlerischen Wert," Langen 88.

17. "Die behandelten Situationsbildchen etwa unterscheiden sich wenig von dem zeitgenössichen Bühnenbild. Beide Male ist das Ausschnitthafte des Sehens, der Rahmen um die Situation, das Entscheidende und didaktisch Wertvolle" (Langen 88).

18. This essay does not intend to claim that Goethe is proto-Brechtian!

19. The very suggestive theory of a tyrannical mother from whom Werther flees is only outlined by Spann: "As far as can be ascertained, none

of the commentators in the past have realized that Werther did not leave home in the way that one would expect of a man in his twenties, but that he had, literally, run away from his widowed mother. In fact, he communicates with her only about business matters and money; he does not notify her about the important events in his life, e.g., the acceptance of a position at court and his resignation half a year later. He does not even leave a last note for her before his suicide, but includes the few words: 'Liebe Mutter, verzieht mir!' in the last note to his friend.... As soon as his father died she had taken her son, still a child, away from the little town he calls 'lieb und vertraulich' in order to lock herself up in the city which to Werther is 'unertraglich' ... Werther too shows his protest in his attire: a simple blue coat, a yellow waistcoat, breech and riding boots" (77).

20. The theme of "empty embrace" has been studied by Fetzer who shows the differences between the two empty hugs at the end of *erstes Buch* and of *zweites Buch*, and compares them to the unsuccessful hug which Werther tries to give to Lotte after they kiss. Fetzer views Lotte not as a woman, rather as the projection of the woman whom Werther wants to see in her, hence his title: "Schatten ohne Frau" ("Shadows without Woman"). I propose that Fetzer's point can be taken further by postulating that Lotte's shadow is the only part of her that appears on "stage." She *is* merely a projected image (cfr. letter of 20 Jan., 1772: "Wie ich herein trat, überfiel mich Ihre Gestalt, ihr Andenken, o Lotte!" ["The moment I entered, your image came to my mind—O Lotte—your memories!"], or *incipit* of letter of 6 Dec., 1772: "Wie mich die Gestalt verfolgt!" ["How her image haunts me!" transl. Lange 65]).

21. "They walked down the avenue. I stood gazing after them in the moonlight, then threw myself on the ground, and wept, sprang up, and ran out on the terrace, and there below in the shade of the linden trees I saw her white frock gleaming as she disappeared near the garden gate. I stretched out my arms, and she vanished" (transl. Lange 41). "Sie gingen die Allee hinaus, ich stand, sah ihnen nach im Mondscheine und warf mich an die Erde und weinte mich aus und sprang auf und lief auf die Terrasse hervor und sah noch dort unten im Schatten der hohen Lindenbäume ihr weißes Kleid nach der Gartenthür schimmern; ich streckte meine Arme aus, und es verschwand" (*WA* I, 19: 86).

22. "Was ist der Mensch, der gepriesene Halbgott! Ermangeln ihm nicht eben da die Kräfte, wo er sie am nöthigsten braucht? Und wenn er in Freude sich aufschwingt oder im Leiden versinkt, wird er nicht in beiden eben da aufgehalten, eben da zu dem stumpfen kalten Bewußtsein wieder zurückgebracht, da er sich in der Fülle des Unendlichen zu verlieren sehnte?" (*WA* I, 19: 140).

23. "... als Lotte den Kutscher halten, und ihre Brüder herabsteigen ließ, die noch einmal ihre Hand zu küssen begehrten, das denn der älteste mit aller Zärtlichkeit, die dem Alter von fünfzehn Jahren eigen sein kann, der andere mit viel Heftigkeit und Leichtsinn that. Sie ließ die Kleinen noch einmal grüßen und wir fuhren weiter." (*WA* I, 19: 28).

"Die klügste setzte sich in eine Ecke, mit dem Rücken gegen das Fenster, und hielt die Ohren zu! Eine andere kniete vor ihr nieder und verbarg den Kopf in der ersten Schoos. Eine dritte schob sich zwischen beide hinein und umfaßte ihre Schwesterchen mit tausend Thränen." (*WA* I, 19: 34).

"Ich nahm das Schnupftuch vor die Augen und verließ die Gesellschaft, und nur Lottens Stimme, die mir rief: wie wollten fort, brachte mich zu mir selbst." (*WA* I, 19: 48).

"Sie gingen die Allee hinaus, ich stand, sah ihnen nach im Mondscheine und warf mich an die Erde und weinte mich aus und sprang auf und lief auf die Terrasse hervor und sah noch dort unten im Schatten der hohen Lindenbäume ihr weißes Kleid nach der Gartenthür schimmern; ich streckte meine Arme aus, und es verschwand." (*WA* I, 19: 86).

"Die Lippen und Augen Werthers glühten an Lottens Arme; ein Schauer überfiel sie; sie wollte sich entfernen und Schmerz und Anteil lagen betäubend wie Blei auf ihr. Sie athmete sich zu erholen, und bat ihn schluchzend fortzufahren, bat mit der ganzen Stimme des Himmels! Werther zitterte, sein Herz wollte bersten, er hob das Blatt auf und las halb gebrochen." (*WA* I, 19: 175).

24. What has been ascribed to Goethe, in this depiction of Werther's death, is to a great extent Goethe's quotation from a letter that Kestner wrote to him, describing details of Jerusalem's death. Goethe did make some significant changes, but the often-cited cryptic ending and the Emilia Galotti reference are straight out of Kestner.

"Morgens um Sechse tritt der Bediente herein mit dem Lichte. Er findet seinen Herrn an der Erde, die Pistole und Blut. Er ruft, er faßt ihn an; keine Antwort, er röchelte nur noch ... Über dem rechten Auge hatte er sich durch den Kopf geschossen, das Gehirn was herausgetrieben ... Der alte Amtmann kam auf die Nachricht herein gesprengt, er küßte den Sterbenden unter den heißesten Thränen. Seine ältesten Söhne kamen bald nach ihm zu Fuße, sie fielen neben dem Bette nieder im Ausdrucke des unbändigsten Schmerzens, küßten ihm die Hände und den Mund, und der ält'ste, den er immer am meisten geliebt, hing an seinen Lippen, bis er verschieden war und man den Knaben mit Gewalt wegriß" (*WA* I, 19: 190–91).

25. *Vergangen vs. Gegenwart, Stadt vs. Natur, Würmchen vs. Allmächtigen, täuschende Geister vs. wohltätige Geister.*

26. See also Furst 149.

27. "All this passes away, but no eternity could extinguish the [glowing life] which was kindled yesterday by your lips, and which now burns within me. She loves me! These arms have embraced her, these lips have trembled upon hers. [This mouth stammered on her] She is mine! Yes, Charlotte, you are mine forever!" (transl. Lange 82, with some corrections by me) ["Alles das ist vergänglich; aber keine Ewigkeit soll das glühende Leben auslöchen, das ich gestern auf deinen Lippen genoß, das ich in mir fühle! Sie liebt mich! Dieser Arm hat sie umfaßt, diese Lippen haben auf ihren Lippen gezittert, dieser Mund hat an dem ihrigen gestammelt. Sie ist mein! du bist mein! ja, Lotte, auf ewig" (*WA* I, 19: 179–180)].

And, as Lotte's correctly observes: "O why were you born with that excessive, that ungovernable passion for everything that [you ever touch]? ... I fear, I fear that it is only the impossibility of possessing me that makes your desire for me so strong" (transl. Lange 72, with a correction by me) ["O, warum mußten Sie mit dieser Heftigkeit, dieser unbezwinglich haftenden Leidenschaft für alles, was Sie einmal anfassen, geboren werden! ... Ich fürchte, ich fürchte, es ist nur die Unmöglichkeit mich zu besitzen, die Ihnen diesen Wunsch so reizend macht." (*WA* I, 19: 156–57)].

## Works Cited and Consulted

Abbott, Scott. "The Semiotics of Young Werther." *Goethe Yearbook* 6 (1991): 41–65.

Batley, Edward. "Werther's Final Act of Alienation: Goethe, Lessing, and Jerusalem on the Poetry and the Truth of Suicide." *The Modern Language Review* 87 (1992): 868–878.

Buch, Hans Christoph, ed. *Die Leiden des Jungen Werthers*. By Johann Wolfgang von Goethe. Berlin: Verlag Klaus Wagenbach, 1982.

Cody, Richard. *The Landscape of the Mind: Pastoralism and Platonic Theory in Tasso's Aminta and Shakespeare's Early Comedies*. Oxford: Clarendon Press, 1969.

Doke, Tadamichi. "Zur literarischen Methode der «Leiden des jungen Werther»." *Goethe Jahrbuch* 91 (1974): 11–23.

Dye, R. Ellis. "Werther's Lotte: Views of the Other in Goethe's First Novel." *Journal of English and Germanic Philology* 87 (1988): 492–506.

Ehrentreich, Alfred. "An die Peripherie von Goethes «Werther»." *Goethe Jahrbuch* 100 (1983): 266–271.

Feise, Ernst. "Zur Entstehung, Problem und Technik von Goethes 'Werther'." *Journal of English and German Philology* 13 (1914): 1–36.

Fetzer, John. "Schatten ohne Frau: Marginalia on a Werther Motif." *The Germanic Review* 46 (1971): 87–94.

Flax, Niel M. "Goethe's *Faust II* and the Experimental Theatre of His Time." *Comparative Literature* 31 (1979): 154–166.

———. "The Presence of the Sign in Goethe's *Faust*." *PMLA* 98 (1983): 183–203.

Furst, Lilian R. "The 'Imprisoning Self': Goethe's Werther and Rousseau's Solitary Walker." *European Romanticism, Literary Cross-Currents, Modes and Models*, Gerhart Hoffmeister, ed. (Detroit: Wayne State U.P., 1990): 145–161.

Goethe, Johann Wolfgang von. *From My Life. Poetry and Truth. Parts One to Three*. transl. by Robert R. Heitner. Thomas P. Saine and Jeffrey L. Sammons eds., *Goethe's Collected Works*, vol. 4. New York: Suhrkamp, 1987.

———. *The Sorrows of Young Werther*. transl. by Victor Lange. David E. Wellbery ed., *Goethe's Collected Works*, vol 11. New York: Suhrkamp, 1988.

———. *Werke*. Weimarer Ausgabe. 133 vols. Weimar, 1877–1919.

Gräf, Hans G. *Goethe ueber seine Dichtungen*. 9 vol. Frankfurt a/M: Rütten & Loening, 1902.

Graham, Ilse. "Goethes eigener Werther." *Jahrbuch der deutschen Schillergesellschaft* 18 (1974): 268–303.

Kowohl, Carla Sabine. "Genesi e struttura de *I dolori del giovane Werther*." *Humanitas. Rivista bimestrale di cultura* n.s. 37 (1982): 434–454, and 592–622.

Kuzniar, Alice A. "The Misinterpretation of Self: Werther versus Goethe." *Mosaic, A Journal for Interdisciplinary Study of Literature* 22/2 (1989): 15–28.

Langen, August. *Anschauungsformen in der deutschen Dichtung des 18. Jahrhunderts: Rahmenschau und Rationalismus*. Darmstadt: Wissenschaftliche Buchgesellschaft, 1965. (Unveränderter reprografischer Nachdruck der Ausgabe Jena, 1934.)

Lederer, Max. "Goethe und das Theater." *Neophilologus*. (1936): 202–212.

Molnar, Géza von. "Confinement or Containment: Goethe's *Werther* and the Concept of Limitation." *German Life & Letters* n.s. 23 (1970): 226–234.

Müller-Salget, Klaus. "Zur Struktur von Goethes *Werther*." *Deutsche Philologie* 100 (1981): 527–544.

Nolan, Erika. "Goethes «Die Leiden des jungen Werthers»: Absicht und Methode." *Jahrbuch der deutschen Schillergesellschaft* 28 (1984): 191–222.

Rickes, Joachim. "Das 'Gewittermotiv' in Goethes *Werther* — motivtheoretisch betrachtet." *Wirkendes Wort* 42 (1992): 406–420.

Ryder, Frank G. "Season, Day, and Hour — Time as Metaphor in Goethe's *Werther*." *Journal of English and Germanic Philology* 63 (1964): 389–407.

Schmiedt, Helmut (ed.). *"Wie froh bin ich, da ich weg bin!" Goethes Roman Die Leiden des jungen Werthers in literaturpsychologischer Sicht*. Würzburg: Königshausen & Neumann, 1989.

Siebers, Tobin. "The Werther Effect: The Esthetics of Suicide." *Mosaic, A Journal for the Comparative Study of Literatures and Ideas* 26/1 (1993): 15–34.

Skonnord, John. "Act and Artifact: Narrative Procedure in *Werther*." *Journal of English and Germanic Philology* 78 (1979): 157–177.

Sondrup, Steven. "Wertherism and *Die Leiden des jungen Werther*." *European Romanticism, Literary Cross-Currents, Modes and Models*, Gerhart Hoffmeister, ed. (Detroit: Wayne State U.P., 1990): 163–179.

Spann, Meno. "'Werther' Revisited: Two Hundred Years of a Masterpiece." *Mosaic, A Journal for the Comparative Study of Literature and Ideas* 5 (1972): 73–83.

Vincent, Deirdre. *Werther's Goethe and the Game of Creativity*. Toronto–Buffalo–London: University of Toronto Press, 1992.

Walker, Colin. "Werther, the Good Samaritan and the Pharisees." *German Life & Letters* 41 (1987–88): 393–401.

Wellbery, Caroline. "From Mirrors to Images: The Transformation of Sentimental Paradigms in Goethe's *The Sorrows of Young Werther*." *Studies in Romanticism* 25 (1986): 231–249.

BRIGITTE PEUCKER

# The Material Image
# in Goethe's Wahlverwandtschaften

As its baffled readers may be only too well aware, the *Wahlverwandtschaften* (1809) were written during a period in Goethe's career that is characterized, as Victor Lange puts it, by a "paradoxe Verschränkung von scheinbar widersprüchlichen Kunst- und Denkformen" (337). In my essay I will take up these seemingly contradictory attitudes concerning the nature of the work of art, emphasizing an impulse in art that is antithetical to the attitudes of classicism and that is nevertheless closely tied to it: the question of the relation of the real to representation. As a text, Goethe's novel is constantly at pains to play out this relation, be it in the domain of natural signs that is the landscape garden or in the variety of aesthetic projects that juxtapose the figured presence of the body with the signs used in its representation or ornamentation. Indeed, Goethe's novel might be said to construct a testing ground for theories of representation involving the relation of the image to materiality.[1] From 1796, the time of Goethe's reading of Diderot's *Salon* of 1765 and the "Essay on Painting," through the publication of Goethe's own essays on painting in *Ueber Kunst und Altertum* in 1816–17, Goethe formulates and reformulates his ideas concerning the place of mimesis in the visual arts.

From *The Germanic Review* 74, no. 3. © 1999 by Helen Dwight Reid Educational Foundation.

## I. THE NATURAL ATTITUDE

In the programmatic introduction to his short-lived journal on art, the *Propyläen* of 1798, Goethe is at pains to distinguish between what he takes to be a desirable form of mimesis, one that strives for "Kunstwahrheit," and an undesirable, inferior form of mimesis—one perpetuated by an artist "der einem blinden Trieb folgt"—a mimesis whose aim is the excessive appearance of naturalness (*Schriften* 149). It is this same issue of mimetic adequacy and of the boundaries between art and nature, not surprisingly, that occupies center stage in what Goethe calls a "ein Gesprach, das auf der Grenze zwischen dem Reiche der Toten und Lebendigen geführt wird," a "conversation" with Diderot that Goethe conducts in the interpolated commentary that accompanies his partial translation of Diderot's "Essay on Painting" (*Schriften* 149).[2] The urgency of this eighteenth-century issue is revived for Goethe as he struggles in the *Propyläen* to defend his aesthetics against the romantic attitudes assumed by the Schlegels in the *Athenäum*. It is a moment when he sees himself embattled both by the "imitators"—"die Nachahmer"— and the Romantic "imaginers," or "Imaginanten" (*Schriften* 319).

It is in the *Propyläen*, too, that we find "Der Sammler und die Seinigen," the short epistolary novelette in which Goethe, with the help of Schiller, amusingly distinguishes among a variety of attitudes toward visual representation.[3] The novelette begins with a portrait of the sensibility that Goethe understands by the term "Nachahmer" and recounts the story, humorously portrayed, of a collector whose interests extend only to one kind of art: "ihn erfreute die genaue Nachahmung der natürlichen Dinge" (*Schriften* 263). The collector's desire for representations of the natural world begins with precise sketches of *natures mortes*, of still-lifes of flowers, butterflies, shells: All objects of significance from kitchen, garden, or fields are fixed—"fixiert"—on paper (263). Gradually the collector's preoccupation with images of natural objects evolves into a desire to surround himself with portraits of beloved family members and friends, then expands to encompass the need for life-sized representations of his family and of himself: "akkurat wie er sich im Spiegel sah" (264). Later, he insists that all family members be painted in their most natural, characteristic stance, amid the objects by which they are customarily surrounded, thus combining the genres of portrait and still-life into a "slice-of-life" painting. Next, the obsession with precise reproduction leads the collector to commission a trompe l'oeil portrait of himself and his wife located behind a false door,[4] executed in accordance with all the rules of perspective, for whose sake a window is moved so that the light falling on the portrait will enhance the illusion.

The collector's desire for the real leads him onward until his mimetic drive—his "blinder Trieb," as Goethe puts it—culminates in the commission of a life-sized wax figure of himself derived from a plaster cast of his living face, clothed in an actual wig and dressing gown, and as his son says, "so stizt der Alte noch jetzt hinter einem Vorhange, den ich vor Ihnen nicht aufzuziehen wagte" (*Schriften* 268). The "Nachahmer," in his obsession with the simulation of life through lifelike representation, is well on his way toward creating the automata that populate Hoffmann's tales and, in so doing, evokes in his son the responses that Freud associates with the uncanny. Interestingly, Goethe's representation of the "Nachahmer" as collector uncannily evokes the real-life painting and collecting practices of a late eighteenth-century American painter, Charles Willson Peale. Peale, as Susan Stewart suggests, in those practices explored "the cognitive boundary between displaying death and displaying life ... through various devices of trompe l'oeil" (42). Two such works in particular recall Goethe's collector. In 1787, Peale had begun to trick visitors to his museum by placing a realistic, life-sized wax figure of himself there (Stewart 44). Later, in 1795, Peale exhibited a life-sized trompe l'oeil portrait of his two sons climbing a staircase—a painting that he insisted be displayed in a doorway and to which a real step was added as an extension of the painted step. Had Goethe known Peale's work, it would probably have met with the same fascinated and slightly horrified disapproval that we find in his attitude toward the projects of his fictional "imitator."

Goethe also looks with scorn on the strict imitation of nature elsewhere in the *Propyläen*, notably in "Über Wahrheit und Wahrscheinlichkeit der Kunstwerke." This dialogue, constructed around a debate between a "Zuschauer" and an "Anwalt des Künstlers," concerns a work of art, a theater set on which theater boxes with spectators have been painted. It is here, in particular, that Goethe's dialogue takes on the character of a dispute with Diderot, for what the painted figures disrupt is the self-forgetting of the spectators whose activities they mirror. As the "Zuschauer" would have it, the "real" spectators in their boxes are incensed at being confronted with facsimiles of themselves in the act of viewing, since this representation offends against the dictum of naturalness that should, according to the "Zuschauer," extend to all aspects of stage productions. The "Zuschauer" speaks in what we might call the voice of Diderot and claims that the self-conscious artifice of the set creates a space in which theatricality will necessarily flourish.[5] The advocate of the artist, on the other hand, argues against the primitive nature of a sensibility that demands strict mimesis from the work of art, claiming that works of art need not seem real ("wahr scheinen"), but need have only the appearance of reality, "einen Schein des Wahren" (*Schriften* 176–77). Indeed, in this wordplay itself the advocate of the artist points to the necessary action of the *Geist* that must figure in both the creation of genuine art and its reception. The witty specularity of the painted spectator figures is likened to the play of verbal wit, underlining the contention that both linguistic and visual signs are arbitrary, and hence calling into question the eighteenth-century notion that the signs of painting are natural.

As we might conclude from his engagement with "Naturwahrheit" and "Kunstwahrscheinlichkeit" in the translation of the "Essay on Painting," Goethe seems to have misunderstood Diderot's notion of the "natural" in art as tantamount to the obsessive realism that Goethe satirizes in his imitator.[6] We can infer that Goethe, like the advocate of the artist, believes that "das Kunstwahre und das Naturwahre völlig verschieden sei und, dass der Künstler keineswegs streben sollte, dass sein Werk eigentlich als ein Naturwerk erscheine" (*Schriften* 178). Once more the artist is enjoined against the making of exact copies. Indeed, in the dialogue between spectator and advocate, one of the examples used to illustrate the grave limitations imposed on the work of art by realism alludes to Pliny's famous account of the contest between Zeuxis and Parrhasios, confined to a brief allusion to "die Vögel, die nach des Meisters Kirschen flogen" and to the (canonical) suggestion that only such inferior creatures as birds can be fooled into believing the fruit to be real (*Schriften* 179). During the contest with Parrhasios, Zeuxis is said to have created a bunch of grapes so true to nature that it lured a flock of birds out of the sky to taste the fruit.[7] Zeuxis's still-life, a trompe l'oeil of the first order, tricked the birds into attempting to enter the space of the painting to taste the fruit—grapes, not cherries, as Goethe would have it (Bryson, *Looking at the Overlooked* 30). Although Goethe is mistaken in equating Diderot's attitude toward the natural with that of his own "Nachahmer," a pronounced interest in bringing the real into the space of representation (in the form of the beholder's fictive entry into the painting) and in bringing the represented into the space of the real world figures importantly in Diderot's *Salons*.

Lest his reader should miss his point, Goethe further satirizes the hapless birds who sought refreshment in Zeuxis' painting—and any beholders who confuse representation with the real—in what he calls "a more recent story," which I quote in full:

Ein grosser Naturforscher besass, unter seinen Haustieren, einen Affen, den er einst vermisste, und nach langern Suchen in der Bibliothek fand. Dort sass das Tier an der Erde, und hatte die Kupfer eines ungebundenen naturgeschichtlichen Werkes um sich her zerstreut. Erstaunt über dieses eifrige Studium des Hausfreundes, nahte sich der Herr, und sah zu seiner Verwunderung und zu seinem Verdruss, dass der genäschige Affe die sämtlichen Kaefer, die er hie und da abgebildet gefunden, herausgespeist habe. (*Schriften* 180)

Much to the naturalist's chagrin, the ape is not engaged in reading the text; he is engaged in eating its illustrations, thereby aptly illustrating his incapacity to understand the nature of signs.

As a preoccupation of the literary imagination, the tantalizing gap between word and thing has had a long history, one that suggests that the desire to forge a merger between the "real" and representation has been one of the aims of writing from its beginnings. An awareness of the disjunction between the factuality of the real in general and the inability of language not only to represent it but somehow to cross over into the domain of the real informs fiction and poetry alike. In the visual arts, trompe l'oeil effects aim for the kind of ontological boundary crossing that is suggested in the moments when writing aspires to invade, to incorporate, or to be a thing: It is the desire to join the realm of the real with that of representation that engenders trompe l'oeil in painting. The Zeuxis and Parrhasios story, recounted in Pliny's *Natural History* and cited through the centuries, attests to a parallel fascination with this problem on the part of the visual arts and the writing about them, launching what Norman Bryson calls "the natural attitude" (*Vision and Painting* 3).

The story of Zeuxis is one that Diderot undoubtedly had in mind in his evocation of Chardin's still-lifes in the *Salon* of 1763, which Goethe may not have known (Mortier 264–65). Of these paintings Diderot writes: "you have only to put out your hand and you can pick up those biscuits and eat them, that orange and cut it and squeeze it, that glass of wine and drink it, those fruits and peel them" (*Selected Writings* 150). It is as though, Diderot continues, the still-lifes were painted with the substance of the things themselves: "Oh, Chardin! It is not white or red or black you mix on your palette, it is the very substance of things themselves" (*Selected Writings* 150). Clearly, what is at issue in these anecdotes is not merely the question of realistic representation, of tricking the eye. Satirically in the case of Goethe's ape, playfully in Diderot's description, the situations recounted here have a significance beyond the question of the beholder's entry into the space of representation. What is figured in each of these narratives via the metaphor of ingestion is nothing less than the anxious attempt to redeem these *natures mortes* by means of the rhetorical claim that they are not representations of natural objects but natural objects themselves; what is figured additionally is the attempted union of the beholder with the image. It is not merely the question of the realism of Zeuxis's painting that is intriguing, not simply the fact that it launches the "natural attitude" toward painting, a point of view that stresses painting's "reduplicative mission" (Bryson, *Vision and Painting* 3). Rather, Pliny's narrative is so essentially fascinating because it provides us with an early instance of one of the drives that fuel the visual and verbal arts alike: the drive to merge the real with the represented. Most obviously operative in theater, which uses the living body as the vehicle of dramatic performance, this drive finds its satisfaction in the *frisson* generated when life and art or, more broadly, reality and art, purport to be continuous. It is this fascination with the relation of the image to the real—and with the materiality of the image—that the *Wahlverwandtschaften* variously play out.

## II. THE REPRESSION OF THE PICTURESQUE

This juxtaposition of the image with the real is one of the primary features of picturesque aesthetics. It is evident, for instance, in the confusion as to whether the picturesque as a category should properly be confined to descriptions of paintings (the position of Richard Payne Knight), or whether it is founded in the nature of things (the position of Uvedale Price). In Price's famous and amusing "Dialogue," much is made of the manner in which its fictional participants, two of whom are based on Price and his opponent Knight, compare real scenes with paintings in a collection that they view—a device, as one scholar notes, "which permits that double comparison of art and nature which is somehow involved, essentially or accidentally, in every conception of the picturesque" (Hippel 279). During the course of this "Dialogue," the exponents of Knight and Price are at pains to compare the image and the real in varying degrees.

Beyond its earliest definition as a painterly view of nature, the picturesque is the site of territorial interpretative struggles from the 1780s to roughly 1810. By descriptive rather than analytical means, Price, Knight, and William Gilpin—though by no means in agreement—developed the notion of the picturesque from what is certainly its origin in Addison's Uncommon. The picturesque, like Addison's earlier term, is associated with an interest in variety, as when Gilpin, echoing Addison, says of the Lake District that its picturesque landscape "strike[s] the mind with a thousand opposing ideas" (Watkin 48). And it is primarily irregularity—irregularity of contour, of lighting and of surface—that is thought to provide such variety. Through the writings of Uvedale Price especially, the picturesque comes to be defined by its tactility, its dependence on variegated textures as the greatest source of its visual interest. One frequently cited example refers to the picturesque quality of the rough and shaggy coats of goats; the cow, too, is considered picturesque, especially, as Gilpin puts it, "in the months of April and May, when the old coat is coming off" (Hussey 119).

The interest in the shaggy coats of animals evinces a concern with natural process that lurks just under the surface of descriptions of picturesque natural and painterly scenes, a concern specifically with the "effects of age and decay" that establishes the temporal axis of the picturesque (Martin Price 281). It is in part their connection with decay and process that explains the overwhelming fascination of the picturesque with ruins, structures on which time has wrought its texture-creating effects. We find it in the combination of natural and artificial that lends ruins their peculiar status as "sacred things ... rooted for ages in the soil" (Hussey 196). At once the product of art and nature, the ruin as structure is created by man, but gradually, as it is transformed by natural process, the ruin takes on a life of its own. As Uvedale Price puts it, "The more broken, weather-stained, and decayed the stone and brickwork, the more the plants and creepers seem to have fastened and rooted in between their joints" (qtd. in Hussey 179). Natural growth had, of course, already been read as the "ornament of Time" in Gilpin's description of Tintern Abbey, where Time is seen to work as a colorist and where mosses and lichens are said to "give those full-blown tints which add the richest finishing to a ruin" (qtd. in Hussey 117). It has been pointed out that the picturesque interest in the effects of natural process not only includes animals and such objects as ruins, but also extends to the aging process in human beings (Martin Price 282). As a focus of interest for the picturesque sensibility, inanimate object and person are often interchangeable. Indeed, Uvedale Price writes with equal fervor concerning "incrustations" on the surface of ruins and potential "incrustations" on the teeth of a parson's daughter (Hussey 74).

Autumn is the season most appropriate to the picturesque, "the painter's season," as Uvedale Price puts it, with his taste for the autumnal tints of the Venetian school, of Titian and Gorgione (qtd. in Hussey 43). But the passage of time will reduce the picturesque beauty of the parson's daughter, for example, to a state beyond the mere threat of "incrustations," a state that exceeds the boundaries of the picturesque. Autumn and twilight clearly emblematize human aging in its progress toward death, but the subliminal awareness that death is the culmination of natural process tends in most cases to be aestheticized by the theoreticians of the picturesque, covered over by the values of art. In Price's *Dialogue*, a carcass in a butcher shop is redeemed because it displays "the blended variety of mellow tints" reminiscent of a similar image in Rembrandt (qtd. in Hussey 77).[8] Similarly, though much earlier, in 1763, Diderot's description of Chardin's "Gutted Skate" ends with an exhortation to painters to learn from Chardin to "redeem the distastefulness that is present in certain natural objects" (*Selected Writings* 150). Interestingly, Diderot's admiration for the textures of Chardin's paintings, for their areas of thick layering or *impasto*, anticipates the interest in such texturing by painters who exemplify the picturesque for theorists of the next generation. Texture is, of course, a quality that we tend to associate with objecthood. As a consequence, when the emphasis on texture is carried over into painting by way of *impasto*, we can read in this technique the unrealizable desire to lend the two-dimensional image the three-dimensional quality of the object.

The emblematizing of death forms an integral part of the power of the picturesque. As we know, the picturesque design in landscape gardening and in architecture called for the building of suitable ruins, should none be available, though not all men of fashion took the extreme measures taken by Mr. Tyers, proprietor of Vauxhall. As part of his "garden of ideas," Mr. Tyers had a "Valley of the Shadow of Death" built on his estate, equipped with "coffins instead of columns, and skulls agreeably scattered about" (qtd. in Hussey 159). As early as 1752, the architect William Chambers made a drawing in which he depicted one of his proposed buildings as a ruin, surrounded by natural growth. This building, a structure eroded by Time, was appropriately designed as a mausoleum (Watkin 56). As Ann Bermingham puts it, the "love of the ruined and dilapidated" that characterizes the picturesque is often accompanied by an "elegiac mood and graveyard melancholy" (70).

The tension between the image and the real is also present in the central claim of landscape gardeners that their art paints in natural signs. When the characters of the *Wahlverwandtschaften* undertake to landscape the estate, their projects are reminiscent of Repton, who wished to imitate nature so successfully in his gardens that the eye could not distinguish between the natural and the artificial. Goethe's novel mildly satirizes this aim in the figure of an English traveler always equipped with his *camera obscura* who epitomizes the spectatorial attitude toward nature and who, "als er die

Gegend vorher nicht gekannt, und was man daran getan, von dem, was die Natur geliefert, kaum zu unterscheiden wusste" (197).[9] But when Goethe's characters consult works on landscape design with engravings of original and "improved" scenes reminiscent of Repton's Red Books, the nature of the projects that they will undertake tells us that these drawings are primarily in the mode of Capability Brown, to whose insistence on smooth contours advocates of the picturesque objected so strenuously.[10] In the manner of Capability Brown, Goethe's characters join three small lakes into one larger one, cut away an angle of a cliff to create "eine schoen geschwungene Wendung," (23–24) and clear the undergrowth out from under clumps of trees.

Perhaps because Humphry Repton's landscape gardens are allowed to accommodate the picturesque in a limited way (Hippel 225), one picturesque locale in the emblematic landscape of the novel remains unimproved: The old wooden mill hidden in a crag with its surrounding undergrowth and moss-covered rocks. As a wilderness, it is a region of danger in the narrative, the place that first evokes in Eduard the desire to clasp Ottilie in his arms, the place where he persuades her to remove the portrait of her father that hangs around her neck. In laying aside the portrait, Ottilie lays aside the paternal order, causing Eduard to feel "als wenn sich eine Scheidewand zwischen ihm und Ottilien niedergelegt hätte" (56). The mill's collapsed wall metaphorically creates a picturesque "ruin" and it is here, in the "unimproved," "uncontrolled" landscape of the picturesque that Ottilie first symbolically strays from what she takes to be her "proper path" and allows the sequence of events that culminates in three deaths to unfold. In his essay on the *Wahlverwandtschaften*, Walter Benjamin reminds us that the mill is traditionally emblematic of the underworld (71), and we might add that it is a site of danger and death in the German romantic lyric as well.

It is also no doubt in a struggle with the picturesque that Charlotte, who initiates the interest in landscape architecture, makes the somewhat astonishing "improvement" that raises protest later on: In accordance with what the narrator suggests are the demands of sensibility, she levels the grounds of the churchyard, removes all the grave markers, arranges them in orderly fashion along the church wall, and sows the resulting field with clover. Charlotte's intention, we are told, is to make the churchyard a place "auf dem das Auge und die Einbildungskraft gerne verweilten" (15), to give it "eine heitere und würdige Ansicht" by creating a decorative surface "mit verschiedenen Arten Klee besät, der auf das schönste grünte und blühte" (127). Charlotte's bold gesture replaces the rough and rugged picturesque with the smooth contours, gay colors, cheerfulness, and fertility of the landscape of the beautiful. In Goethe's novel, in which even the smallest detail is made to do a great deal of work, it should come as no surprise that a character who undertakes a project such as Charlotte's should also be unusually aware of "den Grünspan kupferner Gefässe" (30), of the incrustations and deposits that signal the threatening aspect of natural process and the effects of time. No elegiac sentiment, no churchyard melancholy, is to be allowed the spectator of Charlotte's churchyard scene: rather, the scene suggests a pastoral idyll with the pastor and his wife presiding, as the text tells us, as Philemon and Baucis.

Many of Charlotte's neighbors are outraged at the radical separation of grave marker from body that this "improvement" accomplishes. The grave markers themselves, having formerly served the double function of commemorating the site of natural process below and of standing over and against that process, are now arranged and ordered and have become aesthetic objects on display, signs divorced from their referents. The presence of death in this scene is confined to an awareness of the "et in arcadia ego" (Faber 105) that pastoral seeks to contain under the smooth surface of green meadows. Death is, as Benjamin suggests, consigned to the depths, banished "in die Tiefe" (67). In Goethe's text, the picturesque in its relation to time and to death is successfully repressed: the verdigris on copper pots is rubbed off, and the decaying body is covered over, unmarked. When visible, the human corpse takes on the more enduring qualities of the work of art. The fear of death—the desire to stay its effect, to preserve the body—is repeatedly attached to the problem of representation in this novel. Here, at least in part, is one reason for Goethe's prohibition against the making of exact copies, for they produce the uncanny effects that underline rather than cover over the relation of representation to death.

## III. DEATH MASKS; CONTACT RELICS; ACHEIROPOETOI

The architect's pronouncement concerning death masks, whose metonymic relation to the body is traditionally said to give them something of the status of "natural objects," is a case in point, as is the architect's somewhat macabre collection of "Nachbildungen und Entwürfe von alten Grabmonoumenten" (133). Although the architect himself is something of a copyist, then, be concedes that although no form of art may produce a more exact copy than that produced by a death mask, death masks are, among all forms of representation, the least likely to lend the impression of living forms—

lebende Formen"—to the portrait busts produced by using them (130). Further, the debate in this novel concerning the function of portraits as monuments and, more grotesquely, the art object that Ottilie's corpse—preserved under glass—becomes, attest to an excessive preoccupation with death that is only partially naturalized as a fashionable concern of the period with its origins in the picturesque.

Like Charlotte, who transforms grave markers into decorative objects, the architect is anxious to divorce his extensive collection of gravemound artifacts from their ritual significance. Unearthed, arranged neatly for display, these artifacts no longer retain the status of natural object that they metonymically acquired in the grave, but are aestheticized, "cleansed" of their connection to the body that had naturalized them, and now function as works of art.[11] The architect's picturesque interest in monuments and memorials is grounded in his self-conscious awareness of the distance that exists in the modern period between the mourner and the body of the beloved. Because it is no longer possible "die Reste eines geliebten Gegenstandes eingeurnt an unsere Brust zu drücken" or "sie unversehrt in grossen, wohlausgezierten Sarkophagen zu verwahren" (129), the architect agrees with Charlotte that the separation of body and memorial should be acknowledged openly. To this end, he suggests that "gut ausgeführte Monumente" or "Denkzeichen, Denkschriften" should be placed "in schönen Hallen um die Begräbnisplaetze," marking—and yet distancing—death by aesthetic means (130). Predictably, Charlotte and the architect also agree on a related topic: For both of them, the relation of a portrait to its subject is severed at the moment of its completion.

Later in the novel, in a pantomime devised by Charlotte's daughter Luciane, the architect enacts the distance he perceives between memorial and body, comparable to the distance between representation and its object, in a telling way. In the pantomime, accompanied by the mournful strains of a funeral dirge, Luciane represents Artemisia carrying an urn containing the ashes of her husband Mausolus, the man for whom the first mausoleum was built and named.[12] Behind her walks the architect—also *playing* an architect—carrying a blackboard on which he is expected to draw the mausoleum that is to house the funeral urn with its ashes. After the architect has done so reluctantly, "Artemisia" asks him to place the urn on top of the monument by drawing it there. Clearly, the pantomime continues the discussion of the relation of representation to death, for the funerary urn, an artifact, figuratively contains the remains of the body. As a prop in a pantomime, the urn is raised to a higher level of artifice in the aesthetic space of the stage on which the performance takes place; the urn then symbolically enters yet another aesthetic space, when it is transposed into a chalk drawing on the blackboard, achieving a still greater degree of aestheticization and increased distance from the body.

The transposition of the urn into an image of an urn once again dramatizes the (figured) bringing of the body into representation. The effect is rendered problematic when the mausoleum, designed as a memorial, with permanence in mind, is drawn in chalk, an irony of which at least one spectator is dimly aware: "es tut mir leid, sagte jener, dass die Zeichnung so vergänglich ist" (148). In the performance, represented object and the means of representation—urn and drawing in chalk—exist in a state of extreme tension with one another, and the so-called union of body and image takes place at many removes.

But the architect's central project is the restoration of a picturesque, semi-ruined side chapel of a Gothic church "als ein Denkmal voriger Zeiten und ihres Geschmacks" (132). It is here that Ottilie functions as the site of unease concerning the body's relation to representation. Like many eighteenth-century heroines in this regard, Ottilie can properly be said to die into representation: She is anorexic, becomes increasingly mute as the novel progresses, and lives, as it were, in her diary entries. Further, the architect, while decorating this chapel, brings Ottilie almost literally into his painting when he paints her features within the outlines of the many tracings from ancient pictures with which he embellishes the chapel walls. Ottilie, confronted with the mirror images of her face in the figures who populate these frescoes, experiences a profound crisis of identity: It seems to her "als ob sie wäre und nicht wäre, als wenn sie sich empfände und nicht empfände," suspended as she is between her body and the paintings (140). Fittingly, it is the museum-space of the chapel, with its auratic glow and atmosphere, that will later house Ottilie's body.[13]

As a corpse, Ottilie under her glass-lidded coffin is aestheticized once more and thus exemplifies the most extreme solution to the problem of bringing the real—the body—into the space of representation. Goethe's narrative has contrived to accomplish what the architect sketched out in the pantomime of Artemisia and the urn: The side chapel, in its hybrid status as museum and mausoleum, is said to contain the body not only as a portrait, but also literally, behind glass, in place of a portrait. As we might expect, then, this is a body strangely insusceptible to the effects of time and decay: Ottilie's beauty remains intact, despite its picturesque location. Like the space in which it finds itself, the body, too, is a hybrid: It is a relic, an icon, and a lasting work of art. Although Goethe himself is committed to organicist doctrines concerning the work of art, unlike Diderot he is at pains to ensure that the real is fully transformed by art and, further, that the aesthetic and the religious remain distinct from one another. How, then, do we understand the conclusion of this novel, with its aestheticized corpse and its "nazarenische(s) Wesen" (Benjamin 139)?

To take up this question, let us return briefly to the architect's negative reaction to the death mask with its uncomfortable proximity to the body. As a "contact image," the death mask closely approaches the status of *acheiropoetoi*, or images not made by human hands, the most famous example of which is the sudarium of St. Veronica, the cloth with which she reputedly wiped sweat and blood from the face of Christ on his way to Calvary. As a reward for Veronica's service, a perfect imprint of the face of Christ is said to have appeared on her cloth, and hence the sudarium came to be western Christianity's most sacred relic, its "true image" or *vera icon*. In the context of early Christianity, *acheiropoetoi* derive their importance precisely from the fact that they are not manufactured, a characteristic that sets them apart from pagan images or idols (Koerner 80). As Joseph Koerner puts it, the sudarium is "simultaneously a cult object and an implied aesthetic," for it "brings forth a theology of the sign.... as perfect match between image and model, *signum* and *res*" (86). Art historians have seen in the story of the Veronica, as it is called, a "fitting myth of origin for German painting" (Paecht 107), and Koerner in particular anchors his analysis of Dürer's self-portraits in this image. Dürer, of course, was venerated as a painter both in his own time—on the day after his death, a group of artists exhumed his cadaver and used it to make a plaster cast of his features (Koerner 249)—and during the Romantic period, when the writings of Wackenroder and Tieck turned him into a cult figure, an artist imitated by his would-be acolytes, the *Nazarener*.

Like the Veronica, the death mask is the imprint of the face itself; molded on its features, it brings the body's markings into the space of representation. As a cast, the death mask is the negative of these features and, interestingly, provokes the same reaction in the architect concerning their use in the production of portrait busts that we find toward the physionotype in France of the 1830s. Although the physionotype would greatly facilitate the production of busts, its consequent resemblance to its living model was said to be merely a "ressemblance matérielle," without life (Buddemeier 60), one that could never compare with the transformative powers of the portrait to suggest the human spirit. It is this same conviction concerning the superiority of the portrait that causes Goethe's architect to react as he does to the death mask, with a feeling of repugnance at the close link between the image and the real on which it is based—an attitude not unlike the one expressed by Goethe toward the tastes of his collector and the appetite of the ape. The architect, like the advocate of the artist in "Über Wahrheit und Wahrscheinlichkeit," also believes in the importance of the transformative action of the *Geist* in matters of representation.

Perhaps we might say, then, that Ottilie's body as work of art occupies an ontological position similar to that of the Veronica, the *vera icon*: Not the product of the human hand, the Veronica is the "true image" of early Christianity precisely because it is at once image and body, *signum* and *res*. Both the "Anzeige zu *Über Kunst und Altertum*" that appeared in the *Morgenblatt für gebildete Stände* some years later, in March 1816, and the essay entitled "Heidelberg" that appeared in *Über Kunst und Altertunt* during that same year attest to Goethe's interest in and familiarity with various painterly representations of St. Veronica (*Schriften* 656–67; 676–708). As a work of art, Ottilie's body behind glass might very well appeal to the taste of Goethe's imitator, the collector with the penchant for the real in art: Indeed, in "Der Sammler und die Seinigen," we learn that the collector's daughter, "noch jung und schön," was painted in her coffin shortly after her death (*Schriften* 268).

How, then, to explain the novel's seemingly positive attitude toward Ottilie's body, with its power, for instance, to make the fragmented body of Nanny whole? Heinrich Meyer's "Neudeutsche Religiös-patriotische Kunst," known to have been written in close consultation with Goethe, takes a distinctly negative view of the regressive "Hang zum Altertümlichen" that exemplifies old-German taste, with its "in Gartenanlagen erbaute Ruinen ... samt dem ganzen gotischen Spitzen-und Schnörkelwesen" (*Schriften* 716). Indeed, Goethe's attitude toward "neo-Catholic" religious art is well known; his comments concerning the "klosterbrudisierende, sternbaldisierende Unwesen" of romantic art frequently cited (Bollacher 36). How uncharacteristic, then, as Thomas Mann points out, "mitten in protestantischer Sphäre eine Heilige zu kreieren, zu deren Leichnam das lutherische Landvolk sich wundergläubig in die Kirche drängt" (qtd. in Lillyman 365). Not only does the "work of art" that is Ottilie's corpse exemplify the union of image and the real, constituting a "material image" that aspires to be at once sign and thing, but it is in other ways a "Zwitterwesen" as well. As Benjamin points out, as a character in the novel Ottilie transgresses generic boundaries: "in der Tat sind in Ottiliens Gestalt die Grenzen der Epik gegen die Malerei überschritten" (Benjamin 115).

## IV. THE STAGING OF PAINTING

The works of art favored by his collector are repugnant to Goethe also because they are "Mischwerke," mixed media rather than generically distinct works, arguably theater props as much as they are paintings or sculptures. As mixed media, products of generic boundary crossings, for Goethe they are symptomatic of decadence in art. The history of collecting that we see in Goethe's "Sammler" re-enacts the history of art as Goethe describes it in the introduction to the *Propyläen*:

> Indem man die flacherhobenen Werke immer höher und höher machte, dann Teile, dann Figuren ablöste, zuletzt Gebäude und Landschaften anbrachte, und so halb Malerei, halb Puppenspiel darstellte, ging man immer abwärts in der Kunst, und leider haben treffliche Künstler der neuern Zeit ihren Weg auf diese Weise genommen. (*Schriffen* 149)

In the *Wahlverwandtschaften*, Luciane is criticized for accompanying her songs and recitations with gestures and hence, as the narrator puts it, "unpleasantly" combining the lyric and the epic with the dramatic. Luciane's pantomime as Artemisia also includes music and drawing, but she outdoes herself in the tableaux vivants, positioned as they are between painting and drama, object and event. As Goethe puts it, using the Horatian trope of the monstrous text, tableaux vivants are "Zwitterwesen zwischen der Malerie und dem Theater" (qtd. in Holmström 232). It is in the "lebende Bilder" or "natürliche Bildnerei" of the tableau vivant, of course, that the body is most effectively brought into painting (159). Interesting in this regard is a satirical passage concerning tableaux vivants in a review of the *Wahlverwandtschaften* published in 1810 by Böttiger and Schiltz and quoted by Holmström:

> Everyone pretends to be delighted with this dumb living-dead drama, in which the petrified actor finds himself vastly interesting, while the spectator tries with cries of appreciation to conceal his dissatisfaction and his yawns. Now that we have thus learnt to use living people instead of dead colours and brushes when describing moving scenes, we must also venture the hope that we may soon see the notes of a Haydn symphony fixed, or baked into a pastry so that the tongue, too, can savour them. (qtd. in Holmström 216–17)

The "living-dead drama" that is the tableau vivant is obsessively interested in "making real" and, by way of the metaphors of these reviewers, suggests a materialism of the sort that we find in Heine.

This is not the place to focus in detail on the paintings chosen as a basis for the tableaux vivants performed by Luciane and her friends. Suffice it to say that all three of them—Van Dyck's "Belisarius," Poussin's "Esther Before Ahaseurus," and the Terborch—were in fashion during this period, all were available as engravings, and all are mentioned in Diderot's *Salons*, though Wille's engraving from Terborch occurs only in the *Salon* of 1767.[14] We know that Goethe himself probably owned all three of the engravings in question and, further, that engravings of this kind often did not correspond very closely to the paintings on which they were based (Trunz 203). The relation of painting to engraving is especially intriguing in the case of the "Paternal Admonition," by Wille, close friend of Diderot and teacher of Tischbein and Hackert, whose engraving reinscribes the scene painted by Terborch—or Terburg—within the ethos of the bourgeois tragedy. To render the work as a domestic scene, Wille altered the ages of the women in the painting—in the Terborch they are both young—to suggest a daughter and her mother, and he replaced a young soldier with the paternal figure of his title (Trunz 215). Interestingly, in the case of this last tableau the narrator takes care to mention that it is based on the engraving of a painting referred to as "die *sogenannte* väterliche Ermalmung von Terborch" (italics mine) and then goes on to describe the father as one who "*scheint....* seiner Tochter ins Gewissen zu reden" (italics mine; 160). Goethe's narrator hints at an ambiguity concerning the subject of Terborch's painting: Although we do not know whether Goethe was aware of the ideologically motivated changes that Wille introduced into his engraving, the narrator's tongue-in-cheek tone in these passages suggests that he may have been.[15] In fact, according to art historians, Terborch's painting probably depicts the interior of a brothel (Binstock 42).

Luciane's tableaux vivants are said to represent "das Bild als Wirklichkeit," suggesting that she shares the impulse that propels Goethe's collector. As exemplified by her attachment to her pet ape, Luciane's "mode of reference is mimetic" (Brodsky 1165). When her mother, Charlotte, attempts to comfort Luciane for her ape's absence, she offers to send to the library for "einen ganzen Band der wunderlichsten Afferibilder" (149) to take the real ape's place, thereby evoking the ape of "Über Wahrheit und Wahrscheinlichkeit" who mistakes images of insects for the real thing. Luciane, then, is doubly marked as mimic or "Nachahmer," someone whose mimetic drive makes her the object of mockery. Unlike Luciane's tableaux, those in which Ottilie participates offer "die Wirklichkeit als Bilde" suggesting a mimetic relationship somewhat more favored by Goethe. We know from Goethe's writings that he originally connected tableaux vivants generically with Neapolitan cribs (Holmström 211), and Ottilie, in her tableaux, figures as the madonna in two representations of the *crèche*, neither of which is based on a specific painting. But much about Ottilie's tableaux, including the virtual absence of spectators, suggests that they conform to Diderot's ideal dramatic *tableau* and therefore approach as closely as possible the idea of nature as art.[16] Hence, they, too, remain problematic.

Further, the very fact that Ottilie occupies the role of the madonna undermines the supposedly uncontrived and unstudied "naturalness" of these tableaux in a variety of ways. Goethe's known attitude toward the madonnas of the *Nazarener* and toward the religious themes of romantic art in general makes this choice of subject a questionable one—not to mention the fact that Ottilie's virginity is under siege in this novel and that the child that she holds stands in for Charlotte's unborn child whose body bears the emblematic traces of two imagined adulterous acts. How fitting, then, that Ottilie's representation as madonna mirrors another aesthetic debate of the period. An important focus of eighteenth- and early nineteenth-century interest in the madonnas of Raphael was the question of whether the woman who sat for them was really his mistress and what effect, if any, the "fallen" body of the model had on the status of these paintings as religious icons. Kleist takes up this issue, for example, in "Brief eines Malers an seinen Sohn," published in 1808, where, in a "väterliche Ermahnung" of another kind, the father advises his son not to be concerned that the feeling he entertains for the madonna that he is painting is "unrein und körperlich" (873). In this opinion, the father in Kleist's fictive letter is unlike Ottilie's teacher, who comes upon her tableau unexpectedly and takes against "diese Vermischung des Heiligen zu und mit dem Sinnlichen" (174).

If there is ambiguity about the subject of the Terborch painting, then indeed Luciane, who represents the young woman who is either admonished by a father (Wille) or employed as a harlot (Terborch), is placed in a compromising position. In both instances, then, in Luciane's most successful tableau vivant and in Ottilie's, there may very well be a "hidden meaning," a subtext very much in keeping with the genre itself, present in the "attitudes" from which it develops with their "recondite use of concealed quotations from classical pictorial art" (Holmström 216).[17] Definitely in Ottilie's case, and possibly in Luciane's, what is at issue is the juxtaposition of the image and the real, of a woman's chaste body with a fallen one. But the use of the body as a vehicle in tableau vivant is in and of itself problematic: Its very lack of motion enhances its erotic lure, its libidinal pull on the spectator (Lyotard 356). The motionless body is the source of a titillation produced by an aesthetic illusion that is never complete, that remains always partial.

The *Wahlverwandtschaften* themselves are said to have established the fashion for tableaux vivants as the embodiment of painting by human actors (Nemec 78; Holmström 216), and among the various sources cited for these were the exotic performances of Emma Hart, the future Lady Hamilton, that Goethe and various other travelers to Naples witnessed and wrote about (Holmström 211; Puskar 404). Her so-called "attitudes"—representations of classical works of art—held her spectators spellbound, as did the poses inside a life-sized black box framed in gold, by means of which she evoked ancient and contemporary painting (Holmström 110ff). Spectatorial interest in "attitudes," referred to as a "mimoplastic" art, was fed in part by the widespread enthusiasm for "body language" in theater, as evinced by Diderot's writings on gesture and pantomime. Although in the narrative of Goethe's novel the tableaux are clearly *Gesellschaftsspiele* like Emma Hart's entertainments, something more is also at stake here.[18] Goethe's familiarity with Diderot's dramas and with Diderot's ideas concerning theatrical *tableaux*,[19] as well as Goethe's knowledge of the *Salon* of 1765 and the "Essay on Painting,"[20] suggest that in Diderot's writings we have a more serious source for Goethe's interest.

The effect that Emma Hart achieved in representing sculpture played on Pygmalion's sculpture of Galatea coming to life, for Hart's spectators were acutely aware that at any time her living body could break out of its self-imposed immobility. On the other hand, by framing the body as an aesthetic object and placing it against a funereal backdrop of black velvet, she played on the killing off of the human body of which Herder accuses painting (Herder 12–13). Interestingly, the figures that Emma Hart most often reproduced by such means were said to be from Pompeian murals and thus were images doubly connected with death, images that embalm time. Arrayed in a white tunic, hair flowing, and with the aid of a variety of shawls, Emma Hart arranged her body in a series of poses, thus creating shifting— not moving—three-dimensional pictures characterized by an alternation between prolonged immobility and sudden movement, an alternation that emphasized the tension between the painterly subject of each representation and its human vehicle.

Tableau vivant, then, as a staging of painting, achieves the effect that the drawing of the mausoleum in Luciane's pantomime strives for but cannot attain: It successfully brings the living body into painting, collapsing as far as possible the distance between signifier and signified suggested by the chalk image of the mausoleum. In so doing, tableau vivant plays on two related uncanny effects: the arrested motion or "freezing"—hence death—of the human body, on the one hand, and the embodiment or "bringing to life" of the inanimate image on the other. Not surprisingly, Goethe's narrator comments on the uncanny effect these tableaux have on the spectators:

> Die Gestalten waren so passend, die Farben so glücklich ausgeteilt, die Beleuchtung so kunstreich, dass man fürwahr in einer andern Welt zu sein glaubte; nur dass die Gegenwart des Wirklichen statt des Scheins eine Art von ängstlicher Empfindung hervorbrachte. (159–60)

Once again we find the disquieting union of the image and the real, functioning in this instance both as a reminder of and a protection against death.

## V. THE IMITATOR

Let us now return briefly to Goethe's imitator and his collection. In their sheer number, his commissioned objects constitute a barricade between the imitator as collector and the real world that they portray. By means of the still-life paintings with which he surrounds himself, the imitator creates a surrogate world more impervious to the effects of time than his own. "Die Angst vorm Tode, die jede andre einschliesst," suggests Benjamin, is one that especially pervades Goethe's texts, "denn der Tod bedroht die gestaltlose Panarchie des natürlichen Lebens am meisten" (84). From Goethe's point of view, the trompe l'oeil painting behind the door and the wax figure of himself that the imitator commissions are disturbing in part because they reduce art to its function as memorial and because, in so doing, they lay bare the desperation with which we seek to sustain life.

The story of the imitator is an allegorical narrative. It suggests that the passion for mimesis is, at its most extreme, a desire to bring the body literally into the space of representation. The motivation behind such a desire is paradoxical: It lies, of course, in the need to memorialize life through art, but it also involves the attempt to create an intimate relation between image and thing, to take up the signified into the signifier and hence to bridge the Kantian gap between representation and things-in-themselves. Though Goethe's overt aesthetics militate against such a bridging, in *Die Wahlverwandtschaften*, as we have seen, he plays to and with certain tastes of the period that gain their impact by these means. It may be that Goethe's experiments with representation in this novel were begun as acts of imitation, as satire, and thus all the more easily became the vehicles of an authentic anxiety. This is an issue that the tone of Goethe's novel will continue to obscure.

## NOTES

1. This is perhaps not so surprising in the period after Schiller's death in 1805, when a rigorous classicism no longer seems to hold sway over Goethe's sensibility. See also Thomas Fries, whose work on the *Wahlverwandtschaften* takes up the question of "das Wirklichwerden von Bild und Zeichen" (130) and J. Hillis Miller's chapter on this novel in *Ariadne's Thread*. My own essay has its origins in several related conference papers presented in 1992–93 and is an elaboration of an argument I put forward in *Incorporating Images*, 107–14.

2. Goethe probably first read both Diderot's *Salon* of 1765 and the "Essai sür la Peinture" in August 1796, approximately a year after they were first published (Mortier 270). The decision to translate the essay was connected to his project of writing a general introduction to the visual arts.

3. Schiller collaborated in the writing of this piece (Gearey 253).

4. Here Goethe refers pointedly to the architectural meaning of the trompe l'oeil as false door or window.

5. See Michael Fried's well-known reading of Diderot's attitudes toward theatricality.

6. See Dieckmann's elucidation of the mimetic relationship between nature and art in Diderot.

7. Of interest here is not so much that Goethe either chooses to omit or is unaware of the second part of the story, which establishes Parrhasios as the clear victor of the contest by means of his painting of a curtain, a trompe l'oeil effect of even more consummate realism that causes Zeuxis to demand that it be pulled to reveal Parrhasios's painting, but that Goethe seems unaware of the variant of this story that supports his own point of view. In this variant, Zeuxis is said to have represented a child carrying a bunch of grapes that, like the other painting, attracted birds. When one of the beholders of the painting suggested that the representation of the child could not be lifelike because it did not frighten the birds away, Zeuxis is said to have "removed the grapes and kept what is best in the picture rather than what was most life-like" (Bann 32).

8. It should be noted, however, that this moment contains some self-irony.

9. Goethe himself, of course, sketched a design for an English garden in 1776 (Faber 96) and, inspired by Prince Leopold von Anhalt-Dessau's park at Woerlitz, laid out the park at Weimar two years later (Watkin 171).

10. Werther, however, had an eye for the picturesque—to which his sketch of village children in a composition complete with fence, barn door, and broken wagon wheels will attest (*Leiden* 49).

11. Peter McIsaac's "Exhibiting Ottilie" covers some of this ground. The focus of McIsaac's essay is different from mine, however: McIsaac's reading is interested in the way in which art inculcates social values and, in the case of the tableaux vivants, in the gender specificity of the cultural values that they represent. Although I find McIsaac's reading to be of interest, it could be enhanced by a more thorough understanding of the history and nature of tableaux vivants and of their function in the context of Goethe's writings on art.

12. It should be noted that in the *Salon* of 1765, which Goethe knew, Diderot describes Deshays's charcoal sketch "Artemisia at the Tomb of Mausolus." As Diderot writes, "Deshays composed this sketch in the final moments of his life; death's grip had chilled his hand and made the charcoal difficult to control, but the eternal, divine kernel retained all its energy." Though Deshays's sketch does not closely resemble the scene portrayed by Goethe, it seems likely that it inspired the choice (*Diderot on Art* 1: 50).

13. Benjamin points out the double identity of this space as both museum and mausoleum (68).

14. Mortier suggests that it is possible that Goethe did know the *Salon* of 1767, perhaps in one of its transcribed, underground manifestations (264). The painting once ascribed to Van Dyke is now thought to have been the work of Luciano Borzone (Trunz 205).

15. Interesting in this regard is Aloïs Riegl's reading of what he terms the "novelistic" character of Terborch's paintings: "Der Auffassung der Terborschen Novellen liegt etwas Ätzendes, Sarkastisches zugrunde: der Meister spottet über die geheimen Leidenschaften seiner Mitmenschen und fordert den Beschauer auf, das gleiche zu tun" (274).

16. See Suzanne Guerlac for a discussion of the topic of mimetic reciprocity between art and nature in Diderot.

17. We also find "hidden meanings" in the "charade-tableaux" in Thackeray's *Vanity Fair*, where the human body is used to enact verbal solutions to riddles, as in the game of charades as we know it today.

18. Of course Goethe himself arranged tableaux vivants, monodramas, and related theatrical events at Weimar, including the staging of Rousseau's "Pygmalion" in 1772 and of his own "Proserpina" in 1814. Rousseau's piece is a monodrama; Goethe's is a "Mischwerk" including tableaux and a monodrama. The subject matter of these pieces is curiously suggestive in the context of our theme, representing as they do the "birth" of a woman from an inanimate sculpture, and the "death" of a living woman as she eats of the pomegranate (Holmström 104ff).

19. See Humboldt's letter to Goethe from Paris stressing the close proximity of French acting to pictorial art. Goethe reworked this letter and used it in the *Propyläen* (Holmström 103).

20. Both were first published in Germany in 1796. As Martin Meisel points out, Baron Grimm added a description of the performance of tableaux vivants to the *Salon* of 1765 (Meisel 47).

## WORKS CITED

Bann, Stephen. *The True Vine: On Visual Representation and the Western Tradition*. Cambridge: Cambridge UP, 1989.

Benjamin, Walter. "Goethes *Wahlverwandtschaften*." *Gesammelte Schriften*. Eds. Rolf Tiedemann and Hermann Schweppenhäuser. Vol. 1:1. Frankfurt am Main: Suhrkamp, 1974. 59–140.

Bermingham, Ann. *Landscape and Ideology: The English Rustic Tradition, 1740–1860*. Berkeley: California UP, 1986.

Binstock, Benjamin. "Aloïs Riegl in the Presence of *The Nightwatch*." *October* 74 (1995): 36–44.

Bollacher, Martin. "Wilhelm Heinrich Wackenroder: *Herzensergiessungen eines kunstliebenden Klosterbruders*." *Romane und Erzählungen der deutschen Romantik*. Ed. P. M. Lützeler. Stuttgart: Reclam, 1981. 34–57.

Brodsky, Claudia. "The Coloring of Relations: *Die Wahlverwandtschaften* as *Farbenlehre*." *MLN* 97 (1982): 1147–79.

Bryson, Norman. *Looking at the Overlooked: Four Essays on Still Life Painting*. Cambridge, MA: Harvard UP, 1990.

———. *Vision and Painting: The Logic of the Gaze*. New Haven: Yale UP, 1983.

Buddemeier, Heinz. *Panorama, Diorama, Photographie: Entstehung und Wirkung neuer Medien im 19. Jahrhundert*. München: Wilhelm Fink, 1970.

Diderot, Denis. *Diderot on Art*. 2 vols. Trans. John Goodman. New Haven: Yale UP, 1995.

———. *Selected Writings*. Ed. Lester Crocker. New York: Macmillan, 1966.

Dieckmann, Herbert. "Die Wandlung des Nachahmungsbegriffs in der französischen Asthetik des 18. Jahrhunderts." *Poetik und Hermeneutik I: Nachahmung und Illusion*. Ed. Hans Robert Jauss. München: 1964. 28–59.

Faber, Richard. "Parkleben: Zur sozialen Idyllik." *Goethes "Wahlverwandtschaften": Kritische Modelle und Diskursanalysen zum Mythos Literatur*. Ed. Norbert W. Bolz. Hildesheim: Gerstenberg Verlag, 1981. 91–168.

Fried, Michael. *Absorption and Theatricality: Painting and Beholder in the Age of Diderot*. Chicago: U of Chicago P, 1980.

Fries, Thomas. "Die Reflexion der Gleichnisrede in Goethes *Wahlverwandtschaften*." *Die Wirklichkeit der Literatur: Drei Versuche zur literarischen Sprachkritik*. Tübingen: Niemeyer, 1975. 90–130.

Goethe, Johann Wolfgang von. *Die Leiden des jungen Werther*. Stuttgart: Reclam, 1948.

———. *Die Wahlverwandtschaften*. Stuttgart: Reclam, 1956.

———. *Essays on Art and Literature*. Ed. John Gearey. New York: Suhrkamp, 1986.

———. *Schriften zur Kunst*. Zürich: Artemis, 1954.

Guerlac, Suzanne. "The Tableau and Authority in Diderot's Aesthetics." *Studies on Voltaire and the Enlightenment* 219 (1983): 183–94.

Herder, Johann Gottfried. "Plastik." *Herders Sämtliche Werke*. Ed. Bernhard Suphan. Berlin: Weidmann, 1892. 73–154.

Hipple, Walter John. *The Beautiful, the Sublime, and the Picturesque in Eighteenth-Century British Aesthetic Theory*. Carbondale: Southern Illinois UP, 1957.

Holmström, Kirsten Gram. *Monodrama, Attitudes, Tableaux Vivants: Studies in Some Trends of Theatrical Fashion, 1770–1815*. Stockholm: Almquist and Wiksell, 1967.

Hussey, Christopher. *The Picturesque: Studies in a Point of View*. London: Frank Cass and Co., 1967.

Kleist, Heinrich von. *Sämtliche Werke und Briefe*. Ed. Helmut Sembdner. München: Hauser, 1961. Vol. 2.

Koerner, Joseph Leo. *The Moment of Portraiture in German Renaissance Art*. Chicago: U of Chicago P, 1993.

Lange, Victor. "Goethe im Glashaus: Klassizistische Kunstmassstäbe, altdeutsche Kunst, und neudeutsches Künstlerwesen." *Heidelberg im säkuldren Umbruch: Traditionsbewusstsein und Kulturpolitik um 1800*. Ed. Friedrich Strack. Stuttgart: Klett-Cotta, 1987. 337–51.

Lillyman, William J. "Monasticism, *Tableau Vivant*, and Romanticism: Ottilie in Goethe's *Die Wahlverwandtschaften*." *JEGP* 81.3 (1982): 347–66.

Lyotard, Jean-Francis. "Acinéma." *Narrative, Apparatus, Ideology: A Film Theory Reader*. Ed. Philip Rosen. New York: Columbia UP, 1986. 349–59.

Meisel, Martin. *Realizations: Narrative, Pictorial, and Theatrical Arts in Nineteenth-Century England*. Princeton: Princeton UP, 1983.

McIsaac, Peter. "Exhibiting Ottilie: Collecting as a Disciplinary Regime in Goethe's *Wahlverwandtschaften*." *German Quarterly* 70 (1997): 347–57.

Miller, J. Hillis. "Anastomosis." *Ariadne's Thread: Story Lines*. New Haven: Yale UP, 1992. 144–222.

Mortier, Roland. *Diderot in Deutschland, 1750–1850*. Stuttgart: J. B. Metzler, 1972.

Nemec, Friedrich. *Die Okonomie der "Wahlverwandtschaften."* München: Wilhelm Fink, 1973.

Peucker, Brigitte. *Incorporating Images: Film and the Rival Arts*. Princeton: Princeton UP, 1995.

Price, Martin. "The Picturesque Moment." *From Sensibility to Romanticism: Essays Presented to Frederick A. Pottle*. Ed. Frederick W. Hilles and Harold Bloom. Oxford: Oxford UP, 1965. 259–92.

Puskar, Norbert. "Frauen und Bilder: Luciane und Ottilie." *Necrophilologus* 73.3 (1989): 397–410.

Riegl, Aloïs. *Das holländische Gruppenportrait*. Wien: Österreichische Staatsdruckerei, 1931.

Stewart, Susan. "Death and Life, in that Order, in the Works of Charles Willson Peale." *Visual Display: Culture Beyond Appearances*. Ed. Lynne Cooke and Peter Wollen. Seattle: Bay Press, 1995. 30–53.

Trunz, Erich. "Kupferstiche zu den 'Lebenden Bildern' in den *Wahlverwandtschaften*." *Weimarer Goethe-Studien*. Weimar: Hermann Böhlaus, 1980. 203–17.

Watkin, David. *The English Vision: The Picturesque in Architecture, Landscape and Garden Design*. New York: Harper and Row, 1982.

IRMGARD WAGNER

# West-östlicher Divan
## *and Other Late Poetry*

T he task at which Melusine's champion failed is precisely the task Goethe sets himself and his readers in his volume of poems and prose *West-östlicher Divan*: going beyond, crossing the border from the familiar to the foreign, transcendence in many dimensions. As the title states, this is to be an encounter—a conversation and negotiation—between West and East.[1] Most of the poetry, 240 pages in the first edition, about half that in modern editions, was composed in the short space between spring 1814 and autumn 1815. Yet right up to its publication in 1819, Goethe kept writing an even longer prose segment, *Noten und Abhandlungen*, to follow the poems, under the original title "Besserem Verständnis" ("for better understanding").

He presents himself to his readers as a traveler and a tradesman. In the poems he is a traveler seeking to adapt to foreign ways of life and to appropriate the foreign tongue as far as possible. In the *Noten* he is a tradesman who exhibits and advertises his imported wares to best advantage ("Einleitung").[2] Thus the *Noten* offer an introductory course in Persian cultural studies: history, government, daily life, religion, and literature, complete with references for further study, as Goethe in conclusion discusses Orientalist scholars and sources. At a deeper level the essays reflect on the nature and function of culture in a wide range, encompassing relations of power and submission, tradition and innovation, love and war, God and man,

From *Goethe*. © 1999 by Twayne Publishers.

spirit, intellect, and the arts. There is in particular an entire poetology in these *Noten*, a view of literature radically different from the classicist version that Goethe had previously espoused. The imaginary excursion into the Orient gave the Western author a new vantage point from which to evaluate and revise his own theory and practice.

Goethe's project of cultural mediation developed over time. Like his Chinese studies, his interest in Persia originated in an impulse to escape from the chaotic end of the Napoleonic Empire. The very first lines of the poetry cycle point to this origin: "North and West and South are breaking, / Thrones are bursting, kingdoms shaking: / Flee, then, to the essential East" (*Works*, 1:203, lines 1–3). When his publisher, Cotta, gave him a translation of poetry by the fourteenth-century Persian Hafis, it was to serve as diversion in the small-town spa close to home, Bad Berka. Here Goethe had withdrawn while the European powers were sorting out Napoleon's future after his resignation from the throne in April 1814. And then the unexpected happened. Hafis hit like a flash of lightning, reigniting Goethe's lyric genius that had lain dormant for decades and that now began pouring forth poem after poem. The strange new voice, speaking from afar in time and space, captivated the acknowledged grand master of German poetry to the point of identification. *Unbegrenzt* (*Unbounded*; *Works*, 1:205) presents in Goethe's new, witty style the relation between the German poet and his Eastern model and "twin" (16), Hafis.

The opening poem, *Hegira* (*Works*, 1:203), tells how and why the twinning came about. Although the impulse was indeed one of flight, the flight takes direction toward origins: the poet's origin in the time of youth and lyric poetry ("youthful bounds ... spoken word," 15–18) and humankind's origin in the Eastern cradle of faith. From rationalist sophistication ("brains racked and riven," 12) of aged Europe, the poet turns back to seek pure beginnings in the East, in a quest of rebirth, renaissance. The fifth stanza recalls Mignon's song of longing, reminding us of that earlier escape in search of renaissance—Goethe's Italian journey—but with a decisive difference. This time the goal is not classical Rome and Greece, the homeplace of European culture. The fourth stanza evokes the exemplary foreign: oases, deserts, and caravans trading coffee and spices. The spring of classical poetry, Helicon, has been displaced by Khizr's spring (6). Goethe's readers, educated in the classical tradition, would be utterly bewildered; they had no idea who or what Khizr was.[3] And instead of the moving pathos of Mignon's lines, we find the hallmark of the new poetry Goethe had discovered in Hafis: the intellectual play of associating incongruous elements, the sublime with the ludicrous. Poetry serves "for the stars to hear, / Robber bands to quail with fear" (29, 30).

Incongruity pairs the sacred and the profane in the sixth stanza: Saint Hafis and the tavern, holy poetry and the lust of wine and women. And the last stanza proclaims that precisely this is Goethe's new poetological program. Poetry claims to be a higher discourse, a discourse on spirit enabled by ecstatic experience, in particular the ecstasies of love and wine. The difference from classicist doctrine is apparent. Instead of ascetic abstraction and separation of the ideal and sublime from the real and sensual, this poetry finds the sublime within the sensual, in the real and banal of everyday life: the holy poet in bars and spas and paradise in a woman's hair and perfume.

The poetological program structures the volume in its 13 titled segments or "books." The two first books on poetry and the poet (*Buch des Sängers* {*Book of the Poet*} and *Buch Hafis* {*Book of Hafis*}) lay out the orientation, as the Western author responds to his Eastern model, Hafis. Two books on love (*Buch der Liebe* {*Book of Love*} and *Buch Suleika* {*Book of Suleika*}) mark the main body of the volume, framing four shorter books of reflections on the wide horizon of life including politics, power, and a poet's peeves (*Buch der Betrachtungen* {*Book of Reflections*}, *Buch des Unmuts* {*Book of Distemper*}, *Buch der Sprüche* {*Book of Proverbs*}, and *Buch des Timur* {*Book of Timur*}). A chapter on the ecstasies of wine and desire in the shape of a beautiful boy (*Schenkenbuch*) leads to the final sphere: paradise (*Buch des Paradieses* {*Book of Paradise*}) through another set of reflections on religious matters (*Buch der Parabeln* {*Book of Parables*} and *Buch des Parsen* {*Book of the Parsee*}).

The most famous poem of the entire cycle, *Selige Sehnsucht* (*Blessed Longing*; *Works*, 1:206), states the poetic program in poetic terms. Despite its place in conclusion of the programmatic first book on poetry, *Selige Sehnsucht* is commonly read as a love poem. Love, however, is here merely metaphor and way station on the progress proper: the path of poetic transformation. Goethe here reworked a Hafis poem of similar length, which is indeed a love poem.[4] The change of theme must be taken seriously. Love is the central trope, a poetic aid to understanding spiritual transformation. Goethe also recycles two recurrent symbols of Persian poetry: the candle or lamp and the moth burning. For Western culture, where sun or fire worship is unknown and fire instead signifies damnation and annihilation, the meaning of emancipation and transfiguration intended in these symbols might be inaccessible. Goethe makes it accessible by presenting the sun-fire religion of ancient Persia in the *Noten* and in the poems of *Buch des Parsen*.

The poem *Selige Sehnsucht* and the transformative process it enacts pass from paradox, from juxtaposition of contrasts—"bliss" and "longing," "alive" and "death by fire"—to synergistic union. The heart of the poem, the site of that union, is the sexual experience of passion, procreation, and renewed desire for ever higher union in stanzas 2 and 3. The lyric *thou*, differentiated from the *I* of the speaking voice (3), seduces the reader to identify with the subject of this central experience: we all love to love. Then hits the shock of line 16: "Moth, you meet the flame and die." Instead of glorified human life at its highest, literally flying high in stanza 4, *thou* is a moth burned to death. "Schmetterling," however, also refers us to the butterfly law of metamorphoses, from caterpillar through pupa to winged creature: model of transfiguration. Death is one more metamorphosis in the chain of life.

And it is an unending chain, a cycle in which every end is a new beginning. "Die and dare rebirth!" in the last stanza is a radical restatement of the truth hidden within the tired concept of rebirth. Every true change presupposes death; it means the ultimate and absolute giving up of whatever there is now: identity, our living self. The imperative form makes it a challenge and turns the death wish of the beginning (4) into obligation. Radical change is the only way toward being truly alive, toward being of this planet and knowing it as our home. Otherwise humans will remain bewildered strangers in a world they do not see through (19–20). For it is ever the essential human task, and particularly the poet's task, to enlighten, to make life transparent to truth, a task that can be completed only through transcendence and transformation.

That there are far more who will not take this view and this step is stated in the first stanza. The poem is a word to the wise, not to the crowd. The encounter with aristocratic and meritocratic Persian culture could only reinforce Goethe's elitism in postrevolutionary Europe. He gives it ample rein in the poems of *Buch des Unmuts*, for which he offers nice apologies in the *Noten* but no excuses. The Eastern model of unabashed self-esteem appeals to him far more than the hypocrisy of the Western virtue of "Bescheidenheit" (modesty, self-denial, *HA*, 2:199, line 10). Immodesty is a necessary corollary of being a poet; the very act of creating poetry is what the Greeks would have called hubris. But Goethe is no longer in the classicist mold; thus he brashly proclaims the overboldness of poetic speech in "Dichten ist ein Übermut" ("Writing poetry is an arrogance").[5] In the Eastern world Goethe has found once more the proud assertiveness of *Prometheus*, the signature poem of his Sturm und Drang days.

If in *Selige Sehnsucht* love was *only* a metaphor, it was, however, to signify a central theme of the work: poetry, like love, is creative power. The *Divan* as a whole demonstrates that love is a most fertile soil for creativity. The largest group by far are the love poems in *Buch der Liebe* and *Buch Suleika*. More than that, the book owes its very existence to love. For when Goethe, captivated by Hafis, had decided to compete with his twin in "love, drink, and song"[6] there happened to him, after a summer of wine, partying, and poetry on the banks of the Rhine and Main, an extraordinary love experience. The story of Goethe and Marianne Willemer deserves to be read on its own. Glorified for generations as a tale of the power of mutual inspiration between congenial partners in passion and poetry, for today's readers, and not just women, the story holds a deep ambivalence. In the end, Goethe included four of Marianne's poems, edited of course, in his volume.[7]

For Goethe's own program in the *Divan*, love played a dual role: (1) in providing the ecstatic frame of mind requisite for the higher discourse of poetry and (2) in acting as a most malleable phenomenon, infinitely sprouting words, poetic speech, and imagery. One of the features that so attracted Goethe to Eastern poetry was its wealth of associations, comparisons, and symbols. Everything associates with everything, he states in the *Noten* (*HA*, 2:179). "What makes you great is that you cannot end" begins his praise of Hafis in the poem *Unbegrenzt* (*Works*, 1:205). Love is the site of boundless potential for speech: the paradigm of poetry and playground for spirit. Goethe had long used nature to speak about love, but now he has found a new way of looking at nature, a new attentiveness with the focus on the natural rather than the emotional phenomenon. The bridge between the two, nature and love, is made by spirit: in explicit reflection by means of pathos or irony or in implicit equivalence anticipating the poetic realism of the later nineteenth century.

Another famous *Divan* poem, *Gingo biloba* (*Gingko Biloba*; *Works*, 1:208), uses one tiny detail of nature, "this tree's leaf," to explore the concept of unity and division. Philosophers had meditated on dualism and dialectics from Saint Augustine to Hegel, who just then was at the height of fame. Goethe's brief three stanzas distill centuries of thought in a lucid statement, which nevertheless includes the Eastern inspiration, the esoteric gesture of love—only the two lovers will understand the secret—and the essential nature of this love that exists (only?) in these poems ("my songs," 11). The poem *An vollen Büschelzweigen* (*On Laden Twigs*; *Works*, 1: 210) also takes a close look at a bit of nature, but from a different perspective. Here it is a chestnut kernel, growing, ripening, and finally bursting from its shell. By anthropomorphic sleight of hand the "fruits" of nature (3) come to mean both the swelling of passion to consciousness and insemination ("Schoß"

[16] means lap and womb), as well as the process of poetic production: "my songs" (15).

Goethe is at his most playful in a poem that bears his pseudonym for its title, *Hatem* (*Works*, 1:212), in the game of mythical Eastern lovers he was playing with Marianne-Suleika. *Buch Suleika* is arranged as a dialogue, in which the pair exchange poetry over a period of meetings and separations. In this poem Goethe has encrypted himself in the "Hatem" of verse 11. The rhyme requires a response to "(Morgenr)öte" (9): *Goethe*, of course. The play of self-irony expands over the entire poem and includes grand features of nature evoked in snow-capped summits and volcanoes. The stern mountain face ("jener Gipfel ernste Wand," 10) and snow on the peak poke fun at his advanced age in contrast with the "snakes" of her youthful tawny "curls" (he was 65, Marianne 30). Only in Goethe's Oriental poetology was it acceptable to compare snakes with mountains. In a radical change of style, the last stanza explodes the sophisticated language game by taking the metaphoric volcano literally. A little pile of ashes is all that is left of the aged lover who thought he was an Etna of passion.[8]

*Wiederfinden* (*Reunion*; *Works*, 1:212), the longest poem of *Buch Suleika*, is in a different register. Crafted in stanzas of twice the usual *Divan* length, it maintains a consistently serious tone with a rhetoric of the sublime. Again nature on the grand scale is the setting. Love is part of a cosmic spectacle: the creation of the universe; or, rather, the creation of the universe is part of a love story. The lovers' "reunion" in the first and last stanzas, framing the cosmic scene, is the individual event that first calls forth and in the end replaces universal creation ("Creators of his world are we," 40). It happens merely in the mind, but it is precisely the claim of this poem that the mind of the poet can be the source of creation. And so Goethe rewrites the creation myths of biblical and classical traditions. To the biblical story of "Become!" (13) he adds the pain of division from original union, in a version of the big bang theory (14–16). For the music of the spheres in Platonic cosmology he substitutes his own *Farbenlehre* ("of hues and harmonies a game," 30): light and dark can enter into relationships through the colors, just as "Trüben" (opaque) rhymes with "lieben" (love, 29–32).

The last poem in *Buch Suleika* takes the boldest step yet from love to the divine. *In tausend Formen* (*A Thousand Forms*; *Works*, 1:216), disarmingly playful and elegant, practices idolatry; religious fundamentalism would have to condemn it as blasphemy. Goethe plays on the first syllable of the divine name in Islam, All(ah), and on a ritual of enumerating Allah's names, to place the beloved in *all* the imaginable functions of the divinity: from the conventional "Allerliebste" (2) to extraordinary word creations such as

"Allbuntbesternte" (14) and "Allherzerweiternde" (20). Goethe's religion of the beloved proves superior even to its model, at least in the mind of the poet. Islam gives God many names but does not allow images. Poetry visualizes the word, and the poem realizes names as "forms" in a profusion of images, two to each stanza. In the penultimate stanza, the *All*-beloved fills up all the world and constitutes the totality of outer and inner life: earth and the sky/heaven (*Himmel* means both), light and air: "I breathe you" (20). Because breath turns air into soul, as in the Genesis story, or into heart, as in Goethe's "Allherzerweiternde," the poem's last line follows naturally. God, "Allah," under every one of his names, now means the beloved.

The last *Divan* segment, *Buch des Paradieses*, confirms the link of love and the divine. The higher discourse of poetry, inspired by love, leads to the highest state of human existence: pure spirit in a life beyond this world. The most meditative poem of this group announces the upward dynamic in its title: *Höheres und Höchstes* (*Sublimer and Sublimest*, *Works*, 1:218). Composed in retrospect, three years after the *Divan* experience, the poem offers a summary in conclusion. At a level of abstraction unusual for the *Divan*, it imagines a vision of the afterlife. Goethe attempts to state suprahuman, metahuman ideas in human, imaginable terms and to express religious content in poetic form. At the same time, this is a test to validate the *Divan* program. Is poetry really a higher discourse able to speak on matters of spirit? Have readers of the cycle learned to understand this new language? The challenge goes to Goethe, too, the tradesman who now asks himself whether he succeeded in selling his foreign wares: did he enlighten, did he teach well enough so that now he can speak in these "sublimer and sublimest" terms?

Following a basic *Divan* principle, the beyond is linked to this world, the spiritual to the sensual. The first half of the poem chats in comfortable language on familiar topics: my self in this life: my needs, desires, limitations, likes, and dislikes. This self is not the subjective individual, Goethe, or a Werther self of romantic definition; it is everyone—"der Mensch"—because everyone is his own "liebes Ich" (6, 9). And everyone, says the first half of the poem, wants to remain an *ich*, clings to his or her identity in this and any other world (8). But, says the second half, that is not possible. Any truly other world is utterly foreign, as foreign as East is to West. The East–West theme closes the first half and opens the second half with the most densely written and abstract verses on language as central metaphor. The language of the beyond is far more foreign than "German" is to Islamic paradise (19–20), with many dialects and a secret grammar whose declensions we hear but cannot understand.

To achieve understanding, the human will have to remain a sensate being, but the five senses operating separately and thereby failing to comprehend will have to become one unified sense. Such radical change is possible only by means of transubstantiation: "der Verklärte" ("in Glory," 32). The finite body has become infinite desire, action, and motion directed toward God. God, focus of all desire, is love and the force that links all— everything and everyone. Finally, of course, there is no more everything or everyone. The exclusive identity of the *I*, last seen in verse 37, is displaced by the inclusive *We* of the last line, and this *We* disperses, disappears in the All of divine love.


## Urworte Orphisch

Written in autumn 1817 but published only in 1820 in Goethe's house journal, *Zur Morphologie*, *Urworte Orphisch* (*Works*, 1:231–33) has acquired near cult status, quite in keeping with its title, one might say. Goethe's later poetry tends to be philosophical but also rather brief: a reflexive moment in verse, a variation on his ubiquitous prose *Maximen und Reflexionen* (*Maxims and Reflections*). *Urworte Orphisch* is an exception. It is far longer and far broader; it is a meditation on the principles that structure human life. In his study of Near Eastern culture Goethe came upon the Orphic cult in Egypt and preclassical Greece, which continued to exist as an underground, archaic religion during the classical period. The stanza titles refer to the gods that in Orphic myth surround a newborn, similar to the fairies in *Sleeping Beauty*: representations of the powers that determine human destiny.

As the Orphic myth attempts to explain the enigma of life—the interrelation of character, behavior, and destiny—so Goethe's poem tries to answer the basic question after what drives and controls an individual's life: What makes people act the way they do? What in particular explains exceptional persons such as Napoleon, who never ceased to fascinate Goethe, or, for that matter, Goethe himself? In 1817 Goethe was still working on the *Divan Noten und Abhandlungen*; exploring culture, history, and individual life; and hoping to write some more poems for the *Buch des Timur*, representing Napoleon. He had not yet returned to his autobiography. After the dramatic and traumatic events of the recent past in the public and personal spheres, he was still reorienting himself.

Public events included Napoleon's amazing hundred-day return and final exile, the postrevolutionary turn to antirevolutionary reaction, the shifting power relations in Europe and within Germany, and the accelerating emergence of economic factors in the destiny of nations. Closer to home, in 1817 Goethe had finally resigned as director of the Weimar theater, thereby breaking the last link with Schiller and his own classicist epoch. On the personal side there had been the passion and renunciation of the *Divan* experience, the horrible death of his wife (1816), and the marriage of his only son (1817). The emphasis on the generational sequence and on family and marriage is remarkable in the explanatory remarks on *Urworte Orphisch*, which Goethe published in his other house journal.[9] Even more remarkable is the deep ambivalence of his comment.

The form of the poem signals its superior status. Goethe cast only his very important poems in the long iambic stanza with its constricting rhyme scheme: *ababababcc* (*ottava rima*). The Greek strophe titles erect a ceremonial threshold, proclaiming esoteric and archaic meaning. The style is elevated, predominantly abstract and conceptual, with scant imagery except for the middle strophe, "Eros," which elaborates an allegory of love. Here, style is message. Goethe translates the ancient way of viewing the world figuratively, in myths and gods, into our ways of thought, into nineteenth-century concepts developed to understand life's phenomena. The attentive contemporary of German idealist and romantic philosophy had learned this conceptual language well.

But it is more than a question of language. The poem replaces the old, static worldview with the modern, dynamic view of the world as a field of energies and forces in constant change. The question now is of history: What drives humans as individuals and collectives? What controls our directions? What obstructs or accelerates our course? Goethe here sees human life as a grid of vectors that reinforce or weaken each other's effects. The poem plots the course of a life like a graph through a field of interacting vectors, with the individual a bouncing ball drawn, pulled, kicked, blocked, or diverted hither and yon. Far from offering a new orientation, let alone a certainty in the bewildering modern world, the poem declares human life on principle a system of errors. Goethe's comment is amazingly pessimistic: "Man who has lost his way is lured into new labyrinths; there is no limit to going astray: for *the way is an error*" (*HA*, 1:406; emphasis mine). Dynamic drive versus blockage is the overall design of the poem, in the sequence of topics and strophes as well as within each strophe.

The pattern is prominent in the first strophe, "Daimon." Static forces prevail: the sun standing still, the inescapable law of identity, the individual indelibly minted by origins. Among the factors that shape a personality, the constellation of planets and sun merits special note. Scholars may disagree on Goethe's view of astrology; the least we can say is that the opening image denotes the historical time and place of an individual's life. It matters when and where Napoleon, or Goethe, was born; the historical moment decides to a large degree who a person can become. The accumulated counterforces of growth and development seem preset within eternal limits, foretold by prophets and sybils. But precisely here is a way out of the determinist bind. Truths told by prophets and sybils are myths; the modern truth valid for us will be modified by all that follows in the rest of the poem.

"Tyche" in the second stanza brings immediate change. In direct opposition to *daimon, tyche* is the not-I: what befalls a person from the outside. (In Goethe's usage "Das Zufällige" [coincidence] connotes "that which befalls" a person, in life events as well as in encounters with others.) Humans do not grow up in isolation; they develop through parenting and education and through chance encounters with mentors, friends, and lovers or with strangers and the foreign who become relevant in the way that Italy and Hafis did for Goethe. Tyche is a mobile force that interferes with the essentially stable daimon: self. The first big jolt of tyche signals a leap in development: the exit from self-enclosed childhood and adolescence (Freud's narcissistic period) through love arriving in the next stanza.

In the third stanza, "Eros" is not merely erotic desire but all desire that has the force of eros, that excites enthusiasm and promises ecstasy. It includes ambition to attain a goal, the lust of power, or an artist's desire to create. It means reaching out toward an other, wanting to possess and shape what is outside the self. Love here is a metaphor for self-aggrandizement and for intensified pleasure of the self by expansion into other territories and appropriation of other selves. Such expansionist drive carries the danger of dispersal and dilution. The last fine introduces a countermove of concentration to refocus desire so that an individual's highest potential may be achieved. This concentrated effort in turn entails the next stanza, "Ananke-Necessity."

The fourth stanza, "Ananke-Necessity," is the most abstract in style and teems with provocative paradoxes. It poses the question that drives the poem as a whole: how free are we really? Kant and his disciple Schiller had spent their lives trying to save human freedom; Goethe's answer is highly skeptical. All our efforts at liberation, all our actions to try to prove our free will amount, ultimately, to narrower space in the prison of our existence. The elaborate play with modal verbs reflects on the real-life impact of action. No action is experientially neutral. All our acts circumscribe arbitrariness (*Wollen* and *Willen* versus *Willkür*, 2–4). Whatever we choose to do will limit our choices of future action, It is here, in this interaction of modalities, that ethics, morals, and laws originate ("sollten," 3, and "Muß," 6). Freedom has to be negotiated with the irreducible conditions of human life.

"Necessity" ends, logically, in total blockage. The last stanza, entitled "Elpis-Hope," begins in a world of iron walls, locks, and rock-solid barriers of eternal duration. But then, in the fourth line, the locks fall away. The figure of hope is Goethe's addition to the Orphic tradition, which knew only the four gods of the previous stanzas. In this, more than in anything else in the poem, consists the modern turn: there is always hope. Remarkably, Goethe's comment is silent on the last stanza. Except for implying that ethics and religion could not exist without hope, he leaves it to the reader to reflect on what hope means: "every fine mind will gladly undertake to formulate a comment in moral and religious respects" (*HA*, 1:407). A final comment on the poem as a whole might point out that hope emerges, ultimately, as the crucial tool of empowerment and liberation. It took the course of history from Orphic antiquity to Goethe's modern era to discover hope as the defining glory of being human: the ability to always again believe in new beginnings.

### MARIENBADER ELEGIE

The great elegy generally known as the *Marienbader Elegie* (1823), may well be Goethe's most astounding poetic feat; its power is evident in its reception history. For Goethe scholarship the *Elegie* stands as an uncontested summit and a continuing challenge to interpretation. The poem's exceptional standing stems from three factors: its sheer length of 23 six-line stanzas, the immediacy gained from its origin in an intensely personal experience, and the artistry that translated this experience into a universal dimension. The old poet's last love story, his unrequited attraction to the very young Ulrike von Levetzow over three Bohemian spa summers and his rejection, need not be elaborated here. When he received the final no, after having resolved for his part—at age 74—to embark on a radically new life should he be accepted, he composed the *Elegie* on the long journey home, and he composed himself by doing it. This is part of the *Elegie*'s unique character and a large part of its powerful impact: here language is action, and the poem enacts a healing process.

The *Elegie* (*Works*, 1:246–52) presents three major aspects. It is a poem about love; it represents the experience of a tremendous loss; and it is a performance of mourning. The poet speaks in personal and particular terms about his love for a childlike girl, yet he also says what all love is, can be, and can do. Love in the *Divan* was quite different. Stylized after the Hafis model, love was at bottom impersonal and instrumentalized in the service of aesthetic ecstasy. In the *Elegie* love is one-sided, an activity solely of the poet's soul. Poetic love does its usual life-intensifying magic: time disappears (stanza 3),[10] absolutes become reality (stanza 2), and desire finds total fulfillment (stanza 2) or, when denied, creates total misery (stanzas 4 and 5). But beyond that, love reveals a potential special to this poet—Goethe, surely one of the most thinking poets we know—at this stage in his long, productive life.

Love has the power not merely to inspire (*begeistern*) but to inspirit ("begeisten," 11.5): to revitalize, to motivate, and to give the gift of spirit as in the miracle of Pentecost. The lover is newly aware of himself (stanza 10), but also—and more importantly—released from the rigid enclosure within the self ("Selbstsinn," stanza 15). His imagination is freed from the bonds of anxiety imposed by past experience (stanza 12); being in love means living entirely in the present moment, to the fullest possible extent (stanzas 16 and 17). At its farthest reach love is religion. In stanzas 13 and 14, Goethe attempts a definition of religiosity and equates it with love. What stands out is the simplicity of the feeling on the one side (stanza 13; end couplet of stanza 14) and the complexity of the explanation on the other. Love shares with religiosity an essentially enigmatic nature. In love as in religion we become aware that we do not understand ourselves, which is precisely the challenge of love and religion: we attempt to "unriddle" ("Enträtselnd," 14.4) ourselves in the presence of and through an other.

All of this—and much more—is lost when love is lost. This more is what the *Elegie* describes when it explores how a tremendous loss affects us. There is, of course, the general misery to be expected: "gloom, remorse, self-mockery, clouds of care" (5.5), indifference to the splendors of nature (stanza 6), haunting by the beloved's image (stanzas 7–9), and the body's protest in tears and life-threatening torment (stanzas 19 and 20). But again, as in the poet's love, there are aspects of loss that go beyond the conventional to the tremendous, the exemplary. in the last four stanzas, after the accumulated details of love and loss have been spelled out, this side emerges as loss of reality and loss of self. "I've lost it all, earth, heaven, self" (23.1). The poet, whose talent it is to speak his pain (the *Elegie*'s motto evokes *Torquato Tasso*), has lost the power of speech (19.2). In exploring why he cannot speak he finds that he has lost the essence of spirit: willpower and the ability to think, to go beyond mere images to concepts (20.6, stanza 21). Thus he has lost access to the world: to his friends, whom he sends away; to the rest of humankind, who still are connected to each other and to the world; and to all of nature: the universe. Nothing makes sense anymore (stanza 22).

How does Goethe resolve the contradiction between what the poet says and the fact that he can still say it? The poem, despite the poet, makes magnificent sense. The solution lies in the third major aspect of the *Elegie* as a performance of mourning. Psychoanalytical views of mourning emphasize four points. First, to achieve healing over time, the mourner must keep going through his or her loss over and over again. Second, it is the work of mourning to retell in detail the story of lost happiness in order to commit the events to memory, to take them out of the present and place them in the past. Over its 138 lines the *Elegie* probes into past bliss and present misery. The difference between past and present ("nun") is emphasized repeatedly, as required in mourning. A third requirement is the telling to someone: the reader of the poem or, explicitly, the "good companions" who have listened to the narrative (stanza 22). Finally, mourning is a ritual, a performance with formal requirements. Poetic form in itself, with its demands on style and meter, meets this requirement. The *Elegie* is particularly formal in using the ceremonial stanza (*ababcc*) that Goethe reserved for special occasions (see *Urworte Orphisch*), in its demanding synthesis of affective and intellectual abstraction, and in its rhetoric of high seriousness. Translating feeling into form, this poem traces a path from the personal to the universal dimension.

## CHINESISCH-DEUTSCHE JAHRES- UND TAGESZEITEN

Goethe's cycle of 14 short poems, *Chinesisch-deutsche Jahres- und Tageszeiten* (1827), deserves to be better known. Once more, now 77 years old, Goethe ventured out toward a foreign culture and created from the encounter, as he did in the *Divan*, a new type of poetry. He started the year 1827 by reading Chinese novels (in French translation); then he reviewed a volume of Chinese poetry (in English translation) and offered prospective readers a sample by translating two poems into German. Next, like the Chinese sage of his cycle, he withdrew to his garden cottage outside the city for a very productive summer. Part of the harvest were the 14 poems, which transplant the Chinese model into German nature and culture. Each poem, in an average eight lines, presents one impression, reflection, or dialogic exchange of thought in Goethe's new style, which he called "geistig schreiben" (writing with spirit) (I).[11] We might call the new poetry emblematic, where meaning is immanent in the emblem, inscribed in the phenomenon depicted.

Like bamboo or peach trees and blossoms in Chinese pictorial poetry, plants are the favorite emblems here. White, star-shaped daffodils with red hearts wait for spring (11). A field of wildflowers bursts into extravagant fireworks of verbal virtuosity; desire is fulfilled at the apex of the sun's course in June: "Wunscherfüllung, Sonnenfeier, / Wolkenteilung bring' uns Glück!" ("Wish-fulfillment, sun celebration, / Cloud division bring us luck!" III.7–8) Throngs of thistles and nettles—very unpoetic plants these—crowd out the poet's vision in summer (VI). The rose, by contrast, is the flower of flowers, emblem of emblems in the German tradition from the Baroque mystic Angelus Silesius to the modernist R. M. Rilke.[12] In Goethe's cycle the rose is the anchoring point. Present in 3 of the 14 poems (IX, X, and XI), the rose stands for absolutes (X) and for the eternal law of growth, bloom, and waning that governs all being through passing seasons and time: "Es ist das ewige Gesetz, / Wonach die Ros' und Lilie blüht" ("This is the eternal law / directing the bloom of rose and lily," XI.8–9).

The outstanding poem is VIII: "Dimmrung senkte sich von oben" ("Twilight Down from Heaven," *Works*, 1:260). Twice as long as the others and placed at the center of the cycle, it marks a long moment of balance, when spring and summer turn into fall. The first strophe balances downward with upward movement as twilight descends and the evening star ascends, as fogs rise and the darkness of the lake draws the gaze into its black depth in another extraordinary word creation: "Schwarzvertiefte Finsternisse" ("darkened deeps more black than ever," VIII.7), all coming to rest and balance in the reflection on the lake's surface: "Widerspiegelnd ruht der See" ("mirroring calmly lies the lake," VIII.8). The second strophe similarly balances distance and closeness between the faraway moon and the nearby water, until the moon's image, "Luna," joins the reflected twigs in a shadow play on the lake.[13] Finally, outer and inner worlds interconnect in the closing lines: "Und durchs Auge schleicht die Kühle / Sänftigend ins Herz hinein" ("Through the eye the coolness sliding / Touches with a calm the heart," VIII.15–16). Here visual perception, physical sensation, and emotion are all at one, in calm equivalence. Man, having opened his eyes to take in what the previous lines depicted, is in perfect balance, at peace.

## NOTES

1. *Works*, vol. 1, *Selected Poems*, translates the title somewhat obscurely as "The Parliament of West and East." References for this chapter's poetry are to this edition, with exceptions noted. Numbers in parentheses refer to lines.

2. References for *Noten und Abhandlungen* are to *HA*, 2:126–264, here 127.

3. In Hafis's poetry, Khizr is a green-clad old man, guardian of the source of life.

4. See, for the text of the model, Hans Albert Maier, *Goethe, West-östlicher Divan* (Tübingen: Niemeyer, 1965), 111.

5. Not in *Works*, vol. 1. See the poem *Derb und tüchtig* (*Coarse and Efficient*) in *HA*, 2:16.

6. Hegira is quoted from *Works*, 1:203, here line 5.

7. All in *Buch Suleika: Hochbeglückt in deiner Liebe* (*Supremely happy in your love*), *Was bedeutet die Bewegung?* (*What means the motion?*), *Ach, um deine feuchten Schwingen* (*Oh, for your moist wings*), and *Wie mit innigstem Behagen* (*With intensest well-feeling*).

8. The *Works* translation of the last line is inadequate. A better reading would be "Oops! he burned up on me."

9. *Über Kunst und Altertum*, 1820. See *HA*, 1:403–7.

10. For this long poem, first numbers refer to stanzas and numbers after a period to the lines within the respective stanza.

11. Roman numerals refer to the number of the poem within the cycle and arabic numerals to lines within a poem. The *Works* selection prints only one poem of this cycle (VIII). References are to *HA*, 1:387–90.

12. For Rilke's interest in this cycle see Lee, *Studies in Goethe's Lyric Cycles*, p. 176 and n. 17.

13. Shadow play was a Chinese entertainment much imitated in Europe at the time.

# Chronology

| | |
|---|---|
| 1749 | Johann Wolfgang von Goethe born in Frankfurt on Main on August 28. His parents are Katharina Elisabeth Textor Goethe and Johann Caspar Goethe. |
| 1765-68 | Studies law at the University of Leipzig. |
| 1768-70 | Seriously ill, returns home to recover. |
| 1770-71 | Finishes law studies at Strasbourg University. |
| 1771-75 | Opens a private law practice in Frankfurt. Writes for the review journal *Frankfurter Gelehrte Anzeigen*. |
| 1773 | Publishes the drama *Götz von Berlichingen*. |
| 1774 | Publishes *Clavigo: Ein Trauerspiel* (later translated as *Clavidgo: A Tragedy in Five Acts*) and *Die Leiden des jungen Werthers* (later translated as *The Sorrows of Young Werther*). |
| 1775 | Becomes engaged to Anna Elisabeth Schönemann, the daughter of a wealthy banker. Travels to Switzerland. Engagement broken in September. Visits Weimar in November at the invitation of the young Duke Carl August. |
| 1776-86 | Becomes the duke's close friend, the general court wit, and organizer of court theatricals. In 1776, awarded the rights of citizenship and assigned administrative duties in Weimar government. Enters intense relationship with Charlotte von Stein, the wife of a court official, that continues for 12 years. Begins studies in geology, botany, and anatomy. |
| 1777 | Sister Cornelia dies at the age of 26. |

1782            Father dies after years of senility.

1786-88         Travels to Italy, Sicily, and Venice. Studies architecture, sculpture, botany, and anatomy. In 1788, returns to Weimar. Begins relationship with Christiane Vulpius.

1787-90         Publishes *Goethe's Schriften* (his collected works) in eight volumes, most notably containing *Iphigenie auf Tauris* (later translated as *Iphigenia: A Tragedy*) and *Egmont: Ein Trauerspiel in funk Aufzugen*, both published in 1787 (later translated as *Egmont*), *Torquato Tasso* and *Faust: Ein Fragment*, both published in 1790.

1789            Son, named August, is born.

1791            Appointed director of Weimar Court Theater. Begins work on optics.

1792            Accompanies the duke on campaign in France against the revolutionary army. Receives a house as a gift from the duke.

1792-1800       Publishes *Goethe's Neue Schriften* in seven volumes, which most notably includes the comedy *Der Groß-Cophta*, published in 1792, and *Reineke Fuchs*, published in 1794. In 1793 he publishes *Der Bürgergeneral*.

1794            Meets Schiller and develops productive relationship. Writes for Schiller's journal *Die Horen* from 1795 to 1797.

1795-96         Publishes *Wilhelm Meisters Lehrjahre* (later translated as *Wilhelm Meister's Apprenticeship*).

1798            Publishes *Hermann und Dorothea*. Buys farm, which he sells in 1803. Begins publishing his own journal, *Die Propyläen*, as a successor to Shiller's.

1804            Publishes *Die näturliche Tochter*.

1806-10         Marries Christiane Vulpius in 1806. Publishes 13-volume set of his work from 1806-1810, with *Faust* appearing in 1808 as a part of the set. In 1808 his mother dies. In 1809 publishes *Die Wahlverwandtschaften*. In 1810 publishes *Zur Farbenlehre* (later translated as *Goethe's Theory of Colours*).

1811-13         Publishes *Aus meinem Leben: Dichtung und Wahrheit* (later translated as *Memoirs of Goethe: Written by Himself*). Starts Chinese studies in 1813.

| 1816-17 | Wife dies in 1816. Publishes *Italienische Reise* (later translated as *Travels in Italy*). In 1817 resigns from Weimar Court Theater. |
| 1819 | Publishes book of poetry, *West-östlicher Divan*. |
| 1821 | Publishes *Wilhelm Meisters Wanderjahre*, first version (later translated as *Wilhelm Meister's Travels*). |
| 1822 | Publishes *Campagne in Frankreich 1792/Belagerung von Mainz* (later translated as *The Campaign in France in the Year 1792*). |
| 1827-42 | Publishes 60-volume collection of his work, which most notably includes *Novelle* (later translated as *Goethe's Novel*) in 1828, a revised and enlarged edition of *Wilhelm Meisters Wanderjahre* in 1829, *Faust: Eine Tragödie* in 1832, and an expanded edition of *Dichtung und Wahrheit* in 1833. |
| 1830 | Death of Goethe's son in Rome. |
| 1832 | Dies on March 22. |

# Contributors

HAROLD BLOOM is Sterling Professor of the Humanities at Yale University and Henry W. and Albert A. Berg Professor of English at the New York University Graduate School. He is the author of over 20 books, including *Shelly's Mythmaking* (1959), *The Visionary Company* (1961), *Blake's Apocalypse* (1963), *Yeats* (1970), *A Map of Misreading* (1975), *Kabbalah and Criticism* (1975), *Agon: Toward a Theory of Revisionism* (1982), *The American Religion* (1992), *The Western Canon* (1994), and *Omens of Millennium: The Gnosis of Angels, Dreams, and Resurrection* (1996). *The Anxiety of Influence* (1973) sets forth Professor Bloom's provocative theory of the literary relationships between the great writers and their predecessors. His most recent books include *Shakespeare: The Invention of the Human*, a 1998 National Book Award finalist, and *How to Read and Why*, which was published in 2000. In 1999, Professor Bloom received the prestigious American Academy of Arts and Letters Gold Medal for Criticism.

HANS RUDOLF VAGET teaches German at Smith College. He is the author of a book on Goethe as well as the editor of the Oxford World's Classics edition of *Goethe's Erotic Poems*. He also has written two books on Thomas Mann.

EHRHARD BAHR teaches Germanic languages at California State University at Los Angeles. He is the author of *The Novel as Archive: Or the Genesis, Reception & Criticism of Goethe's* Wilhelm Meister's Wanderjahre. He is also the editor of other titles.

ERNST BEHLER has taught at the University of Washington. He has written *German Romantic Literary Theory* and is the author and editor of other titles as well.

WOLFGANG WITTKOWSKI has been Professor of German at the State University of New York at Albany. He has written and edited a number of books and has written numerous articles on German literature, literary theory and reception, and other topics. He has been the organizer of the Goethe Symposium held in Albany every other year since 1980.

DONNA DIETRICH attended the University of Florida, and HARRY MARSHALL has been Assistant Professor of German there. He has published articles on Goethe, Kleist, and Elisabeth Plessen.

HANS REISS has taught at the University of Bristol. He has published *Goethe's Novels* and has written and edited other books as well.

JOHN GEAREY has taught at The City College of New York. He is the author of *Goethe's Faust: The Making of Part I* and the editor of *Goethe, The Collected Works: Essays on Art and Literature.*

TOBIN SIEBERS is Professor of English and Comparative Literature at the University of Michigan. He has written and edited a number of books. Some of those he has written are *The Ethics of Criticism* and *The Romantic Fantastic.*

SIGRID LANGE has taught at the University of Jena. She has written a book covering Goethe, Schiller, and Kleist and has published other pieces on them and other topics as well.

HARALD WEINRICH has been Professor of Romance Languages and Literatures at the Collège de France. He has written more than 200 books and articles. One of his more recent titles is *Lethe: Forgetting & Memory in Literature.*

DAVID CONSTANTINE has taught at the University of Oxford. He is the translator of Goethe's *Elective Affinities* for the Oxford World's Classic Series. He has written books of poetry and also has edited a number of books.

ILONA KLEIN teaches French and Italian at Brigham Young University. She has published a book in German.

BRIGITTE PEUCKER teaches Germanic Language and Literature at Yale University. She has published *Lyric Descent in the German Romantic Tradition* as well as other work.

IRMGARD WAGNER is Professor of German at George Mason University. She has published widely on Goethe, Hölderlin, Kleist, Kafka, and the theory of literature and history. She is the author of *Critical Approaches to Goethe's Classical Dramas: "Iphigenie," "Torquato Tasso," and "Die natürliche Tochter."*

# Bibliography

Adler, Jeremy. "Modelling the Renaissance: Intertextuality and the Politics of Goethe's Tasso." *Publications of the English Goethe Society* 63 (1994): 1-48.

Bahr, Ehrhard. *The Novel as Archive: The Genesis, Reception, and Criticism of Goethe's "Wilhelm Meisters Wanderjahre."* Columbia, S.C.: Camden House, 1998.

Batley, Edward. "Werther's Final Act of Alienation: Goethe, Lessing, and Jerusalem on the Poetry and Truth of Suicide." *The Modern Language Review* 87, no. 4 (October 1992): 868-78.

Bennett, Benjamin. *Goethe's Theory of Poetry: "Faust" and the Regeneration of Language.* Ithaca, N.Y.: Cornell University Press, 1986.

Berman, Russell A. "Faust, Germany, and Unification." *South Central Review* 12, no. 2 (Summer 1995): 1-15.

Blackall, Eric A. *Goethe and the Novel.* Ithaca, N.Y.: Cornell University Press, 1976.

Boyle, Nicholas. *Goethe: "Faust Part One."* Cambridge, England: Cambridge University Press, 1987.

———. "The Politics of *Faust II*: Another Look at the Stratum of 1831." *Publications of the English Goethe Society* 52 (1981-82): 4-43.

Brown, Hilda M. "Goethe in the Underworld: Proserpina/Persephone." *Oxford German Studies* 15 (1984): 146-59.

Brown, Jane K. *"Faust": Theater of the World.* New York: Twayne, 1992.

———. *Goethe's "Faust": The German Tragedy.* Ithaca, N.Y.: Cornell University Press, 1986.

Brown, Jane K., Meredith Lee, and Thomas P. Saine, eds. *Interpreting Goethe's "Faust" Today.* Columbia, S.C.: Camden House, 1994.

Burckhardt, Sigurd. *The Drama of Language.* Baltimore: Johns Hopkins University Press, 1970.

Chambers, Ross. "On the Suicidal Style in Modern Literature." *Cincinnati Romance Review* 6 (1987): 9-41.

Friedenthal, Richard. *Goethe: His Life and Times.* Cleveland: World Publishing, 1963.

Gearey, John. *Goethe's* Faust: *The Making of Part I.* New Haven: Yale University Press, 1981.

Gerald, Gillespie. "Classic Vision in the Romantic Age: Goethe's Reconstitution of European Drama—*Faust II.*" In Gillespie, Gerald, ed., *Romantic Drama.* Amsterdam: Benjamins, 1994.

Graham, Ilse. *Goethe: A Portrait of the Artist.* Berlin & New York: De Gruyter, 1977.

Gustafson, Susan. "Goethe's 'Clavigo': The Body as an 'Unorthographic' Sign." In Kelly, Veronica, ed., and Dorothea von Mucke. *Body & Text in the Eighteenth Century.* Stanford, Calif.: Stanford University Press, 1994.

Hadas, Moses, trans. *Goethe the Poet.* Cambridge: Harvard University Press, 1949; reprinted, 1970.

Hoelzel, Alfred. "The Conclusion of Goethe's *Faust:* Ambivalence and Ambiguity." *German Quarterly* 55 (1982): 1-12.

Kuzniar, Alice A., ed. *Outing Goethe and His Age.* Stanford, Calif: Stanford University Press, 1996.

Lange, Victor, ed. *Goethe: Twentieth Century Views.* Englewood Cliffs, N.J.: Prentice-Hall, 1968.

Larkin, Edward T. "Goethe's *Egmont:* Political Revolution and Personal Transformation." *Michigan Germanic Studies* 17, no. 1 (Spring 1991): 28-50.

Lee, Meredith. *Studies in Goethe's Lyric Cycles.* Chapel Hill: University of North Carolina Press, 1978.

Leppmann, Wolfgang. *The German Image of Goethe.* Oxford: Clarendon Press, 1961.

Littlejohns, Richard. "The Discussion between Goethe and Schiller on the Epic and the Dramatic, and its Relevance to Faust." *Neophilologus* 71 (1987): 388-401.

Maertz, Gregory. "Carlyle's Critique of Goethe: Literature and the Cult of Personality." *Studies in Scottish Literature* 29 (1996): 205-26.

Morgan, Peter. *The Critical Idyll: Traditional Values and the French Revolution in Goethe's "Hermann und Dorothea."* Columbia, S.C.: Camden House, 1990.

Muenzer, Clark S. *Figures of Identity: Goethe's Novels and the Enigmatic Self.* University Park: Pennsylvania State University Press, 1984.

Peacock, Ronald. *Goethe's Major Plays.* Manchester, England: Manchester University Press, 1959.

Prandi, Julie D. *"Dare to Be Happy!": A Study of Goethe's Ethics.* Lanham, Md.: University Press of America, 1993.

Reed, T. J. *The Classical Centre: Goethe and Weimar 1775-1832.* London: Croom Helm and New York: Barnes & Noble, 1980.

Robertson, Kim. "Poetry or the Truth of theTears." *Germanic Notes and Reviews* 27, no. 2 (Fall 1996): 94-6.

Rowland, Herbert. "Chaos and Art in Goethe's *Novelle.*" *Goethe Yearbook* 8 (1996): 93-119.

Schweitzer, Chrisoph E. "Sarah Austin's Assessment of Goethe's Character and Works and of Weimar." In Hoffmeister, Gerhart, ed. *A Reassessment of Weimar Classicism.* Lewiston, N.Y.: Mellen, 1996.

Shaffer, E.S. "George Eliot and Goethe: 'Hearing the Grass Grow.'" *Publications of the English Goethe Society* 66 (1996): 3-22.

Stephenson, R.H. "Goethe's Prose Style: Making Sense of Sense." *Publications of the English Goethe Society* 66 (1996): 3-22.

Vazsonyi, Nicholas. *Lukacs Reads Goethe: From Aestheticism to Stalinism.* Columbia, S.C.: Camden House, 1997.

Wagner, Irmgard. *Critical Approaches to Goethe's Classical Dramas: "Iphigenie," "Torquato Tasso" and "Die Naturliche Tochter."* Columbia, S.C.: Camden House, 1995.

Wellbery, David E. "Morphisms of the Phantasmatic Body: Goethe's *The Sorrows of Young Werther.*" In Kelly, Veronica, and Dorothea von Mucke, eds. and intro. *Body and Text in the Eighteenth Century*. Stanford, Calif.: Stanford University Press, 1994.

———. *The Specular Moment: Goethe's Early Lyric and the Beginning of Romanticism*. Stanford, Calif.: Stanford University Press, 1996.

Wilkinson, Elizabeth M., and L. A. Willoughby. *Goethe: Poet and Thinker*. London: Arnold, 1962.

Williams, John R. "Faust's Classical Education: Goethe's Allegorical Treatment of Faust and Helen of Troy." *Journal of European Studies* 13 (1983): 27-41.

# Acknowledgments

"Introduction," by Harold Bloom. From *The Western Canon: The Books and School of the Ages*, pp. 203–208. © 1994 by Harold Bloom, reprinted by permission of Harcourt, Inc.

"Goethe the Novelist. On the Coherence of His Fiction," by Hans Rudolf Vaget. From *Goethe's Narrative Fiction*, edited by William J. Lillyman: pp. 1–20. © 1983 by Walter de Gruyter & Co. Reprinted by permission.

"Revolutionary Realism in Goethe's *Wanderjahre*," by Ehrhard Bahr. From *Goethe's Narrative Fiction*, edited by William J. Lillyman: pp. 161–175. © 1983 by Walter de Gruyter & Co. Reprinted by permission.

"*Wilhelm Meisters Lehrjahre* and the Poetic Unity of the Novel in Early German Romanticism," by Ernst Behler. From *Goethe's Narrative Fiction*, edited by William J. Lillyman: pp. 110–127. © 1983 by Walter de Gruyter & Co. Reprinted by permission.

"Goethe's *Iphigenie*: Autonomous Humanity and the Authority of the Gods in the Era of Benevolent Despotism," by Wolfgang Wittkowski. From *Goethe in the Twentieth Century*, edited by Alexej Ugrinsky: pp. 77–81. © 1987 by Hofstra University. Reprinted with permission of Greenwood Publishing Group, Inc., Westport, CT.

"Thoas and Iphigenie: A Reappraisal," by Donna Dietrich and Harry Marshall. From *Goethe in the Twentieth Century*, edited by Alexej

Ugrinsky: pp. 61–65. © 1987 by Hofstra University. Reprinted with permission of Greenwood Publishing Group, Inc., Westport, CT.

"Goethe's *Torquato Tasso*: Poetry and Political Power," by Hans Reiss. From *The Modern Language Review* 87, part 1 (January 1992): 102-111. © 1992 by The Modern Humanities Research Association. Reprinted by permission of the publisher.

"*Faust II* and the Darwinian Revolution," by John Gearey. From *Goethe's Other Faust* pp. 14–30. © 1992 by the University of Toronto Press. Reprinted with permission of the publisher.

"The Werther Effect: The Esthetics of Suicide," by Tobin Siebers. From *Mosaic, a journal for the interdisciplinary study of literature* 26, no. 1 (Winter 1993): 15-34. © 1993 by *Mosaic*. Reprinted by permission.

Reprinted of material "The 'Other Subject' of History: Women in Goethe's Drama," by Sigrid Lange in *Impure Reason: Dialectic of Enlightenment in Gemany* by W. Daniel Wilson and Robert C. Holub by permission of the Wayne State University Press. © 1993 by Wayne State University Press.

"Faust's Forgetting," by Harald Weinrich. From *Modern Language Quarterly* 55, no. 3 (September 1994): 281-296. © 1994 by University of Washington. Reprinted by permission.

"Rights and Wrongs in Goethe's *Die Wahlverwandtschaften*," by David Constantine. From *German Life and Letters* XLVII, no. 4 (October 1994): 387-399. © 1994 by Basil Blackwell Ltd. Reprinted by permission.

"Goethe's *Die Leiden des jungen Werthers*: An Epistolary Novel, Or A Stage Drama in Disguise?" by Ilona Klein. From *European Romantic Review* 7, no. 2 (Winter 1997): 134-158. © 1997 by European Romantic Review. Reprinted by permission.

"The Material Image in Goethe's *Wahlverwandtschaften*," by Brigitte Peucker. From *The Germanic Review* 74, no. 3 (Summer 1999): 195-213. Reprinted with permission of the Helen Dwight Reid Educational Foundation. Published by Heldref Publications, 1319 Eighteenth St, NW, Washington, DC 20036-1802. © 1999.

"*West-östlicher Divan* and Other Late Poetry," by Irmgard Wagner. From *Goethe*. © 1999 by Twayne Publishers: 132–146. Reprinted by permission of the Gale Group.

# Index